D0450161

Foreword by Egyptologist Joann Fletcher

WHO KILLED KING TUT?

USING MODERN FORENSICS TO SOLVE A 3,300-YEAR-OLD MYSTERY

MICHAEL R. KING and **GREGORY M. COOPER**
with Don DeNevi

Preface by Harold Bursztajn, MD

 Prometheus Books

59 John Glenn Drive
Amherst, New York 14228-2197

Published 2004 by Prometheus Books

Inquiries should be addressed to
Prometheus Books, 59 John Glenn Drive, Amherst, New York 14228–2197
VOICE: 716–691–0133, ext. 207; FAX: 716–564–2711
WWW.PROMETHEUSBOOKS.COM

08 07 06 05 04   5 4 3 2 1

Library of Congress Cataloging-in-Publication Data

King, Michael R.
    Who killed King Tut? : using modern forensics to solve a 3,300-year-old mystery / Michael R. King and Gregory M. Cooper with Don DeNevi.
        p. cm.
    Contents: Tutankhamen's tomb : inscrutable, dismaying; Tutankhamen in the Sunlight—An invitation to unravel an ancient riddle—Egypt : where old paradoxes and new personalities meet, satisfying our itch for history—Tutankhamen's tomb triumphs over time, chronology of main events—Considering the first clues : using victimology to establish Tut's lifestyle; Victimology of Tutankhamen; Background information; Our approach to investigative analysis—It's murder, reasonable suspicion rules out death by accident, suicide or natural causes; Suicide?; Death by natural causes?; By Accident?; Murder?—Zigzagging across Egypt, soaking up the sun, listening to the experts and collecting clues—Two cops in a crypt : tracking four main suspects—Amarna and Minya, Amarna—Radiographs don't lie : myths and theories about Tutankhamen's demise—The unusual suspects : discovery of Horemheb's tomb; Maya; Ankhesenamun; Ay, the Great Manipulator—Why Ay? : presenting the indictment—Conclusion : the curse of the Mummy Tut
    ISBN 1–59102–183–9   *3 //? 4 7 8 /*   *10/04*
    1. Tutankhamen, King of Egypt—Death and burial. 2. Egypt—History—Eighteenth dynasty, ca. 1570–1320 B.C. 3. Forensic sciences. I. Cooper, Gregory M. II. DeNevi, Don, 1937– III. Title.

DT87.5.K525 2004
932'.014'092—dc22

                                                        2003026116

Printed in Canada on acid-free paper

To Bonnie, the love of my life. Thank you for your love, your strength, and your support. To my children, Whitney, Cliff, and Skyeler. Thank you for your example of goodness. I am a better person because I have lived with you.

—Mike King

To the pursuit and discovery of truth and adventure and to my hope that the young King Tut may finally rest in peace.

—Greg Cooper

The mystery of his life still eludes us—the shadows move but the dark is never quite dispersed.

Howard Carter, discoverer of Tut's tomb, in 1924

CONTENTS

8 **CONTENTS**

PREFACE

Greg Cooper and Mike King in their forensic inquiry into the death of King Tut have not only contributed to opening the road to solving an ancient mystery, but they also provide forensic investigators with a road map for the future as to how to avoid the most common pitfalls of expert judgment under conditions of uncertainty. While the psychology of expert decision-making under conditions of uncertainty is still in its infancy, there is a growing recognition of the need for awareness of its pitfalls. This recognition cuts across the variety of disciplines whose experts collaborated with Cooper and King in their grand inquiry and culminated in the award of a 2002 Nobel Prize for economics to Daniel Kahneman of Princeton University.

My own first book that focused on the heuristics and pitfalls of medical decision-making (H. J. Bursztajn, R. I. Feinbloom, R. M. Hamm, A. Brodsky, *Medical Choices, Medical Chances: How Patients, Families, and Physicians Can Cope with Uncertainty*, New York: Delacorte, 1981; New York: Routledge, Chapman & Hall, 1990) was in part inspired by a chance encounter at Harvard in the late 1970s with Kahneman's now deceased longtime collaborator, Amos Tversky. What I subsequently learned about medical decision-making pitfalls, integrated with the psychodynamics of motivation, has served as a foundation not only for educating physicians in training about expert decision-making but also whenever I am asked to serve as an expert on experts advising the judiciary on standards for reliability of expert analysis and forensic inquiry.

It is therefore all that much more delightful to be asked to write this preface to Cooper and King's remarkable forensic inquiry across space and time. The fundamental principles followed by Cooper and King in their inquiry are modeled on the Sherlock Holmes approach to inquiry. They thereby avoid the all-too-common pitfalls that dog so much of expert judgment:

1. Avoiding premature cognitive commitment to a static model of risk. It would have been all too easy for Cooper and King to jump to conclusions and stop asking questions early on. Yet, as their hundred-question approach to victim profiling noted in their chapter 5 illustrates, they were not reluctant to continue to ask questions as to what it meant to be growing up as King Tut, the son of a powerful, feared, and now dead revolutionary leader. Nor were they reluctant to recognize that as people grow they change their minds. To be King Tut as a compliant boy at the age of seven or eight, needing the protection of a powerful regent, Ay, after his own father's death, might mean something very different than to be King Tut, a seventeen- or eighteen-year-old far more likely to be eager to take the reins of power from that regent. Thus, their analysis of risk for King Tut being murdered is dynamic rather than static: "As the sliver of shade grew ever bigger and we turned our eyes to the setting sun, we summarized our thoughts and understanding and determined that King Tut was probably a 'low-risk' victim during his early reign, but as he developed physically, emotionally, spiritually, and temporally, his level of risk slowly began to creep up because of the circumstances he was living in, the situations he found himself dealing with almost daily, and the ever-changing environment" (p. 119).

Cooper and King's use of a dynamic model of risk has wide applications beyond forensic inquiry. Experts, regardless of discipline, in a variety of contexts affecting public policy, have much to learn. For example, a stark contrast to Cooper and King's dynamic approach to analyzing risk was the static model of risk espoused by policy analysts who stubbornly argued for a policy of containment of Saddam Hussein. What such a model overlooked was the possibility that the longer Hussein remained in power, the greater the risk of weapons of mass destruction being transferred. Moreover, a static model of risk overlooked the impact that leaving Saddam in power longer would have in encouraging a race among terrorists throughout the world to seek to outdo Saddam Hussein's regime of terror and defiance of the United Nations by increasingly targeting in ever-more destructive ways America and its allies.

2. Avoiding omniscience. Cooper and King chose to work with a team of experts and avoided the "my discipline knows all" fallacy of narrower minds. By doing so, they were remarkably open to considering insights from a range of disciplines to build a biopsychosocial model of who Tut was, what medical conditions he lived with, what was the changing social context in which he lived and died, and who would have what to gain from his life and death. They also questioned throughout the reliability of the evidence they were considering, whether it had been distorted by previous investigators or even planted by those such as Ay, who had an interest in impression management in this world or the next subsequent to Tut's untimely death.

Unlike those experts who make pronouncements with absolute certainty, the inquiry of Cooper and King proceeded mindful of the residual uncertainty that attended any line of analysis and the need for convergent sources of inquiry to establish validity.

Again, a useful contrast to their recognition of uncertainty and avoiding of omniscience is the relative claims for certainty and omniscience put forward by those policy analysts who advocated continued attempts to contain Saddam Hussein. Yet who could have guaranteed that we would know with certainty when Saddam Hussein would choose to export terror or resume genocide? The over-confidence in our ability to know terror in advance led to counsels that if pursued would have increased the risk of catastrophe.

3. Avoiding equating correlation with causation. Cooper and King were not content to settle for a simple reductionistic approach to determining the cause of death. Facts need to be interpreted to move from being correlates to being causes. Interpretation is only possible via a reference to a carefully analyzed model of human behavior rather than any assumed model. This model includes the fact that acts such as murder, while sometimes motivated by gain, can also be driven by the need to avoid loss.

Among the insights garnered from the study of human decision-making under conditions of uncertainty is that human beings will resort to far riskier acts, including murder, to avoid the loss of power than they might to simply gain power. In analyzing who is the most likely suspect, Cooper and King go beyond the simple "Who has the most to gain from King Tut's death?" While any of the suspects being considered might have something to gain from Tut's premature death, only one leaps out as the suspect who would be prime when the question is asked: "Who has the most to lose from Tut continuing to be alive?" The fact that the young Tut suffered from a medical condition that increased his risk of accidental death by itself does not mean that his death was an accident. To distinguish mere correlation from causation, one has to explore alternate hypotheses and consider which hypothesis is not only supported or contrary to the available data but, ceteris paribus, which has the greatest explanatory power. Thus, the very same physical handicap that made accidental death more likely also makes murder more likely. The seventeen-year-old King Tut, likely to be evermore conscious of the constraints imposed by his physical limitations, would also have been that much more eager to exercise political power as a compensation for his physical vulnerability. As with Kaiser Wilhelm of Germany, who with his withered arm was so driven to prove that he could rule with an iron fist that he precipitated the First World War, a condition that increases vulnerability can also increase hunger for power. Tut's likely increasing hunger for power would have come in conflict with those closest to him. Under such circumstances, it is not surprising that the most reasonable inference from the available evidence is not to accidental death but to murder at the hands of him who would have the most to lose by the young King Tut's growing hunger for exercising power.

How expert analysis can go astray is well illustrated by the blaming by some experts of American power or support for Israel for the terrorism engaged in by Islamic fundamentalist theocrats and their secular fascist counterparts. While there is a correlation between the two, Islamic fundamentalist terrorism predates the rise of American power and is far more characteristic of the bloody tribal disputes among warring warlords in the region, which have raged throughout the millennia. Theocratic or secular fascist rulers rule by terror and are terrified of losing power. Remembering that in the free competition of ideas, any fundamentalist theocracy or fascist regime that rules by fear and creates scapegoats for holy wars cannot afford to lose is the best guideline for understanding the motives for those rulers who will take any opportunity and will use any means, including terrorism, to avoid the loss of power.

In summary, Cooper and King began by inquiring into one of history's mysteries. In the course of their inquiry, they avoided some of the most common pitfalls of forensic inquiry and expert judgment under conditions of uncertainty.

They also bring fresh reminders that to avoid the loss of power, theocrats and fascists who rule by murder will murder to rule.

Harold J. Bursztajn, MD
Codirector, Harvard Medical School Program in Psychiatry
and the Law at Massachusetts Mental Health Center

FOREWORD

W ithout doubt ancient Egypt's most famous pharaoh, the name "Tutankhamen" is familiar to just about everyone on the planet. Yet his fame rests almost entirely on the treasures found in his tomb, with the details of his life sketchy at best and his early death one of the ancient world's great mysteries.

Ever since Howard Carter and Lord Carnarvon discovered the king's tomb in 1922 and made him a superstar, Egyptologists have been trying to answer the many questions that surround Tutankhamen and his fascinating family. But with few hard facts to work with, the limited information that does exist has been endlessly reinterpreted and disputed as scholars go around and around in circles in their attempts to work out what exactly happened at this most intriguing point in history.

In trying to understand the circumstances surrounding Tutankhamen's death in particular, it was clear that more information was seriously needed in order to move forward. So in the spring of 2000, detectives Greg Cooper and Mike King decided to conduct their own investigations in an attempt to gain a new perspective on this three-thousand-year-old mystery.

I have to admit that when I was first approached to work with Greg and Mike as their Egyptologist, I had serious doubts as to whether they would be able to find anything that had not already been picked over by a century of archaeologists, Egyptologists, and scientists. The events under investigation had taken place some 3,325 years ago, so there would be no untouched crime scene, no fresh clues, no "smoking gun," and certainly no living witnesses! In fact, I had serious misgivings whether or not my input would be of any help whatsoever. What on earth could I tell them that would be of any use after such a long period of time?

Fortunately, my fears were put to rest when I finally met Greg and Mike, neither of whom are stereotypical American cops any more than I was a standard British academic! We immediately hit it off and as we fell into easy conversation, they began to tell me about the way they went about their work, using their long years of experience in criminal profiling and intelligence gathering. As I listened to the way in which they had approached some of their former cases, I began to understand just exactly how they could provide answers so long after an event. Their methods are based on human nature, which as Greg explained to me, "remains just the same whether a crime was committed yesterday or thousands of years in the past." And once I realized this, things began to make sense.

Arriving in Egypt, we began a long tour around the country, inspecting tombs, temples, and museums, where my job was basically to act as a kind of interpreter of all things ancient Egyptian. As I deciphered the meaning behind the wall scenes, texts, and statues, I tried to fill in as much of the historical background to Tutankhamen's life as possible, and although there are plenty of variations, which can be found in the bibliography, I tried to provide them with the most likely scenario based on the evidence and punctuated with a whole lot of perhapses, likelys, and maybes.

It seems most likely that Tutankhamen was born around 1342 BCE at Amarna, the city founded by the so-called heretic king

Akhenaten after he broke with the powerful religious leaders in Egypt's traditional religious capital Thebes (modern Luxor). And because Tutankhamen is named on inscriptions from Amarna as "son of the King," it seems logical to assume that he was the son of King Akhenaten. But as Akhenaten's chief wife, the famous Nefertiti, was mother of six daughters and no sons, it is generally assumed that Tutankhamen was the son of one of Akhenaten's minor wives, the most likely candidate being a woman named Kiya.

Raised amid the splendid surroundings of the Amarna royal palace, the baby prince was actually named "Tutankhaten" at birth, meaning "living image of the Aten." The Aten was a form of the sun god Akhenaten chose to worship in place of Egypt's traditional gods after he closed down their temples and took over their vast revenues. Yet this was far more than a religious move, since the temples of ancient Egypt were also administrative centers that employed thousands of people. Their closure caused mass unemployment and social unrest, and for all its opulence, Akhenaten's reign brought his country to the brink of economic ruin. Diplomatic correspondence of the time also shows that Egypt's neglected empire abroad was starting to fragment as pleadings from her allies were simply ignored.

It was long thought that this apparent dislike of military activity was a reflection of the king's pacifist tendencies, with Akhenaten regarded as a benign character whose reclusive lifestyle was meant to keep the troubles of the world at bay. And although many people still regard him as the world's first monotheist and a man before his time, more recent evidence has led some to view Akhenaten in a very different light. He now seems to have been something of a religious extremist, a military dictator who cared little for his people and surrounded himself with yes-men and high-profile bodyguards until his death around 1336 BCE, after some seventeen years on the throne.

And such is the uncertain nature of the whole Amarna Period that we don't even know for certain who succeeded him. For a long time it was thought Akhenaten's successor was a mysterious prince named Smenkhkare, while others believe there is strong evidence that a woman took the throne, with Nefertiti perhaps the most likely candidate. Whoever this successor was, his or her rule was short-lived, and in 1333 BCE the throne passed to Prince Tutankhaten and his half-sister Ankhesenpaaten (Ankhesenamun), Akhenaten's third daughter, to whom Tutankhaten was married in time-honored fashion as a way of keeping power in the hands of the ruling family.

But with Egypt still in crisis at home and abroad, the young king and his equally youthful queen clearly had a hard task ahead of them. As children, they must have been guided by their key officials, notably the vizier (prime minister) Ay and General Horemheb, who seem to have worked together for the good of the country. While Horemheb began to win back Egypt's territories abroad, as shown in wonderfully vivid wall scenes we inspected at length in his tomb at Saqqara, Ay would have been involved in stabilizing the country and restoring order. This was begun by abandoning the city of Amarna and returning to the traditional religious capital Thebes, a move marked in the most public way possible when the new king changed his name from Tutankhaten to Tutankhamen, or "Living Image of Amun," the god whom his father Akhenaten had tried so hard to destroy.

As part of this policy of reconciliation, Tutankhamen reopened the temples his father had closed down, and as he says himself, was kept busy "making monuments for the gods, building temples anew and replenishing their offerings on earth." In fact, Tutankhamen seems to have spent most of his reign traveling up and down his country restoring the traditional religion, the administration, and the military, a lifestyle that is actually supported by the large amount of specially made portable furniture found in his tomb, including folding stools, camp beds, and carrying cases, all displayed in Cairo Museum.

And like all pharaohs, Tutankhamen began preparations for his afterlife while still a young man, drawing up plans for a tomb in the western branch of the Valley of the Kings, close to that of his illustrious grandfather, Amenhotep III. With his own father Akhenaten now an unpopular figure, Tutankhamen wisely chose to ignore his true paternity and instead stressed links with an earlier generation, declaring himself Amenhotep III's rightful heir. And like his grandfather, Tutankhamen was keen to portray himself as an active figure, wielding the same impressive array of weapons that were found in his tomb and again that can be seen in Cairo Museum.

The small crypt (pictured) of Tutankhamen probably escaped serious looting because it was placed under the tomb of Ramses VI (copyright: Griffith Institute, Oxford).

This is all a far cry from the popular image of the tragic little boy manipulated by all around him, and although certainly a child at his accession, Tutankhamen's ten-year reign would nevertheless have seen him develop as a young man not so easily controlled. Although we can never know what kind of man he would have turned out to be, his early years had shown much promise, and from what little evidence we have, Tutankhamen begins to emerge as a competent king in a role he had been trained for since birth.

But then by around the age of twenty, he was dead. With no direct evidence to suggest how Tutankhamen had met his death, murder is often suggested. Many theories have been put forward over the years, ranging from an infected mosquito bite to a bash on the head, or that ancient version of a young man in a fast car, a fatal chariot accident. Yet with no new information available from the world of Egyptology, it certainly seemed appropriate to start looking elsewhere in the search for clues.

And this is exactly what Greg and Mike did, using their specialized skills to provide new information about Tutankhamen's life and death, supported by evidence from some of the world's leading experts in clinical psychology, forensic medicine, and behavioral profiling. The two also scrutinized the original autopsy reports and x-rays of the king's mummy and drew on the modern techniques of facial reconstruction to recreate the young king's original appearance, which took pride of place in a special exhibition at London's Science Museum. Where Carter and Carnarvon had given us the idealized face of the golden death mask, Greg and Mike's investigations allowed us to finally see the real face of Tutankhamen, no longer an ancient Egyptian god-king but a real human being as vulnerable as the rest of us. And just how vulnerable this book will reveal.

Dr. Joann Fletcher
Egyptologist
Great Britain

ACKNOWLEDGMENTS

O ur sincerest appreciation goes out to the many people who assisted us in this magnificent voyage. To you, our hats are tipped! Above all, our thanks to the man with the vision, Anthony Geffen, executive producer, Atlantic Productions, and his producer, the lovely Kate Botting. In alphabetical order, we also sincerely thank Dr. Richard Boyer, Dr. Harold Bursztajn, Harry Chapman, Prof. Alan Dershowitz, the Discovery Channel, Mr. Emad Abd-el Hamid, Simon Farmer, Dr. Todd Grey, Dr. Zahi Hawass, Ms. Sue Hutchison, Lance Kneeshaw, Dr. Malek, Adrian O'Toole, Jonathan Partridge, Mr. Rashidy, Dr. Robin Richards, Dr. Ernst Rodin, Nicola Wicks, and Patricia Wrobel.

And finally, we offer a few words of special tribute to our foremost collaborators:

Dr. Joann Fletcher, an Egyptologist from the United Kingdom, our new friend and personal guide to the tombs of Egypt, enthusiastically supported our formal criminal analysis, believing as we do that it will durably change forever the paradigm by which we view King Tutankhamen.

Meanwhile, Dr. Don DeNevi, a closely reasoning and formidably intelligent author from the San Francisco Bay area, demanded we navigate the rigors of clear writing with grace, integrating critical speculation with meticulous academic inquiry and scholarly research.

Thanks to all of the above we are confident in shedding new light not only upon the lives of a young pharaoh and his aggregate of most trusted aides but also his untimely, tragic death.

M.K.
G.C.

INTRODUCTION

On Sunday, December 3, 1922, almost a month after an ordinary native workman clearing away topsoil in Egypt's Valley of the Kings and Queens at Thebes unearthed a crude 4.75-inch by 7.5-inch step cut in the soft stone, leading to the discovery of King Tutankhamen's tomb, the astounding event was officially announced to the world. And, in fewer than two hundred words in the lower right-hand corner on page 12 of the London *Sunday Times*, the article read:

THE EGYPTIAN FINDS

LORD CARNARVON, who has done much already for Egyptian archaeology—more, perhaps, than any Englishman of our times— has been rewarded during the week with a splendid find, nothing less than the tomb of King Tutankhamen, over three thousand years old. It was uncovered in the famous Valley of the Tombs of Kings, which was supposed by nearly all experts to have yielded up its last treasures several years ago. How important the discovery may prove to be, and what light it will throw on the art and religion of the 18th Dynasty, Egyptologists must be left to explain. But the veriest layman can appreciate the drama of such a find, the years of skilled and happy, patient labour that went to its achievement, and the glimpse of an ancient and ornate civilization thus allowed to our modern eyes. Three thousand years from now what will the excavator bring to light in England that will show what manner of people lived here in 1922? Where will he look for the lost monuments of our greatness, and will they reward him when he finds them?

Hardly an electrifying announcement of what was to become the greatest ancient Egyptian discovery of all time. But in the days and decades that followed, as hundreds of thousands gazed in awe, wondering about the heights and depths of Tut's culture and civilization, and after all the gold and jewels appraised, and the millions upon millions of glorifying adjectives uttered and printed, one fact remains: a sickly, crippled kid died under extremely suspicious circumstances, and an attempt was made to conceal the details of his untimely death and even his very existence.

Sure, it happened thirty-three hundred years ago. Why should we care now?

Because any unsolved killing is a blot on all the hearts and souls of a good humanity, and all ineffable mysteries sooner or later must be solved by someone.

In Tutankhamen's case, why not Mike King and Greg Cooper, two law enforcement specialists in forensics and understanding of criminal behavior?

In the mid-1960s, Mike King, who was born in Salt Lake City, loved *Adam-12*, a popular weekly television police series, so much that it led to a career in law enforcement. By the age of ten, Mike was also in awe of Sergeant Friday of *Dragnet*, especially of how he interviewed and interrogated criminals. "Although Friday was special, he couldn't compare to the powerful images of Starsky and Hutch, to say nothing of Harry Callahan and the other great action cops of the period," he said recently. "I simply grew up wanting to be one of them."

Accepted into the three-officer police department of a small town in northern Utah during the late 1970s, Mike experienced one of those rare life-changing events one week before his first wedding anniversary. On August 17, 1979, while responding to a house fire during a terrible rainstorm, Mike was entangled in a 49,000-volt electric utility power line, which literally tossed him to and fro. After bouncing around for some twenty minutes, he was somehow miraculously freed from the wire's grasp. The young officer had to undergo daily visits to the hospital and doctor's office for months, and the damage required years to heal.

Unfortunately, while on medical leave, Mike was fired "for not having what it takes to be a police officer." After several months of sulking over the abrupt termination, he decided to apply to the Ogden City Police Department, the largest in the northern part of the state, in which four new positions were available. Since more than two hundred other well-qualified candidates were also applying, Mike feared the worst, especially because he would be required to pass a physical agility test. As his feet had been severely burned by the high voltage, Mike's soles began to bleed while running the obstacle course, which included climbing fences and walls as well as crawling through large pipes. In order to pass, the candidates needed to complete the endurance test in two minutes, twelve seconds. Mike reached the finish line in three minutes, thirty seconds.

Sgt. Gary Greenwood invited the young man to rest then try again. Indicating he would, Mike thanked him and hobbled over to his 1970 Chevy, where he sat on the tailgate, wringing the blood out of his socks. A few minutes later Greenwood walked by, saw the bloody feet, and asked what happened. At that point, the Sergeant recognized Mike as "the cop who was electrocuted." Gary laughed. "Anyone tough enough to run with feet like that can be in my department anytime," said Greenwood, who proceeded to give Mike the break of his career: he changed the agility test score to two minutes, eleven seconds, just enough to qualify. To this moment, King is eternally grateful to that kind man who knew a good cop when he saw one.

After a thoroughly difficult, frank, and honest interview before a command staff hiring committee, Mike was offered the second of the four available positions. In the years that followed, the Ogden police department tested his mettle by assigning him to the most challenging field patrols. It was then nonstop action for the young officer—bar fights, high-speed chases, shootouts, and murders. After riding police motorcycles while on patrol between 6:00 P.M. and 4:00 A.M. for a year or so, he was assigned to the tactical and SWAT teams, driving unmarked cars and wearing plain clothes in order to handle felonies in progress. But during all this exciting work, it was the knowledge he gained in the endless training sessions that he loved the most.

In January of 1986, after the chief of the Ogden police department disbanded the Tactical (TAC) Squad, Mike joined newly elected Weber County Attorney Reed M. Richards as administrative assistant and investigator. This allowed King not only to continue his career in law enforcement but also to take advantage of his skills in program development, networking, and resourcing. Reed immediately assigned his administrative assistant to improve the relations between the chiefs of police and county sheriffs in the Ogden area, as well as to develop grant proposals for the office.

Perhaps the most dramatic case Mike ever worked on for Reed dealt with an investigation of the Zion Society, a one-hundred-fifty-member group sexually abusing children in ritualistic ways. Twelve arrests and seven hundred sixty felony counts for sexual abuse of children followed, resulting in all the defendants being convicted, including twenty years to life for the group's leader. Mike's efforts led to the largest, most successfully prosecuted series of cases of organized child sexual abuse in the history of American crime.

When County Attorney Richards was offered the position of chief deputy attorney general for newly elected State Attorney General Jan Graham, Mike, who had followed Reed to the attorney general's office, was asked by the Utah State Legislature to investigate ritual crime in Utah. For more than two years, he poured over one hundred twenty allegations of Satanic ritual crime. Although Mike, who had been promoted to sergeant, and his team were unable to prove long-believed allegations that "Satanists" were raising children to be sacrificed in sexual rituals, they uncovered isolated incidents of ritual-type abuse where child molesters used "Satan" as one of the control mechanisms with child victims. In the process of learning about the criminal mind of such perpetrators, Mike met with several profilers at the FBI Academy's Behavioral Science Unit in Quantico, Virginia. Although all the special agents assigned to the unit were impressive, Kenneth Lanning stood out as the most formidable. His investigative experiences and research work in child serial killers and abductors sparked Mike's interest to the point where he began compiling notes on the common characteristics of the criminals with whom he was dealing.

It wasn't long thereafter that Mike was promoted to lieutenant. When assigned to evaluate the types of programs that would assist law enforcement throughout the state, he was approached by the newly appointed Provo City Chief of Police, Gregory M. Cooper, who at one time managed the FBI's Investigative Support Unit at Quantico. Soon, the two began discussing the possibility of establishing a state profiling office similar to the FBI's. Together, the two traveled the state seeking high-level agency support. Thanks to everyone's enthusiastic endorsement, the Utah criminal Tracking and Analysis Project (UTAP) was born in the fall of 1997.

During their collaborative effort to create UTAP, Greg began mentoring Mike on the "art" and "science" of criminal profiling. Greg's FBI training and Academy insights meshed beautifully with Mike's practical investigative experience at the hometown level to form a unique philosophy. When the legendary John Douglas shared his profiling concepts with him, Mike felt that at long last he was in law enforcement's major league. His education increased on almost a daily basis.

Soon, Greg and Mike were solving some of Utah's most violent serial crimes. Literally hundreds, if not thousands, of hours were spent interviewing offenders across the country. The two focused upon the lives of criminals, the motivations behind their crimes, the manner in which they selected their victims, and how they eluded police. Although Greg was well educated in criminal behavior, Mike was still absorbing all he could about the intricacies of profiling by reviewing crime case after crime case, patiently examining the background of the offenders, the risk levels of the victims, and the specific details of each of the assaults. In short, he was training himself to examine the most minute aspects of each element of a crime.

Requests to train police officers began pouring in from across the nation and abroad. Their reputations as consultants skyrocketed! In perhaps one of the most innovative approaches ever taken in the education of law enforcement officers, Greg and Mike brought along serial killers, arsonists, rapists, and child sexual offenders to the classes and conferences they led: "Our theory is that those of us in law enforcement can read and study all that we want in regard to how serial predators commit their crimes, but until we hear, observe, and learn from the lips of the actual offenders, the ones who are motivated to commit such horrific acts, the written words don't mean all that much. We needed to go to the 'experts' to understand this thought process and personality."

Of course, this new type of in-service training was considered by most as "cutting edge." Heavily shackled with six highly trained officers escorting them, the inmates quietly responded to any and all questions asked by the participants. Such sessions were the only opportunity for ordinary officers and detectives to listen to and observe firsthand the manipulation and evil charisma of these types of offenders. Needless to say, the classes were extremely emotional—and successful.

Throughout such shared experiences, Mike and Greg continued to forge their relationship. They enjoyed each other as friends and professionals. They also relished the synergism that comes from coteaching Criminal Investigative Analysis, the new course they developed together, across America and abroad, twice per month. Invitations to lecture before law enforcement agencies and news organizations across America soon led to their becoming senior analysts for a startup e-company called APBNews. com, offering profiling insights while reviewing cases. Their Web site received more than a million hits per day. In addition, they began appearing regularly on programs aired on MSNBC, Fox, and Court TV. Recently, the two coauthored a manual for police investigators that teaches the principles of behavioral investigative analysis. Titled *Analyzing Criminal Behavior II*, the text is currently being simplified for "A Layman's Guide to Understanding Criminal Behavior."

As a young boy, Greg Cooper fueled his fantasies, like Mike's, by the popular action-packed police shows of the 1960s and 1970s. Yet, he says, somewhere in the deep recesses of his subconscious, there is an explanation for his lifelong obsession with the police, some event that either complemented the dramatizations he saw on TV or preceded them. Recently, he commented,

Perhaps there was some emotionally charged event that I had been exposed to as a child. Astoundingly, the answer finally emerged from the caverns of my subconscious at a very odd moment. I was teaching at a Victims' Advocate Academy conference in Salt Lake City, explaining how I became interested in law enforcement. I had one of those defining moments—I think they call them "AH-HA" moments. An epiphany! I actually had a flashback to when I was six years old. It was as if I were transported through time, and I could feel all of my senses reenact the scene in my heart and in my mind that was to be so deeply profound and influential.

It was about 1960, and my parents were separated, which ultimately led to divorce. I lived in a small, ground-floor studio apartment in Las Vegas, Nevada, with my mom and a fourteen-year-old brother, who basically did what he wanted. I remember in vivid detail what turned out to be a very distinctive day charged with high anxiety, fear, and compassion. It must have been a weekday, probably during the summer because I wasn't at school and my mom was home during daylight. She worked as a waitress at the Flamingo Hotel and was usually gone at night.

I was outside playing on a swing set just across the yard, by myself as usual. I remember my mom opening the door of the apartment just a crack and motioning for me to come to her. She was quite expressive. I wondered why she didn't say anything to me. I ran over to her, and she pulled me through the doorway. The curtains were drawn, and it was dark in the room for lack of sunlight. She turned on a lamp and said that a policeman was coming to the door in a few minutes and, if he found her there, would take her to jail. She briefly explained that it had something to do with "parking tickets." She told me to sneak out the bathroom window and contact the apartment manager, who was a friend, and ask her to come down to our room and tell the policeman that no one lived there.

Just as I was scurrying out the window, there was a knock on the door. My mom looked at me with wide, terror-filled eyes and placed her finger to her lips, motioning for me to be quiet. Another knock came louder, this time followed by a man's voice: "Ms. Cooper, this is Officer [?] with the Las Vegas Police Department. Please open the door; I know you are in there." My mom's face winced, then became deflated, showing an expression of surrender. She told me to come back from the window. I climbed down and stood by her knee as she opened the door to a very large man in a very blue suit with a very big shiny badge. He explained that he had a warrant for her arrest and that she had to come with him. He stated that if she didn't have anyone to leave me with that I would have to come also. I remember getting into the back seat of the police car.

The next thing I remember is that I was escorted to an office area and seated in a chair by a window. A nice lady came over to me and gave me a pencil and paper to draw on. I didn't know where my mom had been taken, but someone explained that everything would be all right and she would be back soon. I felt odd and out of place there but also welcome. A lot of men and women in street clothes were paying attention to me, rubbing my head and talking to me, assuring me everything was going to be fine.

My mom showed up sometime later, and I was gleeful at her return. But much to my disappointment, she explained she would have to stay the night and that a friend of hers who was a policeman was going to take me to his home for the night to stay with his family. I was upset and terrified to think that some stranger, who was probably a friend of the mean guy who took my mom to jail, was now going to take me to his home. My mom assured me that everything was going to be okay.

I remember that when she introduced me to this big, handsome man in plain clothes, he warmly knelt down beside me and shook my hand. He put his arm around me and asked me if I would be his guest and come to his house to meet his wife and children and stay the night. My mom nodded approvingly, which increased my confidence and soothed my anxieties. Mom and I said our good-byes, and she was escorted out of the office. The next thing I remember is that I was in this man's home, being introduced to his wife and older children. I remember the warm atmosphere and the comfort I seemed to be shrouded in.

The last thing I remember is most likely the pivotal event that turned my heart toward this profession. I can vividly reenact in heart and mind a kindness and compassion expressed by this man and his wife that I shall never forget. It was bedtime, and they took me into their bedroom and turned down the bedding, revealing crisp, clean white sheets. The woman lifted me up into the bed, laid me down, and tucked me in. The warmth and security I felt at that moment, after such a disturbing day, seemed to wash away and displace all the fear and anxiety, leaving peace and solitude. Then the big burly man did something that will be branded on me forever—after his wife tightly tucked me in, he came around her, bent down over me, and kissed me tenderly on the forehead.

I doubt that I have ever slept more soundly that I did that night in the house and bed of a stranger. Little did he know the profound effect that he and his wife's sweet and unselfish generosity would have on a little boy who would one day grow up to carry on a legacy of a true "peace officer."

Don DeNevi

"Shall the earth also give back that . . . which has been entrusted to it, and hell shall give back that which it owes."

Carl G. Jung, "Answer to Job"

Chapter 1

TUTANKHAMEN'S TOMB
INSCRUTABLE, DISMAYING

The return of Tut-ankh-Amen into the sunshine after 3,000 years in stifling darkness has a drama both majestic and pathetic. There is a poignant contrast in it. After thirty centuries of peace and silence, he reenters a world that apparently has little changed so far as human nature is concerned.

Algernon Blackwood in 1922

Down the fabled four-thousand-mile Nile, the longest river in the world, past the Delta, Cairo, the Sphinx, the pyramids of Giza, the once-thriving city of Memphis and the lavish necropolis at Saqqara, to the ancient venerable capital of the New Kingdom, Thebes, which then stretched for miles along once fertile, grass-green banks, the colorful landscape was and still is a vast, unforgettable museum of ancient incredibilities. This upper part of Egypt is at all times exciting; at sunset it is sensational, especially during northern Africa's winter months.

The Valley of the Kings. The large doorway right of center is the entrance to the tomb of Ramses VI. At the bottom right is that of Tutankhamen (copyright: Griffith Institute, Oxford).

And in modern times, no matter how wide and newly paved the two-lane highway is on the west side of the Nile opposite the present-day city of Karnak, or how short the distance, it is still a hot, dusty drive from Homer's hundred-gated Thebes to the low, sandy mountains of the Valley of the Kings. But awaiting us at the end of the journey that evening, half-buried in the cliffs, rain-washed rubble, and excavation debris were the tombs and their once-held treasure vaults of the men and women who ruled the known world thousands of years before the birth of Jesus Christ. Regardless of how inundated and often bored we were of the endless assigned readings by the Discovery Channel on the countless pharaohs, the cities they designed and built, their bejeweled mummified bodies in death, and the pomp and circumstance of their funerals, to say nothing of the opulent splendors of their burial chambers, we were jubilant that the sepulcher of teenaged King Tutankhamen (pronounced toot-ang-KAH-men), the pot of gold at the end of the aged Egyptian rainbow, was about to be unsealed for us.

As we traveled in our short-sleeved shirts, wiping the sweat from our brows and commenting about how utterly stifling the Egyptian heat can be, we laughed as we listened to the Egyptian guide and soldier who were traveling with us respond that it was winter and, to them, it was cold.

Each wore the traditional *galabeya* gown as their outer clothing, but underneath they had on thermal underwear, extra shirts, and socks, and they wore winter coats over their *galabeyas*. To us, this was quite interesting. We were visiting Egypt from our mountainous state of Utah, which averages hundreds of inches of snow each year. Our winters had temperatures that could dip below zero. The winter in Egypt was in the nineties and in upper Egypt over a hundred degrees. We talked to our Egyptian friends about the huge amounts of snow we would soon be shoveling in front of our homes, and we told them tales of the 2002 Winter Olympics that would come to our state in the coming weeks.

Greg was a member of the 2002 Winter Olympics Public Safety Command as the chief of police of Provo, where the ice hockey venue would be celebrated. As a lieutenant in the attorney general's office, Mike was assigned to the Central Intelligence Collection and Dissemination unit, CICAD, responsible for the collection and analysis of intelligence. For four years, the state of Utah prepared to receive the world. We were excited about the challenge, and we were excited to remind Egypt that we had that great opportunity. What we didn't really think about was that there isn't a whole lot of snow in Egypt! And there isn't a whole lot of interest in winter sports in Egypt. Most importantly, to such a depressed class of citizens as we were visiting at the time, there was also little interest in the Winter Olympics. Nonetheless, it gave us a great chance to culturally share the differences between our home and theirs.

Accompanying us during that forty-minute drive was Dr. Joann Fletcher, a young British Egyptologist internationally respected for her research and scholarship. Fletcher had been employed by the Discovery Channel not only to provide us with a reign-by-reign history of ancient Egypt from the first human settlement in the Nile Valley (12,000 BCE) to the appearance of Alexander the Great and his dynasty in 332 BCE but also to keep us abreast of the current political climate, especially in light of the events of September 11, 2001, which occurred less than six weeks before our arrival in Egypt.

Cruising along at thirty-five miles per hour, and with a driver at the wheel, we looked across the warm sand dunes and rumpled hills, reflecting upon the tragedy of treasure hunting in early Egypt. Dr. Fletcher commented that at the turn of the nineteenth century, before foreign interest in ancient Egyptian civilization and its antiquities became the rage, there had been numerous intact tombs in the Valley of the Kings. But with the emergence of a new market for anything pharaonic, or pertaining to the funerary, that could be added to European living room "curiosity cabinets," roving gangs of criminal diggers plundered the more accessible crypts. Well into the twentieth century, the illegal excavations continued, despite the Egyptian government's precautions and prosecutions. Visitors and villagers alike felt that all one had to do was poke a hole into the sand and gold, silver, and precious stones would spew forth. Adding to the problem were the countrymen themselves, who for the most part showed few superstitions, little fear, and less sanctity for their once-revered ancestors. Greedily rifling a site, any site, was paramount, regardless of the potential consequences if caught. Thus, hundreds of graves were desecrated and ransacked, leaving the conscientious archaeologist little with which to work. By 1922, so many burial sites had been spoiled and ravaged that if one announced he had discovered and was about to enter a tomb, governmental authorities and museum officials tended to yawn, automatically assuming it had already been looted. So, for everyone involved— current illicit excavator or honest Egyptologist, prudent museum curator or fascinated visitor—treasure hunting in the early part of the twentieth century was replete with painful disillusionment.

As we continued, we could sense that Dr. Fletcher was getting excited about the road we were traveling. She spoke enthusiastically about the canal that once extended along side of us, indicating that the ancient residents had made the same exact directional journey to

Amenhotep's Temple as we were taking. Suddenly, she became very serious and said, "Just keep looking straight ahead for a minute." We sensed that something impressive lay around the next curve, but our imagination was not prepared for the reality that soon jumped out in front of us.

When we rounded a slight bend in the road, towering twin statues of Amenhotep III burst upon us! What an incredible sight! Huge, high statues of Tutankhamen's grandfather, a constant reminder to the people of the Eighteenth Dynasty and beyond of his once-great power, dominion, and leadership. The brilliant blue evening sky served as a backdrop to the statues that dwarfed us as we stopped the vehicle and walked to them for a closer examination. Dr. Fletcher explained how the flooding of the Nile each spring made possible the floating of large barges into the region and the delivery of gifts to their leader. As the overwhelming feelings subsided and we began to discuss the intricate details of the statues, Dr. Fletcher seemed somewhat saddened that our sheer wonderment and excitement of seeing the statues for the first time was waning. Through us, she had been able to vicariously relive her own initial joy of seeing the great twin statues.

As our driver, Ali, approached the Valley of the Kings, our discussion turned to the discovery of the last major intact burial chamber prior to Tutankhamen's—that of Yuya and his wife, Tuya, Tut's great-grandparents and Queen Tiy's parents. Also located in the valley, not far from Tut's tomb, their tomb yielded treasures that stunned the world, artifacts that included beautifully carved wooden chairs decorated with gold designs, pillows covered with linen so perfectly preserved one could sit on them today, and alabaster vases containing liquids still not solidified after thirty-seven hundred years. Situated around two large matching coffins in which husband and wife lay separately and peacefully were wicker trunks; two comfortable beds fitted with springy string mattresses decorated with silver motifs, staffs, and sandals; magical figures holding funeral prayers; as well as hundreds of small gold implements needed by each in the afterlife. Dr. Fletcher commented that to this day the stern features of Yuya and the gentle, feminine smile of Tuya appear so real that they simply seemed asleep. All archaeologists and Egyptologists agreed: no find was as rare or romantic as this.

Entering a remote wadi, a dried-up river valley, Fletcher pointed out all the tombs that remained today. In the denuded burial chambers situated all around us in the barren hills were the pictographs and hieroglyphic inscriptions on their subterranean walls describing the noble deeds of the deceased as well as the national events during the times in which they lived. In short, each crypt, even without its priceless treasures, was a miniature time capsule. In Tut's tomb, because of all its golden treasure and burial significance, this relatively new and smallest of all the valley's recently discovered burial places represented a means of finding out about life in Eighteenth Dynasty Egypt.

TUTANKHAMEN IN THE SUNLIGHT

As we parked in the arroyo and trekked way up the small path in the gathering darkness to the entrance of the tomb cut in the limestone rock, we weighed the words of Algernon Blackwood, a well-known writer at the turn of the century, who, upon learning of Tut's discovery in November of 1922, wrote:

> That kingly figure, blind, deaf, unfeeling, is fortunately unaware of the violent contrast his resurrection emphasizes: the strident chorus of modern voices and his own silence. . . .
>
> And it is an eloquent silence. He emerges from his ancient tomb with dignity, with grandeur, bringing with him into our practical twentieth century a sense of mystery, of star-like leisure, of wonder; something of awe, and a strange forgotten beauty, too. There is about him almost an unearthly touch, not dissimilar, perhaps, to the emotion wakened in Kinglake by the Sphinx, his fellow splendor, so briefly and so adequately described in "Eothen": "Comely the creature is, but with a comeliness not of this earth"—a pregnant sentence that lays upon the mind again, with Tut-ankh-Amen, that singular Egyptian glamour, which is, indeed, a mysterious, almost unearthly spell.[1]

Lord Carnarvon (*left*) and Howard Carter open the door to Tutankhamen's burial chamber (copyright: Griffith Institute, Oxford).

A great deal of nonsense, millions of words of it in fact, poured forth after November 4 of that year, when the first stone step to the grave was sensitively swept off. But not this fine tribute, the best that we've read, by Blackwood. Where others relegated the great discovery to tabloid exaggeration and picture-postcard status, thereby cheapening Tut with sensationalism, writers like Blackwood and Frederick Lewis[2] were the first to truly define him and the discovery, stirring our imaginations by a new spell and lure. For the first time, thanks to them, we gleaned Tutankhamen's undeniable reality, his silence and mystery, his elusive death.

Even that night, descending the twenty-nine steps and slowly proceeding down the low, forty-seven-foot corridor into the tomb's antechamber, it was difficult to describe our emotions. At first we were filled with sheer amazement by where we two ordinary Utah cops were walking. We couldn't believe so many centuries had passed since the solid gold coffin of the young pharaoh had been hand-carried down this same corridor. Suddenly, at once, we felt both an eerie and awesome sensation. Today, because of erosion and deterioration, the public needs a special ticket costing a hundred Egyptian pounds (about £20, or US $30) to enter Tutankhamen's tomb, and only a very select few are allowed to venture beyond the railings that divide the antechamber from the burial chamber or crypt. After all, the mummified remains of a boy-king remain at rest in the stone sarcophagus on the floor of the twenty-two-foot by fifteen-foot burial chamber/crypt beyond the antechamber, adjacent to the treasury room. Not one of us doubted that had these spaces been as completely looted as planned by the two teams of expert graverobbers in the years following the burial in 1327 BCE, leaving no trace of their astonishing riches, including the coffin, the extraordinary gold mask, jewelry, and other art objects and artifacts, the world would not have given a second thought to the crippled young pharaoh whose reign lasted less than nine years, between 1336 and 1327 BCE.

But precisely because the virtually inviolate, well-hidden tomb concealed beneath a few mud-brick houses of the workmen who cut the tomb of Ramses VI finally surrendered what it did, everyone yearned to know more about the young man. Who was he really? What were his character and personality like? Was he a good, kind young man or arrogant, depressed, and miserable? Who were his parents and what were they like? How did they raise him? Whom did he marry and why? And above all, why did he die so young, having barely reached his eighteenth birthday? Was he murdered, as rumored, in the similar manner of several of his predecessors? After all, past behavior predicts future behavior. Was there a pattern before with Tut's progenitors?

Upon entering the antechamber, we gazed at length upon the unmarred wall hieroglyphics that remained untranslated until recently. A hastily painted transcript, part of it unfinished, of Tut's world, his accomplishments and achievements, clearly and beautifully recorded as if an eyewitness to history, surrounded us. We recalled a passage from English archaeologist Howard Carter's diary that described his reaction when he first peeked through a small peephole he punched into the wall of the antechamber from the corridor:

> I inserted the candle and peered in, Lord Carnarvon, Lady Evelyn and Callender standing anxiously beside me to hear the verdict. At first I could see nothing, the hot air escaping from the chamber causing the candle flame to flicker, but presently, as my eyes grew accustomed to the light, details of the room within emerged slowly from the mist, strange animals, statues and gold—everywhere the glint of gold.

When anxious Lord Carnarvon, the English patron who financed Carter's years of exploration, demanded, "Can you see anything?" the archaeologist smiled and said, "Yes, wonderful things."

Later, after the joy of the discovery wore off, Carter realistically appraised the burial chamber and its contents, stating that he was confused. Not about the sarcophagus that appeared to have been placed in the chamber only hours before it was sealed, or the tomb's floor upon which no one had stepped for over three thousand years, and which was still as white and clean as our own bathroom tiles, but by the contents that even at first glance appeared to be in utter disarray. All around were the vestiges of confusion, signs of urgency, not necessarily those of the slapdash or the helter-skelter, but certainly indications to suggest a hurried and unsophisticated effort to lay to rest a pharaoh/god for the eternities. The tomb had been entered at least twice after the burial. "To exaggerate the confusion that existed would be difficult; it was but an illustration of both drama and tragedy. . . . The confusion naturally rendered evidence very difficult to interpret. It was also disconcerting to find that our deductions, no matter how correct they may have been, could seldom be definite," wrote Carter.

Our first reaction was that the tomb was small—so small it was unseemly—for a pharaoh. Fletcher commented that there was no evidence the normal period between death and burial (about seventy days) had not been observed when Tutankhamen was entombed. In fact, she added, the time required to prepare a royal burial is often underestimated not so much for the deceased, but for the gathering or fashioning of his accompanying accouterments. Today, every sixth grader can tell you that from the moment of a pharaoh's death a major effort is undertaken to prepare him for the eternity he will live in the afterlife. Not only does this include his body but also the supplies and equipment to make him comfortable.

Joann commented that, astonishingly, most of the objects and artifacts, long removed from the chamber, had lives prior to Tut's time. In fact, most had not been prepared for burial with him. Some clearly belonged to previous royalty, hinting that the priests had quickly gathered every funerary object in sight and shoved them into an already stuffed chamber.

Furthermore, we were surprised to see that what at first appeared to be patiently painted pictographs were indeed sloppily done. Such amateurism suggested a cover-up at worst or total disregard for the king at least. What intrigued us the most was something about the sarcophagus lid, which didn't seem to match the rest of the sarcophagus. The pattern and images were not uniform. Why? No pharaoh in the history of Egypt was known to have received such a shabby burial—especially when preparation and ceremonies were always critical for someone so significant.

Adding to the confusion was the fact that when Tut and his

tomb were definitely identified, the clearance of the tomb by Carter and his helpers inevitably destroyed vital clues. For instance, the burial chamber was not sealed immediately after its discovery. Crucial exhibits were removed and lost. Despite his meticulous work, Carter overlooked evidence. Even Tut's remains were mishandled, to say nothing of how inadequate the original autopsy was. In fact, Tut's genitals and one rib are still missing.

Dr. Fletcher explained that Carter approached his work as an archaeologist, not as a police officer. The examination of the tomb had to be conducted in that manner. Carter did a marvelous job of cataloging everything in the tomb though, and his meticulous work paid off in our ability to re-create the crime scene nearly a hundred years later. It only makes sense that politicians, curious onlookers with access, and robbers at that time would have kept souvenirs of the find.

Although our initial responsibility was to evaluate the reason for Tut's death—natural causes, accident, suicide, or homicide—it became apparent upon our first visit to the tomb that Tut was not treated the same way as other pharaohs had been after they died. For example, Tut was buried in Ay's tomb in a nobleman's burial area, not a place established for pharaohs. As we considered why this particular pharaoh was buried so quickly, erased from the people's memory, and hidden away, we had to consider all other options equally and fairly.

In short, less than an hour after perusing the sarcophagus and the wall paintings, we perceived that murder was a very real possibility and that someone of importance, a person of high rank who was free to supervise the king's funeral and burial processes unhindered, wanted to stash the victim away forever, erase the fact that he even existed, and downplay any suspicion of foul play. This was not a crypt demonstrating respect, reverence, or love. To the contrary, it was a disrespectful attempt to conceal the life and reign of a pharaoh. Why?

Driving back to our hotel in Karnak late that night, we couldn't help but feel that visiting the death crypt at dusk was one of the most memorable experiences of our lives. We recalled an additional

Blackwood passage: "A total result whose detailed analysis lies hidden in mystery and silence—otherworldly and inscrutable."

NOTES

1. Algernon Blackwood, "The Literary Traveler in Egypt," *Literary Digest International Book Review* (June 1923).
2. See Frederick Lewis's "Egypt the Incredible" in the January 1929 issue of *Women's Home Companion*.

Chapter 2

AN INVITATION TO UNRAVEL AN ANCIENT RIDDLE

For us, criminal behavior is criminal behavior. It doesn't matter if it's today or 3,500 years ago. The statute of limitations on murder never runs out.

Greg Cooper and Mike King in October 2002

To decipher one of Egypt's oldest unsolved mysteries, ending once and for all more than eighty years of speculation, and at the same time investigate an untimely death, even if that death is more than three thousand years old, is not only a challenge for any law enforcement officer but for us, frankly pure, unmitigated fascination. Because there can be no crime more heinous than the systematic murder of a child, uncovering the killer becomes highly motivating.

In America, when a homicide occurs, law enforcers are "on scene" within minutes. With this kind of response time, officers often obtain valuable information from witnesses and victims of the crime. In some cases, the victim is still alive at the time of their arrival and may provide some insight into what happened. Unfortunately, statistical data prove that as the case "cools," law enforcement's ability to solve the case diminishes with each passing day. In the case of Tutankhamen, 1,224,575 days had passed since the death occurred, and that's a long, long time.

Interestingly, when police officers today approach the scene of a gang-related homicide, secrecy and personal revenge often become another obstacle for the enforcers. Gang members are often heard to say, "We'll take care of this ourselves. We don't need police help." It appears that this same "closed lips" policy occurred at the time of Tut's death. Imagine what might have happened to the police officer, or even the commander of the armies, if he had suggested murder and, more importantly, the possibility of murder committed by someone in Tut's inner circle, not just the general public.

In tackling whether Tutankhamen's unexpected demise was unnatural or violent, it makes little difference whether his death is a day, a year, a decade, a century, or even several thousand years old. In fact, a murder 3,325 years old isn't much of a problem, even if all the witnesses and forensic evidence disappeared long ago. The investigative skill needed most for all homicides is an eye for the misplaced detail. You look for statements that don't add up, for the murderer's personality traits or eccentricities that match or don't match the death blow, a behavioral scientist's perspective regarding motivation, a thorough analysis of the method used, and "victimology," a term we use for the study of the essential information about the deceased, such as his or her family, friends, and acquaintances; the victim's normal routine; his special habits; and the like.

Victimology suggests learning everything there is to know about the victim's education, employment, residence, neighborhood, and lifestyle. For example, one of the first questions we ask is whether the person is a low-, moderate-, or high-risk prey. This information is the stuff that feeds our insatiable investigative appetites. And, frankly, we don't mind saying we're pretty good at solving the unsolvable, in light of more than a combined half century of police probing knowledge and experience. Miraculously, our work caught the attention of the London-based documentary filmmakers Atlantic

Productions, which, for reasons of its own, decided to reopen the thick, inactive file on Tutankhamen's unexplained death.

How was it that two retiring American police officers suddenly found themselves in the heart of Egypt, a 1,001,449-kilometer hallowed land replete with forgotten intrigues, assassinations, graves and cemeteries, revenge, and hieroglyphic clues several millennia old?

During the late fall of 2000, Greg was invited by the Open University's Psychological Society (U.K.) to lecture on the art and science of investigative analysis and criminal profiling at its biennial conference at Nottingham University. Anna Thompson, assistant executive producer to Anthony Geffen, a British film producer for Atlantic Productions, happened to read about the forthcoming presentation in the London *Sunday Times* and decided to sit in on the lecture the following morning. She was so impressed with the exhibits and slides that at the conclusion of the talk she walked up to the podium from the audience and bluntly asked Greg if he would be interested in unraveling an ancient Egyptian riddle for a television documentary under development. Cooper laughed and asked for more details.

"Well, our editorial staff would like you to examine some very old material involving a possible murder—a killing, indeed an assassination, that was perpetrated some thirty-three hundred years ago."

Greg, forever the cop, smiled and said, "Of course I'm interested. Go on."

"In a nutshell," Anna continued, "the discovery of King Tutankhamen's tomb by our British archaeologist Howard Carter in 1922 caused an immediate sensation throughout the world. Tut's burial chamber was unlike any that had been discovered previously. The entire crypt with its hundreds of gold, silver, and ivory treasures was virtually intact, including the boy-king's funerary mask. Astonishingly, most graverobbers couldn't locate and loot undoubtedly the richest of all Egyptian burial sites up to that date."

Continuing, Anna asked, "Why did Tut, who had the best medical care in the world's most civilized kingdom, and who was served the best, most healthy fruits, vegetables, grains, fish, and meats, die so suddenly, so mysteriously at barely the age of eighteen? With what I heard today, and with your obvious experience as a former FBI profiler, trained by the best of all possible investigative staffs at the bureau's legendary Behavioral Science Unit, I'm sure you and this Mike King you mentioned can apply modern forensic science to answer most of our questions—or come closer than anyone else has in penetrating the riddle. Will you two gentlemen try?"

Greg responded, "Well, I'm flying back to Utah tomorrow morning. I'll discuss it with Mike, although I'm confident he would agree, as I certainly do. As I mentioned in my presentation, Lieutenant King is the director of the Utah criminal tracking and analysis project. We can fly back here, or you can come over to Salt Lake City and Provo."

After a moment's hesitation, Greg added, "I'm almost certain we can shed new light on this investigation into King Tut's death and determine whether his death was an accident, a natural event, suicide, or even murder. In fact, if it was indeed murder, I think we can evaluate the personalities of the victim, Tut, and those around him and provide a probable suspect in this case."

Anna concluded the brief discussion by saying that someone from Atlantic Productions would be calling him after he returned to Utah in order to set a date and make arrangements for the arrival of a two-person team. Leaving the hotel a few minutes later and hopping into a cab back to his hotel, Greg was dubious he would ever hear from Anna again. Nonetheless, the concept of two detectives using modern-day forensics to solve a thirty-three-hundred-year-old death was very enticing and intriguing.

Less than a month later, while at work in his Provo office, Greg was pleasantly surprised to receive a long-distance telephone call from Anna. After chatting a few moments, she said that her associate and supervisor Kate Botting, an executive producer, and Lance Kneeshaw, the director of the production company, would visit the two within the next thirty days. Greg put a call through to Mike, who was at work in his office in Salt Lake City.

Upon hearing the news that an associate producer and a director from London were flying to Utah to interview the two, Mike was less than thrilled. In fact, he questioned Greg about the reality of such a visit, suggesting that nothing would come of it. Mike had served as chief of staff to the recently retiring attorney general of Utah and was now a lieutenant in the office working white-collar crime cases. Months earlier, a new attorney general had been elected. Mike served as the campaign chairman for the defeated candidate and was now under the careful scrutiny of an administrative assistant who came to the office with only two years of law enforcement experience and the charge to supervise a team of seasoned investigators, most with twenty or more years of experience in the police profession. Mike felt that anything he was doing was being closely evaluated by the new leadership and knew that the higher-ups would not be supportive of a high-profile exposure, even on television. The inherent publicity surrounding such a program would be discomforting at best, and Mike feared his very survival in the office could be seriously threatened.

* * *

In early March of 2001, the two of us met Kate and Lance in the lobby of the Holiday Inn in south Salt Lake City around 9:00 A.M. Unfortunately, Greg was walking on crutches, suffering from gout. But he was determined not to miss this pivotal meeting. When Mike entered the lobby, he looked around at the various people, wondering to himself what an English film producer or director looked like. As he scanned the lobby, studying face after face, he thought that their "profiles" might well be the most difficult of all to conceive. He figured he needed to look for a man and a woman, since he knew they would be traveling together. That allowed him to start excluding individuals. He wondered what clothing they might be wearing and thought they would be dressed casually rather than in business attire. Mike wondered if they would have writing tablets or large briefcases, even suitcases, with them. More importantly, he surmised that they, too, would be scanning the crowd looking for his unfamiliar face. Finally, he wondered if they had crooked teeth similar to the many Englishmen he had watched on television or met in his life.

As he looked around the hotel lobby, a beautiful, dark-haired woman walked into view. She had in her company a good-looking, uptown sort of guy. Mike's confidence soared as he approached the woman and asked, "Are you Kate?"

"Yes." She smiled. "You must be Greg."

"No, I'm Mike King, Greg's partner. It's so nice to meet you. This is Greg."

After a few moments of chitchat, we realized that Botting and Kneeshaw were all business. Completing our pleasantries, the four of us left the hotel en route to the Utah medical examiner's office, where in a conference room we discussed the project, conceiving the best approach to analyze and decipher the mystery. After discussing the different approaches and possible scenarios, Kate asked in no uncertain terms whether we were up to employing current investigative techniques to solve the possible murder of the young king. No sooner had the question left her lips when we responded simultaneously, "YES! We can approach this case just as we do all suspicious deaths." We explained that we would look systematically at the victimology of who Tut really was. Of course, we would need to know more about the political, religious, financial, and emotional status of the people of Egypt at that time. "Above all," Mike said, "it can be done, and we'll do it. This case will be one of the most exciting we've ever worked on. What greater historic adventure can there be?"

As the one-hour appointment turned into three, then four, and five hours, our skepticism dissipated, and with specialized equipment we began the task of sorting through the wealth of books, scholarly papers, photographs, and x-rays, to say nothing of hundreds of pages of interviews with various contemporary experts that Kate and Lance brought with them. Neither of us had ever gazed upon the x-rays of a 3,325-year-old mummy and its skull, let alone that of a famous Egyptian pharaoh.

Both of us were growing increasingly fascinated, indeed intoxicated, as we read each line of the various old autopsy reports. The very thought of working together on such an ancient death was the ultimate challenge to the art and science of criminal profiling that we had worked so hard to bring to law enforcement in Utah and the rest of the United States. The chance to apply the investigative principles and protocols we had designed, utilized, and redesigned was more than we could dream. As Kate and Lance almost forcefully pulled the x-rays, photographs, reports, and documents from our hands at the conclusion of the virtually day-long meeting, we wondered if we would ever see the real crime scene in Egypt. We wanted this job so badly we could almost taste the stale air of Tut's tomb.

Sensing our elation, the two executives asked if we would be interested in appearing in cameo roles of their hour-long documentary. We would be filmed in Egypt, discussing with the audience, the company's staff, and between ourselves the current investigative techniques used to solve the old mystery. Of course, we jumped at the opportunity. After all, it meant flying to and traveling in Egypt to look at the area ourselves! Back in the car, as Greg drove Mike to his office, Mike sighed. "Too bad. Nothing will come of this. It's slim, real slim."

Greg shook his head. "I don't know, Mike. They have put a lot of initial investment into this. They seemed really excited! You never know!"

In mid-May, less than two months after the meeting in Salt Lake City, Kate Botting telephoned Greg to inform him that the staff had completely rewritten the story line for the documentary based upon our meeting. The company's writers were now going to base the entire account on our future investigation *in* Egypt! We were informed for the first time that the Discovery Channel, known for its emphasis on programs dealing with health, travel, animals, and the planets, would host the show. Unbeknownst to us, Kate and Lance had considered more than fifty other homicide investigators from around the world, especially Britain and the United States, before selecting thirty to actually interview. From these, five men and five women detectives were chosen. The selection committee narrowed the choice down to the two of us. We learned this tidbit while having dinner together following our first day of filming in Salt Lake City.

Needless to say, we were jubilant. Atlantic Productions was immediately advised that for the two of us to feel comfortable and confident in launching an investigation of the magnitude the sponsors projected, we would need an understanding as to the following:

1. An agreement that we would engage in a death analysis and not a murder investigation;
2. Since police officers ask questions across many different disciplines in order to fully reveal the truth, we would need to take a multidiscipline investigative approach;
3. And, most important of all, we would need to work hand-in-glove with the world's leading experts in the field, since our knowledge of Egypt and Egyptology, King Tutankhamen and mummification, was nonexistent.

Atlantic Productions and the Discovery Channel agreed immediately, promising that we would be given all the assistance we needed. As a first step, Joann Fletcher, one of the world's most prominent Egyptologists, was made available. She would serve as our "living-day witness" of what the political, religious, financial, and geographical life of Egypt was like more than thirty-three hundred years ago. The cohost companies, to our joy, suggested we actually journey step by step everywhere Tut went, including the temples he lived in, the gardens he walked through—the areas and sites where he traveled. To stray off the beaten track and explore the countryside where Tut vacationed, hunted, and was trained by General Horemheb and his lieutenants meant everything to us in our investigation. To see everything as the boy-king saw it was the frosting on the cake. This meant having access to boats to float across the Nile. It meant hot-air balloons to fly along the Valley of the Kings and around the western branch of the valley, known as the Valley of the Monkeys. It meant driving through the desert, the hot, hilly badlands, in jeeps and trucks. It meant access to autos, buses, camels, trains, and small-engine airplanes. But above all, it meant walking in Tut's footsteps.

All this zigzagging and bouncing around meant that the Discovery Channel and Atlantic Productions would have to clear innumerable obstacles with the Egyptian authorities. As Americans, shortly after the cowardly and reprehensible attack on the twin towers of the World Trade Center, the Pentagon, and the downed passenger jet in Pennsylvania, we would be traveling through certain territory still occupied by hostile groups of the Egyptian jihad who were even then training for terrorist activities throughout the world.

As the Discovery Channel and Atlantic Productions worked to meet our needs, an avalanche of material on Tut descended upon our offices. Almost daily, volumes of recent articles, unpublished papers, old books, and government reports arrived. Mike sat on his Schwinn Airdyne night after night, digesting the detailed autopsy reports, analyzing every piece of literature pertaining to Tut, all the pharaohs, and their political and religious times. After riding his bike, he would climb into his hot tub and spend an additional hour reading and perusing the materials that were delivered that day. By day, Greg continued his position as chief of police for Provo. By night, he devoured all of the information he could digest. We found ourselves e-mailing Egyptologists from around the world, searching Internet sites for more authorities, and watching every documentary on ancient Egypt ever filmed—all in preparation for a land and people, and their ancestors, we would soon be visiting. The two of us, each in our own way, found ourselves waking up night after night wondering about Tut, a kid who a few months earlier meant absolutely nothing to us. Each of us reflected how ironic it was that two homicide detectives who cared so little about ancient Egyptian history were now consumed with it. But this is consistent with all such notorious investigations. Expect it when you least expect it. And you had better be prepared!

All of this preparation led us to "know" Tutankhamen and his inner circle. Many of the challenges we faced could be likened to the challenges faced by many nations today. More importantly, though, as we determined on paper the various possibilities of why the young man died when he did, we realized there was a strange similarity between what may have motivated someone to assassinate the pharaoh at that time, and its equivalent in, say, organized crime today: political assassination, power, greed, control, and dominance.

Then, as we became more and more immersed in Tut's teenage personality, as well as the character of each of the significant men and women around him, we felt the drama of intrigue, murder, and revenge unfold. We sensed the emotions the young pharaoh must have felt as he witnessed his father, Akhenaten, Tut's hero, tutor, and mentor, unexpectedly die. If the information we read regarding the assassination attempts on his father were true, it was possible that Tut also died at the hands of assassins. Not only possible but very plausible. If so, Tut, then, was undoubtedly a scared and intimidated child, his uncertainty increasing when he watched Smenkhkare succeed to Akhenaten's throne, only to live and rule a very short time. While some Egyptologists believe that Smenkhkare was Tut's oldest brother, others are not so sure and identify Smenkhkare as the throne name of Tut's stepmother, Nefertiti. Whatever their identity, the records show that he or she also ruled for a very brief time and then seems to evaporate in the air of ancient history.

Our readings informed us that soon after Smenkhkare's death, Tutankhamen became the pharaoh of the most powerful country in the ancient world. But the nine-year-old boy, we reasoned, was surely incapable of controlling a kingdom and was probably dependent on Ay, Akhenaten's vizier, or prime minister. Obviously, as a young boy, Tut would be easily moldable by the prime minister. According to Dr. Fletcher, Tut's father, Akhenaten, instituted Aten as the form of worship, stripping the Amun priests of their power and authority. Tut, under Ay's guidance, returned the form of worship back to Amun. By doing this, Ay may have convinced Tut that he would quickly earn the hearts and souls of the common people, since they felt more comfortable in returning to worship the traditional Amun. In addition, the prime minister probably persuaded Tut to return the seat of power to Thebes, the current-day Luxor. We felt that after becoming thoroughly knowledgeable of early Egyptian religious holidays and ceremonies, the resettlement staged during the Opet Festival was Ay's greatest achievement since returning the pharaoh and his power base back to Thebes. More importantly for Ay, he personally returned power in the people's eyes to Amun. This strategic ploy conveniently allowed the prime minister to resume the powerful position of high priest over all of the professional priesthood who had once been in power before Akhenaten's rejection of the former polytheistic religion. We reasoned that as Tut ordered the incredible reshifting, he must have felt hypocritical, since he betrayed not only his father in death but also his government and religious beliefs.

Our preliminary readings told us that Ankhesenamun, although only three years older than Tut, appears to have been the more mature of the two. Apparently, the two were married when Tutankhamen was either eleven or twelve years old. Ankhesenamun was the daughter of the exceedingly beautiful Nefertiti, and if the famed Nefertiti was as powerful as most Egyptologists, including Joann Fletcher, believe, she surely would have passed much of her ego, strength, and self-confidence on to her daughter. Imagine the future expectations and promise anticipated by the Egyptian empire when Tut and Ankhesenamun were united. Both had been sired by Akhenaten, a pharaoh, descendant of a long and pure pharaonic bloodline. Enabled with such unblemished genetics and sired by earthly gods, the two showed great promise for an unprecedented empire.

Our initial conclusion about Maya, Tut's treasurer, was that he appears to have been little more than a traditional government bureaucrat who, like many today, punched a clock and did what was assigned. We were certain he was relatively wealthy due to his unique position and the rampant corruption that seemed to go with serving royalty. In fact, his tomb suggests he was arrogant, even a bit pompous—character flaws of someone important and in control of the kingdom's purse strings. Maya served Akhenaten, Tut, and Ay as well. As we explored tomb after tomb, one of the experts we listened to explained that over Maya's tomb was an inscription that read, "In the beginning I was good, in the end I was great." That was an interesting expression of himself, and since the tombs were only meant for the gods, we wondered whom he was trying to impress.

Meanwhile, we learned that Horemheb, the commander of Tut's armies, was a superpatriot who invested all his might in being a good soldier. Initially, we concluded that as head of the army under Akhenaten he was too young to be involved in his death, if indeed Akhenaten was murdered. Interestingly for us, Horemheb may have been away on a military expedition at the time of Tut's demise. Nonetheless, this great general became our very first suspect because history shows that on many occasions the commander of the armies

A wall painting in Tutankhamen's tomb that depicts Ay (*far right*) performing the Opening of the Mouth ceremony on the young king (copyright: Griffith Institute, Oxford).

has the means to overthrow a king and take over his kingdom. The soldier's soldiers were very dedicated and would generally pledge death over forsaking their commander-in-chief. Horemheb, who would eventually become a pharaoh, seemed the most likely candidate as an assassin, if indeed Tut was the victim of a homicide.

Ay, Tutankhamen's vizier, was initially a secondary suspect. This man had been prime minister to both father and son and was nearby at the time of each of their deaths. In fact, after Tut's death, Ay promoted himself to the position of pharaoh before Horemheb could return from his military campaign. Ay was the chief high priest of the Amun priests at the time of their removal from power by Akhenaten. Our readings convinced us that he was a chameleon who played both sides against the middle as he ordered the Amun priesthood to "lay low" and be patient while he orchestrated their return. Whether this included murder, we weren't sure. But we think he may well have convinced Akhenaten that he was the only one who could prevent the Amun priests from disrupting the transfer of government to Amarna in order to change to Akhenaten's Aten worship.

Every mysterious death demands to be resolved. Each case begs the questions, Who is responsible? What happened? Why and how did it happen? What was the motivation? Was this a homicide, a suicide, an accident, or natural causes? These are common questions sparked by our curiosity and drive to understand the unknown and complete the puzzle. We are compelled to connect the dots and watch the picture emerge before identifying the dots. Unfortunately, we have a gnawing need to know *now*. Human nature does not like to delay gratification, and the urge to complete the puzzle can sometimes prompt us to leap prematurely, forcing a square peg into a round hole. We cannot allow ourselves the convenience of shortcuts in such critical matters of life and death.

Recognizing this temptation is the first step to avoiding it and preventing its potential pitfalls. While the foregoing questions are certainly relevant to unraveling the mystery web, they can also divert our energies from an initial course of investigation that may lead us more effectively and expediently to our desired destination—the solution. The primary question to lead us toward that end is "Who is the victim?" The other questions are considered secondary and complementary to the first. By answering this question, we begin to understand in detail who the victim was. We are now prepared to conduct what we call a "victimology," or a study of the victim.

It is important to presume initially that there are no precise answers to the secondary queries. First, they serve us, the investigators, as tools to explore the territory while gathering as much data as possible, which ultimately will lead us to facts and conclusions. This is similar to the physician who employs surgical instruments to conduct exploratory surgery to accurately interpret the patient's symptoms. Before we can isolate the facts, we must approach the mystery with an open and impartial mind. The primary objective is to gather all available data while allowing our minds to accept all the possibilities. Thereafter the investigation proceeds to probabilities. Once the data become factually based, then and only then are we prepared to formulate theories and answers that are consistent, reasonable, and conclusive. The comprehensive response to "Who *was* the victim?" immediately accelerates the investigation. The more information we know about the victim, the more we learn about the offender and the offender's motivation. The victimology also reveals the probabilities of the type of relationship that may have existed between the victim and the offender. The initial purpose of the victimology is to determine the risk level of the victim and the associated probabilities if the victim and offender were strangers to each other or if they knew each other. If they did know each other, what was the nature of the relationship? The victimology also crystalizes the lifestyle of the victim and his or her potential risk of falling prey to certain types of crimes, and it then forms a probable suspect pool.

It is possible that anyone could have been responsible for Tut's untimely death. However, as we evaluate his lifestyle in light of the risk continuum and his environment, situation, and circumstances surrounding the events of his death, general possibilities are eliminated and probabilities emerge, formulating reasonable and sound theories of his likely demise. We concluded that Tut had a low-risk lifestyle, considering the protected and secure environment that he lived in and his exposure to the most prestigious and highly qualified medical services available. All his activities were closely monitored, his food delicately prepared, and the company he kept surely restricted to his closest friends, associates, and family members. Not just anyone would have had access to him—only those whom he, his servants, and his guardians trusted. This leaves us with the conclusion that if Tut were murdered, it was most probable that the likely offender was someone who had immediate and liberal access to him. It would have been someone whom he trusted generally, who was in favor with Tut, and who had typically been in a close circle of elites with whom Tut socialized, lived, and recreated. Given the other scenarios—death by accident, natural causes, or suicide—in the context of the totality of issues we have presented, these theories appear highly unlikely.

As we neared our departure date for Cairo and completed our endless readings, paper evaluations, and preliminary discussions, we gradually narrowed our suspects from the whole Eighteenth Dynasty population to the teenager's inner circle—Ankhesenamun, Maya, Horemheb, and Ay. Now we had to visit the actual crime and burial scenes. Being on site would enhance our abilities to apply the principles of criminal investigative analysis. Sleuthing and searching on Egyptian soil were next on our agenda.

Chapter 3

EGYPT
WHERE OLD PARADOXES
AND NEW PERSONALITIES MEET

*How many illustrious travelers in all ages have sat and gazed upon
the scenes around! And how endless are the speculations in which they
have indulged! . . .*

*It is a perfect wilderness of ruin, almost outrunning the wildest
imagination or the most fantastic dream.*

In Bartlett's "Nile Boat," anonymous poem,
republished in the article "Scenes in Egypt,"
Harper's New Monthly Magazine (June 1850)

D uring our cab drive to the Salt Lake City International Airport that early misty morning in mid-November of 2001, we
barely spoke to each other. Then, approaching the Delta Airlines
check-in with our visas in hand, we looked at each other, and it hit
us—WE WERE REALLY FLYING TO EGYPT!

Soon we were on board Delta Flight 192 to Boston and then,
after flying all day and through the night, we found ourselves

landing smoothly at London's Gatwick Airport. A short shuttle ride connected us to Heathrow, where we were to meet the film crew that would accompany us to Cairo. Although we were exhausted, we enjoyed the early morning ride through the damp English country-side. As we entered Heathrow Airport and made our way to the Egypt Air check-in, we were greeted by the beautiful, eternally enthusiastic Kate Botting, who, after hugging each of us, grabbed us by the arm and led us to the waiting film crew.

The first person we were introduced to was cameraman Jonathan Partridge. Jonathan is a handsome, tall, blonde man. Wearing shorts, and with a carefully guarded smile, he was polite, yet reserved and quiet. Later, we learned about his childhood growing up in South Africa and the many documentary film journeys he had been on during his career. He was always fascinating to listen to late in the evenings.

We were then introduced to Adrian O'Toole, a textbook version, in our opinion, of an English chimney sweep. Affectionately known as "Ado," Adrian was the camera assistant. This young fellow not only covered the fierce fighting in Bosnia but also had witnessed the disruptions of eastern bloc nations and much of the world's ugliness. Talented and cagey at the same time, he saved us from serious trouble with the Egyptian authorities when we videotaped tombs that were off-limits.

Next in line was Simon Farmer, our sound recordist. Simon reminded us of the Beatles in their first appearance on *The Ed Sullivan Show* in 1964 (although we think he is actually from London)—always funny, engaging, and a pleasure to be around.

As we chatted with the film crew, we suddenly heard an incredibly loud and vivacious voice from behind us call out to Kate. We turned to see a young woman with beautiful red hair, a star-shaped jewel in her nose, and solid black clothing from head to foot approach and throw her arms around everyone she saw, including the two guys from Utah!

This, of course, was the fabulous Dr. Joann Fletcher, one of the most amazing women either of us had ever encountered. Dr. Jo, as we called her, was to become one of our closest and dearest friends.

The Atlantic Productions film crew poses outside of Tut's tomb (photo by Mike King).

This fine young woman taught us Egyptian history from her heart and soul. A true scholar, she truly loved everything Egyptian, including the food and drink. We instinctively knew we were blessed and in the best possible of all academic hands.

Within a few hours, and as tired as we were, we found ourselves once again onboard a flight. But this time everything seemed much different. As Egypt Air Flight MS778 left English airspace and flew into Africa's, we looked around and realized that we were the only Americans aboard. We commented that we now understood how a black man must have felt walking into an all-white park in the Deep South during the 1940s and 1950s. Although we appreciated those sitting around us, we felt an uneasiness for the first time. As we looked up into the face of a pretty Egyptian flight attendant as she poured us each a "Lite Coke," we suddenly realized we were not only on the greatest adventure of our lives but possibly the most dangerous.

At 8:45 P.M. on Sunday, November 18, as our jet made its final approach to Cairo's international airport, we looked out our windows to catch our first glimpse of the great pyramids. What a stunning sight! Although the sun had descended and it was dark, huge lights lit the wondrous pyramids in all their glory. Then, a few moments later, the lights of Cairo, a city of more than twenty-two million people, came into view. The great city unfolded like a rolled-up sparkling jeweled carpet for mile upon mile. Soon, the plane touched down safely. We had arrived.

As we exited the plane, Mr. Rashidy, our so-called fixer, greeted us. He quickly shook hands with us, exchanged a few words, asked for our visas, and ordered us to walk immediately behind him as he led us to ten armed guards waiting inside the terminal. Although it had been a day and a half since we left Salt Lake City, and we were most anxious to take a shower and go to bed, we had to endure another two hours clearing customs. Although still early in the evening, the airport was virtually vacant. The empty hallways echoed with our small talk as we patiently answered questions and allowed the authorities to search our suitcases. Then, after clearing customs, we were met by yet another contingent of soldiers and police officers, virtually all of whom were armed with submachine guns. They escorted us to a large bus outside the entrance of the terminal, boarded us with our suitcases, then followed behind as our bus speedily drove through the city to the Gezierah Sheraton Hotel at Tahrir Square in Giza Cairo. Our hotel, overlooking the Nile, was truly beautiful. Although more eager than ever to get some sleep, we joined the film crew in the hotel's restaurant for a very late dinner and the taking of photographs. We supposed we weren't that exhausted after all.

Early the next morning we had breakfast, checked out of the Gezierah Sheraton, and headed for the incredible Saqqara necropolis. With us in the minibus were the crew and a number of armed police. As the bus maneuvered through the streets of Cairo, we were amazed at the way the people lived. The buildings reminded us of those in war-torn Israel and Palestine. What looked "bombed out" was really quite normal. Homes were built with the intention that one day additional floors would be added onto them. We were surprised by the large number of oxen, donkeys, and cattle strolling along the streets and thoroughfares amid varying types of vehicles speeding past and narrowly missing them and their owners. We marveled at city folks pounding small sticks together to make cages for chickens and ducks. We saw women cooking food over open fires in the street, their fuel consisting of little more than weeds, stalks, and small twigs. Seeing them cleaning dishes and scrubbing their clothes in the Nile, less than a few feet from the roadway, was equally touching. We thoroughly enjoyed the colorful clothing everyone wore. And we especially appreciated the wonderful smiles of the children as they swarmed around the bus whenever we stopped. All in all, we felt we were among a relatively healthy, happy people.

SATISFYING OUR ITCH FOR HISTORY

That evening, after a somewhat tiring day touring the Step Pyramid at Saqqara, which is over forty-five hundred years old, we invited Dr. Jo to share a delicious dinner with us. All that morning and afternoon, she had led us and the film crew through the necropolis, lecturing as she walked, never tiring, rarely showing impatience at any of our endless questions. It was obvious the crew adored her. We walked and walked, and she talked and talked. Needless to say, we learned and learned in a way that neither of us had ever experienced before. All of us were allowed to see things that most people, including serious Egyptologists, are not privy to. We rode camels across a nobleman's burial ground and saw skeletal remains, including full skulls, on the surface of the sand.

And as we left the hotel's restaurant and were about to retire to our separate rooms for much-needed rest, Joann startled us by suggesting that we continue the "history lesson" in the hotel lobby. The two cops from Utah reluctantly agreed and ordered bottled water, in keeping with their Mormon belief to abstain from alcohol. As tired as she, too, must have been, Joann still wanted to teach, and we still yearned for more information. "You two sit back and relax while I provide you with a capsule chronology, a few pertinent points, about the ancient past of this great land and its people." Of course, we couldn't resist. And what a marvelous history lesson that woman gave us until the wee hours of the morning.

Dr. Jo began her spontaneous lecture, telling us how Maneho, a third-century Egyptian historian, had compartmentalized the pharaonic period into specific blocks, which came to be recognized as dynasties. A period extending roughly from 3100 to 332 BCE, these sections of history were grouped according to families or their places of general residence.

Further sources used to understand Egyptian chronology include the Palermo Stone, now in Sicily, which lists kings dating right back to the predynastic period. Then there's the evidence from various Kings Lists, including the one at Abydos and others in the British Museum, the Louvre, and in Cairo. Together with art, inscriptions, and astronomical data, these dates can then be correlated.

The Egyptian system of dating their history at "Year 1" with the beginning of each King's reign wasn't unique, since many ancient cultures saw each new ruler as marking a new beginning. The veneration expressed toward each new king, together with the use of Kings Lists, emphasized two important aspects in the Egyptian worldview, namely, the esteem expressed toward the past and the notion of renewal as each pharaoh relived the creation myth.

In Egypt's early history, many of the gods were believed to originate from the position of the stars and were used to form a calendar. The goddess Sopdet (also known as Sothis) represented the Dog Star and was portrayed as a woman with a star on her head. The rising of the Dog Star was always regarded as the beginning of the Egyptian year. Sopdet had a fundamental function in Egyptian mythology, and the Sothic rising took place at the beginning of each solar year, once every 1,460 years. Because we know of two different risings, these help us date ancient Egypt's history, and in turn this has helped create a dating system for much of the Mediterranean, too.

If we fast-forward to the end of the Seventh Dynasty, we have the unification of Upper and Lower Egypt, south and north, under King Ahmose, when the foreign Hyskos rulers were chased out of Egypt and the campaigns against the Nubians were extended. Ahmose was then succeeded by his son Amenhotep I, who coruled with his powerful mother, Ahmose-Nefertari, and both were regarded by most of the Eighteenth Dynasty, and indeed much of the nineteenth, as originators of a royal line, gods in their own right worshiped far and wide.

Yet the main god was Amun, who became the state god during the Eighteenth Dynasty, only to be briefly rejected by Akhenaten and reinstated by his successors.

With Amenhotep I and Ahmose-Nefertari, the Karnak cult center of Amun at Thebes on the eastern bank of the Nile River was embellished, and as we know from our own excavations in the Valley of the Kings at Royal Tomb KV.39, we get the resumption of elaborate building projects on the western bank of the Nile, the traditional land of the dead.

Although kings usually had children by secondary wives, there was also official marriage within the royal family for reasons of policy, with kings marrying their sisters and sometimes their daughters. Many of these princesses became highly influential figures, including Ahhotep, Ahmose-Nefertari, and, of course, Hatshepsut, who was a king's daughter, king's sister, king's wife, and eventually became Egypt's best-known female pharaoh.

Amenhotep I was succeeded by Tuthmose I, whose frequent military campaigns expanded Egypt's empire abroad. His son and daughter, Tuthmose II and Hatshepsut, were married to each other and after Tuthmose II's death, she became regent for her underage stepson Tuthmose III. She then took power herself, adopting male pharaonic titles and regalia, and after a reign of about fifteen years was succeeded by the adult Tuthmose III. Known as the "Napoleon of Ancient Egypt," his long reign greatly increased Egypt's wealth through successful campaigns to North Levant, Palestine, Lebanon, and parts of Syria. The country continued to flourish under his athletic son Amenhotep II, who continued his father's campaigning to bring peace and an improved economy, much of which went straight into the coffers of Amun's priests.

By the reign of his son Tuthmose IV, the priests of Amun had grown so powerful the new king decided to balance their influence by supporting the priests of the sun god, Ra, a political move suggested by Tuthmose's inscription on a large stela set up before the paws of the Giza Sphinx, which by then had come to be known as the very embodiment of the sun god himself:

Now the statue of the very great Khepri [the Great Sphinx] rested in this place, great of fame, sacred of respect, the shade of Ra resting on him. Memphis and every city on its two sides came to him, their arms in adoration to his face, bearing great offerings for his Ka. One of these days it happened that Prince Thutmose came traveling at the time of midday. He rested in the shadow of this great God. [Sleep and] dream [took possession of him] at the moment the sun was at zenith. Then he found the majesty of this noble God speaking from his own mouth like a father speaks to his son, and saying, "Look at me, observe me, my son Thutmose. I am your father Horemakhet-Khepri-Ra-Atum. I shall give you the kingship [upon the land before the living] . . . [behold my condition is like one in illness], all [my limbs being ruined]. The sand of the desert, upon which I used to be, [now] confronts me; and it is in order to cause that you do what is in my heart that I have waited.[1]

And it is from this period that a growing interest in the sun god is cultivated, something Tuthmose IV's son Amenhotep III and his son Amenhotep IV, later known as Akhenaten, convert into full-fledged Aten worship.

A truce having been made with the Mitannians of Syria, Egypt enjoyed a long period of peace and was the most powerful country in the ancient world. Its wealth, once used for military expeditions, was diverted to construction projects, with Amenhotep III dedicating several of his temples to the sun god before eventually declaring himself "The Living Sun God" in his thirtieth year. Although some Egyptologists also believe he made his son Akhenaten co-regent, there is no evidence for this.

Akhenaten's seventeen-year reign, now known as "the Amarna period," was one of the most important in the religious and cultural history of Egypt. Its far-reaching effects continued right into the next dynasty, and the backlash would shape the religious and cultural life of Egypt for decades to come.

The death of Tutankhamen coincided with a large battle being fought against the Hittites. The Hittites lived primarily in what is known today as Turkey and northern Syria. They fought with the Egyptians from time to time. (When we consider later the letter believed to be penned by Ankhesenamun to the Hittite king shortly after Tut's death, when Ankhesenamun asks the king for one of his sons to marry, we recognize the great risk and pressure that she was under.)[2] The Egyptians lost, at Amqa, near Quadesh. It's unclear whether Horemheb was involved in this battle. But if he were, then he may not have been present at the burial of the young king. This is quite unusual, since as military leader he was the most powerful man in Egypt. Instead, it was Ay who arranged the funeral and soon after took the crown. Fragments of a cuneiform letter have been found that suggest that some sort of peace treaty was attempted with the Hittites. The fact that Nakhtim (perhaps a son or grandson of Ay's) was appointed as commander-in-chief suggests that Ay was trying to prevent Horemheb's succession to the throne. Whatever the truth, at some later date the name of Nakhtim was hacked out of inscriptions, probably when Horemheb did finally ascend to pharaoh.

The Amarna period had brought changes to the whole notion of kingship. The Amun priesthood was given increased powers, and despite the fact that the pharaohs of the Nineteenth Dynasty brought prosperity to the country, they were not regarded as divine as they had once been.

For many, Akhenaten had destroyed society. He had denied his people access to their gods; only he and his family had direct access to the divine, and all prayers had to go through them; all routes to the Aten became exclusive.

The tensions between the one and the many gods were resolved in later dynasties by the belief that all gods represented the many manifestations of general divinity. Although kings such as Ay, Seti I, and Ramses II were still part of the traditional kingship mythology, they were now perceived as human, and indeed those of their dynasty, the nineteenth, were commoners by birth. Rather than gods acting through the king, each individual had direct access to their gods. And with the help of the priests of Amun, god had become the king on earth, and much of the power of the real king had been transferred to the god's priests.

Joann concluded her brief history lesson by saying, "Saved for tomorrow are my thoughts on Tut and his tomb—a tomb which really is a magnificent triumph over time. And to help me do that, I'm going to introduce you to one of my favorite people, Howard Carter."

NOTES

1. "Dream Stele" [online], www.touregypt.net/featurestories/tuthmo sis4.htm.

2. Troy Fox, "Who Were the Hittites?" [online], www.touregypt.net/ featurestories/hittites.htm [December 5, 2003].

Chapter 4
TUTANKHAMEN'S TOMB
TRIUMPHS OVER TIME

Grim King of Silence!
Monarch of the Dust!
Embalm'd-anointed-jewell'd-scepter'd-crowned,
Here did He lie in State, cold, stiff and stark,
A leathern Pharaoh, grinning in the dark.

In "Knotsford," Malvern in 1825

Since neither of us knew anything about the rich history or culture of ancient Egypt, and we were therefore in search of simple yet intriguing and authoritative essays on the major pharaohs and their rule, the dynasties, personalities, the commoners, as well as their working and private lives, there was no greater preliminary source than back issues of the *National Geographic* magazine. Where renowned Egyptologists and serious scholars thumb their noses at the popular publication, we pored over and relished every issue we could get our hands on that had anything to do with Egypt—precisely because each article with its numerous black and white, as well as color, photographs, maps, charts, and illustrations were prepared, captioned, and written by renowned Egyptologists and serious scholars of their day. And in nontechnical terms and language we could understand!

Take, for example, an article titled "Daily Life in Ancient Egypt," which appeared in the October 1941 issue, offering laymen like ourselves thirty-two paintings by artist H. M. Herget that illustrated the life, culture, and history of the Egyptians. Thanks to author William C. Hayes, the head of the Department of Egyptian Art at the Metropolitan Museum of Art in New York, we learned that Tutankhamen's name meant "the living image of God, Amen" and was originally written in the scrolls and on wall paintings as Tut-Ánkh-Amūn. Hayes's notes on a few of the symbols and diacritical marks include:

‘ (example Rē‘), a guttural sound unknown in the English language, but corresponding to the Hebrew ‘ayin and the Arabic ‘ain; h (example hotep), an emphatic h corresponding to the Arabic hā; k (example Sakkāreh), a "backward" k rather like our q in "queen" corresponding to the Hebrew gōph and Arabic kāf, hence the map spelling Saqqara; and t (example mastabeh), a thick t, halfway between a sharp t and th spoken with the tongue pressed against the back of the front teeth. Pharaoh, on the other hand, is simple to deal with. We correctly pronounce pharaoh, the title for an ancient Egyptian king, as far'ō, fer'ō, or fā 'rō´. The noun is derived from the ancient phrase per aa which means "great house" and was originally a reference to the royal palace.

In perusing the old *National Geographics*, it was more than the pronunciation that touched us. It was how each of the magazine's articles created a milieu of old Egypt, a colorful appreciation of its social and cultural settings, its beautiful art and architecture, its great pyramids, the riddle of its priceless Sphinx, the thrill of archaeological finds, and the riches of Tut's tomb. Historians like Hayes sensitized us to how the discovery of the boy-king's burial chamber was a unique and authentic chapter in Egyptian history, unaltered and undefiled. In contrast, for the tourist, it meant another place to go and gaze upon. For the hotel and shopkeepers, it meant extra income from the tourists. For the archaeologist, it meant the reward of a life's work, a dream fulfilled. For us, of course, a chance to solve a mysterious death.

* * *

Virtually any kind of historical discovery offers a fable for fascination and imagination. So try then to imagine what it must have been like at midday on November 4, 1922, in the Valley of the Tombs of the Kings at Thebes when one of Carter's workmen brushed away some loose sandy rubble to expose the uppermost of a flight of cut-rock steps leading down into the intact and unbelievably wealthy tomb of Tutankhamen. Eight years would be needed to inspect, catalog, and clear the small tomb of its crowded, wonderful contents. And during that time as many as three hundred to five hundred people, mostly Europeans and Americans, waited patiently in line in the broiling heat for the privilege of seeing the things brought out of the tomb. Again, it was Hayes who reminded us how millions of cubic yards of sand had been moved and sifted in searching for such a fabulously rich tomb—how thousands of Egypt's native population had worked their lifetimes in its multitude of "digs," and hundreds of ships had sailed from its ports and harbors crammed with antiquities for the museums and private collections of the world.

To this day, the discovery of Tutankhamen's tomb exerts a powerful hold on us. But it's not necessarily the shiny gold and sparkling jewels that fascinate. It's how the boy-pharaoh transcended, almost triumphed, over time. Our vivid imaginations crave even more after these three-plus millennia. Tut, really a nobody who survived unmolested in the black silence of a fifth-rate tomb, has become as near immortal as any being in human history. Today, photographs of his face and corpse, as well as x-rays of his head and bones, are viewed by millions on the Internet, in scholarly journals, television specials, and popular magazines. He remains imperishable.

Since all of us have a bit of Ali Baba of the *Arabian Nights* in us, relishing to join in the search of caves and crypts crammed with treasures, let's hop aboard a magical flying carpet waiting to waft us back eighty-plus years to accompany and observe Howard Carter on that warm, sunny Tuesday morning, November 4, 1922, as he watches workmen remove rubble from the sixteen steps leading to the entrance, then descend into the excavation and unseal the several doorways to King Tutankhamen's treasure-laden tomb.

Howard Carter, born on May 9, 1873, in Norfolk, England, had already established for himself an outstanding reputation prior to November of 1922. At the age of seventeen, he accompanied British Egyptologists to Egypt as a draftsman for an archaeological survey conducted by the Egypt Exploration Fund (later "Society"). After considerable experience in the field, he was appointed in 1899 the inspector general of the antiquities department of the Egyptian government. Between 1902 and 1903, he discovered and excavated a number of tombs in the Valley of the Kings, many of which still contained fragments of once-fabulous treasures. From 1907 he worked there on behalf of the fifth Earl of Carnarvon, who was funding his series of "digs" in and around Thebes. Of course, the discovery of Tut's sepulcher would be his crowning achievement. Few realize, however, that equally impressive was his scholarship, exemplified by his ten-year effort at systematically and painstakingly cataloging all the thousands of objects found in the tomb while supervising their transfer to the Cairo Museum. Carter would pass away from natural causes (not from Tutankhamen's curse) on March 2, 1939.

So, for a few moments, there we are in the ancient necropolis of the ovenlike Valley of the Kings, as primitive and undeveloped in 1922 as it was at the dawn of history. We look around and see an archaeologist's hut here and there, the only evidence that modern man has intruded into the rugged, rock-enclosed amphitheater of death chosen for its solitude, silence, and security. Although a crater-like depression behind a range of barren, sand-blown crumbly rock, the Valley of the Kings had to that point yielded surprisingly few tombs containing bodies. In some four hundred years after 1500 BCE, there were only twenty-eight kings.

Probably because he died earlier than expected, the last of a legitimate line, Tutankhamen was buried in a small tomb that may

The corners of Tut's elaborately sculpted, rose-colored quartzite sarcophagus are guarded by the winged goddesses Isis, Nephthys, Neith, and Selket (copyright: Griffith Institute, Oxford).

not have been intended for him, close to the later tomb of Ramses VI, the debris from which effectively hid Tut's tomb so it escaped serious looting. It was supposed to have been prepared for one of his ministers, probably Ay, but Tut died suddenly before his tomb was ready, and this was used instead. Dr. Fletcher indicated that some Egyptologists believe that Tut's original tomb was probably 80 percent complete, since the pharaohs had construction on their tombs begin immediately upon becoming pharaoh. With that in mind, Tut's original tomb, although mostly complete, was still larger than the one he was buried in. A strange sepulcher for Pharaoh Tutankhamen.

After our flying carpet drops us off and continues on its way, we stand there in the morning sun. It is hot and getting hotter. Since Carter is already at the mouth of the tomb, we walk up a steep path. As we look around, we comment that it is no wonder the pharaohs hid themselves in these good-for-nothing hills. There is no question the place is desolate. We pass the tomb of Seti I on our right, then turn toward the lower entrance of the valley. There, we spot a small, white tent, a wooden shelter for the armed guard, the pile of material and stacks of lumber that Carter and other archaeologists use, and the new wall of irregular stones that hides the entrance to Tut's tiny mausoleum.

At this point, a nice-looking man with a warm, congenial smile greets us. After cordial introductions all around, Howard Carter sits us down in the shade of the tomb's entrance wall and enthusiastically describes the finding of the tomb. Exclamations such as "resplendent," "stupendous," "dazzling," "indescribable," and "spellbinding" by those who followed Carter in the days after the discovery mean little compared to the quiet and calm descriptions of his discovery.

What follows, then, are excerpts we plucked from some of the most riveting reading in the twentieth century: Howard Carter's own words of his unearthing and exploration of the tomb of Tutankhamen. First published in installments between 1923 and 1933, Carter's memoirs filled three volumes and were complemented by Harry Burton's photographs. Not only did the famed British archeologist-Egyptologist provide the world with new insights and fresh information about the life and death of the Eighteenth Dynasty pharaoh, but he describes his feelings of astonishment, awe, and reverence as he gazed upon the tomb's extraordinary riches. By quoting a number of extracts from his memoirs, we hope the reader will hurry to the nearest library to check out chapter 5 of Carter's *The Tomb of Tutankhamen*, first published in the United States by E. P. Dutton in 1972.

The Finding of the Tomb

This was to be our final season in the valley. Six full seasons we had excavated there, and season after season had drawn a blank: we had worked for months at a stretch and found nothing, and only an excavator knows how desperately depressing that can be; we had almost made up our minds that we were beaten, and were preparing to leave the Valley and try our luck elsewhere; and then—hardly had we set hoe to ground in our last despairing effort than we made a discovery that far exceeded our wildest dreams. . . .

I arrived in Luxor on 28 October, and by 1 November I had enrolled my workmen and was ready to begin. Our former excavations had stopped short at the north-east corner of the tomb of Ramses VI, and from this point I started trenching southwards. In this area there were a number of roughly constructed workmen's huts, used probably by the labourers in the tomb of Ramses. . . . By the evening of 3 November we had laid bare a sufficient number of these huts for experimental purposes, so, after we had planned and noted them, they were removed, and we were ready to clear away the three feet of soil that lay beneath them.

Hardly had I arrived on the work next morning (4 November) than the unusual silence, due to the stoppage of work, made me realize that something out of the ordinary had happened, and I was greeted by the announcement that a step cut in the rock had been discovered underneath the very first hut to be attacked. This seemed too good to be true, but a short amount of extra clearing revealed the fact that we were actually in the entrance of a steep cut in the rock, some thirteen feet below the entrance to the tomb of Ramses VI, and a similar depth from the present bed level of the Valley. The manner of cutting was that of the sunken stairway entrance so common in the Valley, and I almost dared to hope that we had found our tomb at last. Work continued feverishly throughout the whole of that day and the morning of the next, but it was not until the afternoon of 5 November that we succeeded in clearing away the masses of rubbish that overlay the cut, and were able to demarcate the upper edges of the stairway on all its four sides.

It was clear by now beyond any question that we actually had before us the entrance to a tomb, but doubts, born of previous disappointments, persisted in creeping in. There was always the horrible possibility, suggested by our experience in the Thothmes III Valley, that the tomb was an unfinished one, never completed and never used: if it had been finished there was the depressing probability that it had been completely plundered in ancient times. On the other hand, there was just the chance of an untouched or only partially plundered tomb, and it was with ill-suppressed excitement that I watched the descending steps of the staircase, as one by one they came to light. . . . Work progressed more rapidly now; step succeeded step, and at the level of the twelfth, towards sunset, there was disclosed the upper part of a doorway, blocked, plastered, and sealed.

A sealed doorway—it was actually true, then! Our years of patient labour were to be rewarded after all. . . .

One thing puzzled me, and that was the smallness of the opening in comparison with the ordinary Valley tombs. The design was certainly of the Eighteenth Dynasty. Could it be the tomb of a noble buried here by royal consent? Was it a royal cache, a hiding-place to which a mummy and its equipment had been removed for safety? Or was it actually the tomb of the king for whom I had spent so many years in search?

Once more I examined the seal impressions for a clue, but on the part of the door so far laid bare only those of the royal necropolis seal already mentioned were clear enough to read. Had I but known that a few inches lower down there was a perfectly clear and distinct impression of the seal of Tutankhamen, the king I most desired to find, I would have cleared on, had a much better night's rest in consequence, and saved myself nearly three weeks of uncertainty. It was late, however, and darkness was already upon us. With some reluctance I re-closed the small hole that I had made, filled in our excavation for protection during the night, selected the most trustworthy of my workmen—themselves almost as excited as I was—to watch all night above the tomb, and so home by moonlight, riding down the Valley.

Naturally, my wish was to go straight ahead with our clearing to find out the full extent of the discovery, but Lord Carnarvon was in England, and in fairness to him I had to delay matters until he could come. Accordingly, on the morning of 6 November I sent him the following cable: "At last have made wonderful discovery in Valley: a magnificent tomb with seals intact: re-covered same for your arrival: congratulations." . . .

The day following (26 November) was the day of days, the most wonderful that I have ever lived through, and certainly one whose like I can never hope to see again. . . . There lay the sealed doorway, and behind it was the answer to the question.

Slowly, desperately slowly it seemed to us as we watched, the remains of passage debris that encumbered the lower part of the doorway were removed, until at last we had the whole door clear before us. The decisive moment had arrived. With trembling hands I made a tiny breach in the upper left-hand corner. Darkness and blank space, as far as an iron testing-rod could reach, showed that whatever lay beyond was empty, and not filled like the passage we had just cleared. Candle tests were applied as a precaution against possible foul gases, and then, widening the hole a little, I inserted the candle and peered in, Lord Carnarvon, Lady Evelyn and Callender standing anxiously beside me to hear the verdict. At first I could see nothing, the hot air escaping from the chamber causing the candle flame to flicker, but presently, as my eyes grew accustomed to the light, details of the room within emerged slowly from the mist, strange animals, statues, and gold—everywhere the glint of gold. For the moment—an eternity it must have seemed to the others standing by—I was struck dumb with amazement, and when Lord Carnarvon, unable to stand the suspense any longer, inquired anxiously, "Can you see anything?" it was all I could do to get out the words, "Yes, wonderful things." Then, widening the hole a little further, so that we both could see, we inserted an electric torch.

I suppose most excavators would confess to a feeling of awe—embarrassment almost—when they break into a chamber closed and sealed by pious hands so many centuries ago. For the moment, time as a factor in human life has lost its meaning. Three thousand, four thousand years maybe, have passed and gone since human feet last trod the floor on which you stand, and yet, as you note the signs of recent life around you—the half-filled bowl of mortar for the door, the blackened lamp, the finger-mark upon the freshly painted surface, the farewell garland dropped upon the threshold—you feel it might have been but yesterday. The very air you breathe, unchanged throughout the centuries, you share with those who laid the mummy to its rest. Time is annihilated by little intimate details such as these, and you feel an intruder. . . .

Gradually the scene grew clearer, and we could pick out individual objects. First, right opposite to us—we had been conscious of them all the while, but refused to believe in them—were three great gilt couches, their sides carved in the form of monstrous animals, curiously attenuated in body, as they had to be to serve their purpose, but with heads of startling realism. Uncanny beasts enough to look upon at any time: seen as we saw them, their brilliant gilded surfaces picked out of the darkness by our electric torch, as though by limelight, their heads throwing grotesque distorted shadows on the wall behind them, they were almost terrifying. Next, on the right, two statues caught and held our attention: two life-sized figures of a king in black, facing each other like sentinels, gold kilted, gold sandalled, armed with mace and staff, the protective sacred cobra upon their foreheads.

These were the dominant objects that caught the eye at first. Between them, around them, piled on top of them, there were countless others—exquisitely painted and inlaid caskets; alabaster vases, some beautifully carved in openwork designs; strange black shrines, from the open door of one a great gilt snake peeping out; bouquets of flowers or leaves; beds; chairs beautifully carved; a golden inlaid throne; a heap of curious white oviform boxes; staves of all shapes and designs; beneath our eyes, on the very threshold of the chamber, a beautiful lotiform cup of translucent alabaster; on the left a confused pile of overturned chariots, glistening with gold and inlay; and peeping from behind them another portrait of a king.

Such were some of the objects that lay before us. Whether we noted them all at the time I cannot say for certain, as our minds were in much too excited and confused a state to register accu-

The sealed doorway to Tut's burial chamber, guarded by two life-sized
sentinel statues made of gilded wood (copyright: Griffith Institute, Oxford).

rately. Presently it dawned upon our bewildered brains that in all
this medley of objects before us there was no coffin or trace of
mummy, and the much-debated question of tomb or cache began
to intrigue us afresh. With this question in view we re-examined
the scene before us, and noticed for the first time that between the
two black sentinel statues on the right there was another sealed
doorway. The explanation gradually dawned upon us. We were but
on the threshold of our discovery. What we saw was merely an
antechamber. Behind the guarded door there were to be other
chambers, possibly a succession of them, and in one of them,
beyond any shadow of doubt, in all his magnificent panoply of
death, we should find the Pharaoh lying. . . .

It was curious, as we talked things over in the evening, to find
how conflicting our ideas were as to what we had seen. Each of us
had noted something that the others had not, and it amazed us
next day to discover how many and how obvious were the things
that we had missed. Naturally, it was the sealed door between the

statues that intrigued us most, and we debated far into the night the possibilities of what might lie behind it. A single chamber with the king's sarcophagus? That was the least we might expect. But why one chamber only? Why not a succession of passages and chambers, leading, in true Valley style, to an innermost shrine of all, the burial chamber? It might be so, and yet in plan the tomb was quite unlike the others. Visions of chamber after chamber, each crowded with objects like the one we had seen, passed through our minds and left us gasping for breath. Then came the thought of the plunderers again. Had they succeeded in penetrating this third doorway—seen from a distance it looked absolutely untouched—and, if so, what were our chances of finding the king's mummy intact? I think we slept but little, all of us, that night. . . .

Our first objective was naturally the sealed door between the statues, and here a disappointment awaited us. Seen from a distance it presented all the appearance of an absolutely intact blocking, but close examination revealed the fact that a small breach had been made near the bottom, just wide enough to admit a boy or a slightly built man, and that the hole made had subsequently been filled up and re-sealed. We were not then to be the first. Here, too, the thieves had forestalled us, and it only remained to be seen how much damage they had had the opportunity or the time to effect. . . .

One of the first things we noted in our survey was that all of the larger objects, and most of the smaller ones, were inscribed with the name of Tutankhamen. His, too, were the seals upon the innermost door, and therefore his, beyond the shadow of doubt, the mummy that ought to lie behind it. Next, while we were still excitedly calling each other from one object to another, came a new discovery. Peering beneath the southernmost of the three great couches, we noticed a small irregular hole in the wall. Here was yet another sealed doorway, and a plunderers' hole which, unlike the others, had never been repaired. Cautiously we crept under the couch, inserted our portable light, and there before us lay another chamber, rather smaller than the first, but even more crowded with objects.

The state of this inner room (afterwards called the Annexe) simply defies description. In the Antechamber there had been some sort of an attempt to tidy up after the plunderers' visit, but here everything was in confusion, just as they had left it. Nor did it take much imagination to picture them at their work. One— there would probably not have been room for more than one— had crept into the chamber, and had then hastily but systematically ransacked its entire contents, emptying boxes, throwing things aside, piling them one upon another, and occasionally passing objects through the hole to his companions for closer examination in the outer chamber. He had done his work just about as thoroughly as an earthquake. . . .

Friday, the 17th (of February, 1923), was the day appointed, and at two o'clock those who were to be privileged to witness the ceremony met by appointment above the tomb. . . . One thought and one only was possible. There before us lay the sealed door, and with its opening we were to blot out the centuries and stand in the presence of a king who reigned three thousand years ago. My own feelings as I mounted the platform were a strange mixture, and it was with a trembling hand that I struck the first blow.

My first care was to locate the wooden lintel above the door: then very carefully I chipped away the plaster and picked out the small stones which formed the uppermost layer of the filling. The temptation to stop and peer inside at every moment was irresistible, and when, after about ten minutes' work, I had made a hole large enough to enable me to do so, I inserted an electric torch. An astonishing sight its light revealed, for there, within a yard of the doorway, reaching as far as one could see and blocking the entrance to the chamber, stood what to all appearance was a solid wall of gold. For the moment there was no clue as to its meaning, so quickly as I dared I set to work to widen the hole. . . .

It was, beyond any question, the sepulchral chamber in which we stood, for there, towering above us, was one of the great gilt shrines beneath which kings were laid. So enormous was this structure (17 feet by 11 feet, and 9 feet high, we found afterwards) that it filled within a little the entire area of the chamber, a space of some two feet only separating it from the walls on all four sides, while its roof, with cornice top and torus moulding, reached almost to the ceiling. From top to bottom it was overlaid with gold, and upon its sides there were inlaid panels of brilliant blue faience, in which were represented, repeated over and over, the magic symbols which would ensure its strength and safety. Around the shrine, resting upon the ground, there were a number of funerary emblems, and, at the north end, the seven magic oars the king would need to ferry himself across the waters of the underworld. The walls of the chamber, unlike those of the Antechamber, were decorated with brightly painted scenes and inscriptions, brilliant in their colours, but evidently somewhat hastily executed. . . .

Here a surprise awaited us, for a low door, eastwards from the sepulchral chamber, gave entrance to yet another chamber, smaller than the outer ones and not so lofty. This doorway, unlike the others, had not been closed and sealed. We were able, from where we stood, to get a clear view of the whole of the contents, and a single glance sufficed to tell us that here, within this little chamber, lay the greatest treasures of the tomb. Facing the doorway, on the farther side, stood the most beautiful monument I have ever seen—so lovely that it made one gasp with wonder and admiration. The central portion of it consisted of a large shrine-shaped chest, completely overlaid with gold, and surmounted by a cornice of sacred cobras. Surrounding this, free-standing, were statues of the four tutelary goddesses of the dead—gracious figures with outstretched protective arms, so natural and lifelike in their pose, so pitiful and compassionate the expression upon their faces, that one felt it almost sacrilege to look at them. One guarded the shrine on each of its four sides, but whereas the figures at the front and back kept their gaze firmly fixed upon their charge, an additional note of touching realism was imparted by the other two, for their heads were turned sideways, looking over their shoulders towards the entrance, as though to watch against surprise. There is a simple grandeur about this monument that made an irresistible appeal to the imagination, and I am not ashamed to confess that it brought a lump to my throat. It is undoubtedly the canopic chest and contains the jars which play such an important part in the ritual of mummification. . . .

How much time we occupied in this first survey of the wonders of the tomb I cannot say, but it must have seemed endless to those anxiously waiting in the Antechamber. Not more than three at a time could be admitted with safety, so, when Lord Carnarvon and M. Lacau came out, the others came in pairs: first Lady Evelyn Herbert, the only woman present, with Sir William Garstin, and then the rest in turn. It was curious, as we stood in the

Antechamber, to watch their faces as, one by one, they emerged from the door. Each had a dazed, bewildered look in his eyes, and each in turn, as he came out, threw up his hands before him, an unconscious gesture of impotence to describe in words the wonders that he had seen. They were indeed indescribable, and the emotions they had aroused in our minds were of too intimate a nature to communicate, even though we had the words at our command. It was an experience which, I am sure, none of us who were present is ever likely to forget, for in imagination—and not wholly in imagination either—we had been present at the funeral ceremonies of a king long dead and almost forgotten. At a quarter past two we had filed down into the tomb, and when, three hours later, hot, dusty, and disheveled, we came out once more into the light of day, the very Valley seemed to have changed for us and taken on a more personal aspect. We had been given the Freedom. . . . For ourselves it was the one supreme and culminating moment—a moment looked forward to ever since it became evident that the chambers discovered, in November 1922, must be the tomb of Tutankhamen, and not a cache of his furniture as had been claimed. None of us but felt the solemnity of the occasion, none of us but was affected by the prospect of what we were about to see—the burial custom of a king of ancient Egypt of thirty-three centuries ago. How would the king be found? Such were the anticipatory speculations running in our minds during the silence maintained.

The tackle for raising the lid was in position. I gave the word. Amid intense silence the huge slab, broken in two, weighing over a ton and a quarter, rose from its bed. The light shone into the sarcophagus. A sight met our eyes that at first puzzled us. It was a little disappointing. The contents were completely covered by fine linen shrouds. The lid being suspended in mid-air, we rolled back those covering shrouds, one by one, and as the last was removed a gasp of wonderment escaped our lips, so gorgeous was the sight that met our eyes: a golden effigy of the young boy king, of most magnificent workmanship, filled the whole of the interior of the sarcophagus. This was the lid of a wonderful anthropoid coffin, some 7 feet in length, resting upon a low bier in the form of a lion, and no doubt the outermost coffin of a series of coffins, nested one within the other, enclosing the mortal remains of the king.

Enclasping the body of this magnificent monument are two winged goddesses, Isis and Neith, wrought in rich gold-work upon gesso, as brilliant as the day the coffin was made. To it an additional charm was added, by the fact that, while this decoration was rendered in fine low bas-relief, the head and hands of the king were in the round, in massive gold of the finest sculpture, surpassing anything we could have imagined. The hands, crossed over the breast, held the royal emblems—the Crook and the Flail—encrusted with deep blue faience. The face and features were wonderfully wrought in sheet-gold. The eyes were of aragonite and obsidian, the eyebrows and eyelids inlaid with lapis lazuli glass. There was a touch of realism, for while the rest of this anthropoid coffin, covered with feathered ornament, was of brilliant gold, that of the bare face and hands seemed different, the gold of the flesh being of different alloy, thus conveying an impression of the greyness of death. Upon the forehead of this recumbent figure of the young boy king were two emblems delicately worked in brilliant inlay—the Cobra and the Vulture—symbols of Upper and Lower Egypt, but perhaps the most touching by its human simplicity was the tiny wreath of flowers around these symbols, as it pleased us to think, the last farewell offering of the widowed girl queen to her husband, the youthful representative of the "Two Kingdoms."

Among all that regal splendour, that royal magnificence—everywhere the glint of gold—there was nothing so beautiful as those few withered flowers, still retaining their tinge of colour. They told us what a short period three thousand three hundred years really was—but Yesterday and the Morrow. In fact, that touch of nature made that ancient and our modern civilization kin. . . .

This great gilded wooden coffin, 7 feet 4 inches in length, anthropoid in shape, wearing the *Khat* head-dress, with face and hands in heavier sheet-gold, is of *Rishi* type—a term applied when the main decoration consists of a feather design, a fashion common to coffins of the preceding Intermediate and Seventeenth Dynasty Theban periods. . . .

It was a moment as anxious as exciting. The lid came up fairly readily, revealing a second magnificent anthropoid coffin, covered with a thin gossamer linen sheet, darkened and much decayed. Upon this linen shroud were lying floral garlands, composed of olive and willow leaves, petals of the blue lotus and cornflower, whilst a small wreath of similar kind had been placed, also over the shroud, on the emblems of the forehead. Underneath this covering, in places, glimpses could be obtained of rich multi-coloured glass decoration encrusted upon the fine gold-work of the coffin. . . .

Thus far our progress had been fairly satisfactory, but we now became conscious of a rather ominous feature. The second coffin which, so far as visible through the linen covering, had every appearance of being a wonderful piece of workmanship, showed distinct signs of the effect of some form of dampness and, here and there, tendency for its beautiful inlay to fall away. This was, I must admit, disconcerting, suggesting as it did the existence of former humidity of some kind within the nest of coffins. Should this prove the case, the preservation of the royal mummy would be less satisfactory than we had hoped. . . . I then removed the floral collarette and linen coverings. An astounding fact was disclosed. This third coffin, 6 feet 1¾ of an inch in length, was made of solid gold! The mystery of the enormous weight, which hitherto had puzzled us, was now clear. It explained also why the weight had diminished so slightly after the first coffin, and the lid of the second coffin, had been removed. Its weight was still as much as eight strong men could lift. . . .

The face of this golden coffin was again that of the king, but the features though conventional, by symbolizing Osiris, were even more youthful than those on the other coffins. In actual design it reverted to that of the outermost coffin, inasmuch as it was *Rishi*, and had engraved upon it figures of Isis and Nephthys, but auxiliary to this design were winged figures of Nekhebet and Buto. These latter protective figures, emblematic of Upper and Lower Egypt, were the prominent feature, for they are superimposed in gorgeous and massive cloisonné work over the richly engraved ornament of the coffin—their inlay being natural semi-precious stones. In addition to this decoration, over the conventional collarette of "the Hawk"—again in auxiliary cloisonné work—was a double detachable necklace of large disk-shaped beads of red and yellow gold and blue faience, which enhanced the richness of the whole effect. But the ultimate details of the ornamentation were hidden by a black lustrous coating due to liquid unguents that had evidently been profusely poured over the coffin. As a result this unparalleled monument was not only disfigured—

as it afterwards proved, only temporarily—but was stuck fast to the interior of the second coffin, the consolidated liquid filling up the space between the second and third coffins almost to the level of the lid of the third. . . .

We raised the third coffin contained in the shell of the second, which now rested on the top of the sarcophagus, and moved them into the Antechamber where they were more accessible, both for examination and manipulation. It was then that the wonder and magnitude of our last discovery more completely dawned upon us. This unique and wonderful monument—a coffin over 6 feet in length, of the finest art, wrought in solid gold of $2\frac{1}{2}$ to $3\frac{1}{2}$ millimetres in thickness—represented an enormous mass of pure bullion.

How great must have been the wealth buried with those ancient Pharaohs! What riches that Valley must once have concealed! Of the twenty-seven monarchs buried there, Tutankhamen was probably of the least importance. How great must have been the temptation to the greed and rapacity of the audacious contemporary tomb robbers! What stronger incentive can be imagined than those vast treasures of gold! The plundering of royal tombs, recorded in the reign of Ramses IX, becomes easily intelligible when the incentive to these crimes is measured by this gold coffin of Tutankhamen. It must have represented fabulous wealth to the stone-cutters, artisans, water-carriers and peasants—to contemporary workers generally, such as the men implicated in the tomb robberies. . . .

At such moments the emotions evade verbal expression, complex and stirring as they are. Three thousand years and more had elapsed since men's eyes had gazed into that golden coffin. Time, measured by the brevity of human life, seemed to lose its common perspectives before a spectacle so vividly recalling the solemn religious rites of a vanished civilization. But it is useless to dwell on such sentiments, based as they are on feelings of awe and human pity. The emotional side is no part of archaeological research. Here at last lay all that was left of the youthful Pharaoh, hitherto little more to us than the shadow of a name.

Before us, occupying the whole of the interior of the golden coffin, was an impressive, neat and carefully made mummy, over which had been poured anointing unguents as in the case of the outside of its coffin—again in great quantity—consolidated and

Carter carefully chips away at the rock-hard unguents that had been poured over the gold cloisonne on the third, or innermost, coffin (copyright: Griffith Institute, Oxford).

blackened by age. In contradistinction to the general dark and sombre effect, due to these unguents, was a brilliant, one might say magnificent, burnished gold mask or similitude of the king, covering his head and shoulders which, like the feet, had been intentionally avoided when using the unguents. The mummy was fashioned to symbolize Osiris. The beaten gold mask, a beautiful and unique specimen of ancient portraiture, bears a sad but calm expression suggestive of youth overtaken prematurely by death. Upon its forehead, wrought in massive gold, were the royal insignia—the Nekhebet vulture and Buto serpent—emblems of the Two Kingdoms over which he had reigned. To the chin was attached the conventional Osiride beard, wrought in gold and lapis-lazuli-coloured glass; around the throat was a triple necklace of yellow and red gold and blue faience disk-shaped beads; pendent from the neck by flexible gold inlaid straps was a large black resin scarab that rested between the hands and bore the *Bennu* ritual. The burnished gold hands, crossed over the breast, separate from the mask, were sewn to the material of the linen wrappings, and grasped the Flagellum and Crozier—the emblems of Osiris. Immediately below these was the simple outermost linen covering, adorned with richly inlaid gold trappings pendent from a large pectoral-like figure of the *Ba* bird or soul, of gold cloisonné work, its full-spread wings stretched over the body. As these gorgeous trappings had been subjected to the consecration unguents, their detail and brilliance were hardly visible, and to this must be attributed the disastrous deterioration which we discovered to have taken place in the case of many of the objects. . . .

Although the attributes upon this mummy are those of the gods, the likeness is certainly that of Tutankhamen, comely and placid, with the features recognizable on all his statues and coffins. From certain aspects of the face here recalls his father-in-law Akhenaten, in others, especially in profile, perhaps an even stronger likeness to the great Queen Tiy, Akhenaten's mother, or in other words, as those features gazed at you, there was an incipient gleam of affinity to both of those predecessors.

Those liquid unguents so lavishly used would seem to have been applied as part of the burial ritual for the consecration of the dead king, before his entrance into the presence of the great god Osiris of the Underworld. It was particularly noticeable that, both on the third coffin and the king's mummy itself, the head and feet had been carefully avoided, although some of the same liquid had been poured on the feet (only) of the first outermost coffin. One's thoughts turned, as one mused on the nature of that last ceremony and its intention, to that touching scene "in the house of the leper," when "there came a woman having an alabaster box of ointment of spikenard very precious" and to Christ's words: "she is come aforehand to anoint my body to the burying" (Mark xiv. 8). . . .

The greater part of the flagellum and crozier was completely decomposed, and had already fallen to dust; the threads that once held the hands and trappings in place upon the outer linen covering, were decayed, and in consequence the various sections fell apart at the slightest touch; the black resin scarab was covered by minute fissures, probably the result of contraction; consequently, these external trappings and ornaments had to be removed, piece by piece, and placed in corresponding order and position upon a tray for future cleaning and remounting. The farther we proceeded the more evident it became that the covering wrappings and the mummy were both in a parlous state. They were completely carbonized by the action that had been set up by the fatty acids of the unguents with which they had been saturated.

But, alas! both the mask and the mummy were stuck fast to the bottom of the coffin by the consolidated residue of the unguents, and no amount of legitimate force could move them. What was to be done?[1]

We leave these tantalizing first-hand, eyewitness passages hoping the reader will be engrossed enough to seek out the more lengthy Carter memoirs. All of us are not only present as the archaeologist makes his discoveries but also experience, insofar as humanly possible, his exhilaration, his rush of adrenaline, and later his sobering, contemplative reflections of the wondrous moments. Although more than eight decades old, the twenty-plus lengthy passages suddenly produce in us a deep desire to know the personality of the young man beneath the golden mask. Tutankhamen is now more than just dried-up skin and a pile of bones or the name of some ancient pharaoh who had the misfortune of dying young and whose only claim to fame was that looters were unable to penetrate his burial chamber.

* * *

A long silence had been broken for the first time in over three thousand years by the sound of a small instrument drilling into a sealed doorway followed by a few simple human exclamations as Carter peered into an antechamber. Then, in the weeks and months and years that followed, there was the endless noise of turning a once-sacred and dignified grave into a busy laboratory of stools, tables, and lights, a cataloging center and makeshift warehouse: in short, a booming business and commercial opportunity. Streams of tourists and visitors poured in from all over the world, standing in line and talking excitedly about "Young Toot." Official luncheon party after official luncheon party followed at the tomb's entrance, widened for the occasions. And amid all this hustle and bustle of arriving and departing sand carts, horse carriages, trucks, motor cars, to say nothing of American men and women in riding breeches atop camels eating cold chicken legs, Tut had to be wondering why his subordinates hadn't planned to bury him more carefully.[2]

NOTES

1. Many thanks go to the E. P. Dutton Publishing Company, which graciously and generously granted us permission to quote at length from its *The Tomb of Tutankhamen*, by Howard Carter, published in 1972.

2. For truly fascinating essays on early Egyptian discoveries prior to Howard Carter unearthing Tutankhamen's burial chamber, see the following *National Geographic* magazines: "American Discoveries in Egypt," December 1907; "Reconstructing Egypt's History," "The Resurrection of Ancient Egypt," and "The Sacred Ibis Cemetery and Jackal Catacombs at Abydos," all in the September 1913 issue. Then, of course, the two that inspired us on a more emotional level: "At the Tomb of Tutankhamen—An Account of the Opening of the Royal Egyptian Sepulcher Which Contained the Most Remarkable Funeral Treasures Unearthed in Historic Times," May 1923, and "Daily Life in Ancient Egypt," October 1941.

But no books can compare to Carter's eyewitness accounts of the opening of Tutankhamen's burial chamber and his afterthoughts found in Carter's wonderfully detailed three-volume memoir, which National Geographic compiled into one volume.

Chapter 5

CONSIDERING
THE FIRST CLUES
USING VICTIMOLOGY TO
ESTABLISH TUT'S LIFESTYLE

*Three thousand years have the value of the merest drop in the ocean.
One's hands may reach out and touch the hands which fashioned these
vases, picked this fruit, and baked this bread. The dead noble lying there
in his coffin, a perfectly preserved man, is not a relic of an age of mira-
cles, when the gods walked the earth or sent down their thunder-bolts
from an unremote heaven; but bone for bone, he is the same as the
men of the present day, and his brain has known only the sights and
sounds which we know, altered but in a few unessential details.*
        Arthur R. E. P. Weigall, Chief Inspector of Upper Egypt,
                Department of Antiquities, July 1909

It was in mid-1909 when the late Arthur Weigall reflected on the
approach to a pharaoh's tomb as though he "had come to
awaken the dead, not as angels instructed by the call of the last
trump, but as the degenerate sons of a race that had outlived its mir-
acles and had come with the tidings that the gods were dead."

Almost a hundred years later, we approached Tut's tomb with a much different goal and hope. We sincerely thought it was possible, through the discovery of truth, for the dead to finally rest in peace.

As we left the Cairo Sheraton under the glow of the purple morning sunrise, escorted past the thousands of faces who herded buffalo, goats, and children, our minds raced nearly as quickly as the truck ahead of us filled with Egyptian soldiers who were charged with our safety. While our official motorcade made its way through the city of Cairo and into the desert countryside, we watched the sun rise and another Ramadan day in Egypt begin.

When we arrived at Saqqara for the second time in two days, we were treated with the sight of Egyptian craftsmen chipping rock for the restoration of the pyramids. We were privileged to watch as they swung their heavy tools in order to make the rock yield to their desires. In the distance, the three pyramids of Giza could be seen rising from the desert floor.

As we carefully walked amid the history, we peered into small openings in the sand and stone revealing the treasures of newly discovered tombs. Saqqara was probably the most revered of all Egypt's royal cemeteries, certainly one of the longest used, and one that stretched for more than five kilometers along the Nile. As we slowly strolled through the courtyards, the side-by-side stone mortuary complexes of the rich and powerful, and the famous Step Pyramid, the world's first to replace mud-brick construction with stone, we smiled at each other and said, "Okay. Time to go to work. Let's confer."

In such a simple manner began our serious deliberations regarding King Tut's death.

As pointed out earlier, our investigative approach to a homicide includes a thorough examination of the victim's background in order to appraise the type of suspect we should be looking for. In fact, assessing the deceased's victimology, that is, family, friends, acquaintances, education, employment, residence, neighborhood, lifestyle, and whether the person was a low-, moderate-, or high-risk victim, is standard procedure for any good homicide investigator. Most times, the detective winds up discovering more about the dead person than the unfortunate victim knew about himself.

For us, understanding Tutankhamen's background was absolutely essential to establishing a behavioral pattern or scenario upon which to build a hypothesis. (For a better understanding of the investigative questions we currently employ in a murder case, and those we used in the Tut project, see the summary of our twenty-seven-page investigative approach to Tutankhamen in the appendixes.) By following more than a hundred questions, we can not only establish a criminal personality profile of an unknown suspect but also make an assessment of possible suspects based upon an evaluation of certain background information supplied by local police on a specific suspect, or in Tutankhamen's case, by history itself. To outsmart a cunning Machiavellian-type assassin, if indeed Tut's death was due to murder, was not going to be easy.

Sitting down on a stone railing at the edge of Maya's tomb, leaning as close as we could to the structure for the sliver of shade it provided, we evaluated the facts that we had thus far uncovered.

Although many of our clues to the players of this mystery had been destroyed over the thirty-three centuries that preceded us, we thankfully recognized that without the dogged persistence of Egyptologists like Howard Carter and his staff, to say nothing of the Egyptian government, which continually strives to protect these amazing structures for our glimpses into history, many of our clues would have been destroyed or hidden away by grave robbers, collectors, and locals.

We would later recognize how fortunate we truly were for the systematic way in which the discoverers handled Tut's treasures and artifacts. In addition to clearly inspecting the tomb from an Egyptologist's perspective, Carter carefully categorized the location and description of the items removed. We hoped that the other crypts we inspected received the same care. In some cases we already knew that to be true. In others, tragically, it was the opposite, primarily because of the destructive manner in which the looters and thieves gained access and removed its treasures. We knew that many of our most important crime scene clues had been trampled by Carter's entranced staff during those early days following that eventful November morning in 1922. Furthermore, almost all the artifacts and treasures had been removed, albeit carefully and gradually, by Carter and his staff and taken to Cairo Museum, where they can be seen today. Therefore, the only evidence we would find in our search of Tut's tomb was the construction of the burial chamber. Tut's sarcophagus and the wall painting, as well as the physical artifacts surrounding where the body lay, would also yield clues.

As we surmised earlier, we believed the burial was a rush job. For example, splashes of paint had not been washed off the walls or wiped up from the floors. The broken sarcophagus lid didn't match the sarcophagus itself! The tomb was exceedingly small for a pharaoh, and parts had been recarved and the wall paintings poorly pictographed. The tomb certainly couldn't have been meant for a king. Added to all this is the fact that the spectacular death mask, melded in gold, with quartz, lapis lazuli, carnelian, glass, and faience, had been attached to a gold coffin that had been fashioned for someone else! Even the second death mask in the coffin did not resemble the teenager, and virtually all of the art objects and afterlife hardware had been appropriated from other tombs. Dr. Fletcher showed us where the names of the previous owners of these objects had been etched out.

Was this the way to treat a pharaoh? Hardly. All these points added up to something. As we compared Tut's crypt with those of Horemheb and Ay, it appeared strikingly inadequate. Having examined crime scenes that were both organized and disorganized, we determined that what may have begun as an organized effort to remove Tut from power suddenly became disorganized as those with authority appeared to quickly mummify and entomb the pharaoh in an attempt to erase him from history. These simple facts raised a very significant question. Was Tutankhamen indeed murdered? At first glance, the answer had to be an iffy yes. We now applied our principles of victimology.

VICTIMOLOGY OF TUTANKHAMEN

The victimology we developed during those initial days in Egypt represents a study of the victim in this case, namely, Tutankhamen at the time of his death. It reflects his personality, behavioral characteristics, prejudices, and experience as associated between ages seventeen and twenty. Tutankhamen's childhood and the time when he was orphaned by his father's death was added as supportive documentation when needed.

Background Information

The victim Tutankhamen had been dead for approximately thirty-three hundred years. The following not only is based on the fact and fiction of those who recorded his successes and failures but also represents our impressions based upon many of those opinions and representations. The only information we could use to evaluate the opinions and representations of those living so long ago came from the historical writings. We examined, with the help of Dr. Fletcher and Dr. Zahi Hawass, the statues, paintings, and artifacts from the area where Tut resided. The Egyptologists explained the emotional, financial, religious, and political structure of the time. The manner in which the statues are displayed, the amount of touching allowed, the equivalent physical size of the statues, and the direction in which the subjects look, all teach us who these ancient citizens were; their thoughts, feelings, and emotions; and their strengths and weaknesses.

First of all, Tutankhamen had been known by several names and aliases during his life, for example, Tutankhaten, Tutanhkhamen, Tutankhamen, and King Tut. He was born in the city of Akhetaten, now known as Amarna, Egypt, in the springtime, approximately 1323 BCE. He was the son of the pharaoh, King Akhenaten and his secondary wife Kiya. The city Tut was born into was built by his father after he experienced some type of religious awakening. Before his son was born, Akhenaten officially changed the religious worship system (polytheism) of Amun and many other gods to the monotheistic worship of the one god, Aten. Tut was raised from birth until age nine as a privileged Egyptian of royal blood. He would have had the finest in health and dental care. Tut ate the best foods and played under the watchful eye of employees of the kingdom who were responsible for his safety.

Some historical information suggests the boy's father, Akhenaten, may have suffered from some physical ailments but nothing that appears too dramatic or indeed that can be firmly proven. On the other hand, Tut appears to have suffered from several different handicaps, including the crippling disease of Klippel Feil syndrome. Examinations of Tut's body thirty-three centuries after his death revealed that the pharaoh's cervical spine was fused together into a solid piece, making normal range of motion difficult at best. One might assume that this disease became more debilitating over time, causing numerous problems for him. As the young king matured and his bones began to harden, it's possible that at some point in his puberty he began to feel the effects of the disease. This possibility is supported by the large number of walking sticks found inside Tut's tomb when discovered by Howard Carter.

Tutankhamen's mummy measures 1.63 meters long (5 feet, 3.5 inches). It is difficult to gauge how much his body may have shrunk after death, as the bones and tissues dried out. But he was probably between five feet, five inches, and five feet, eight inches, in height. In evaluating the many wall paintings, statues, and images of Tut, as well as his bone structure, it is assumed that he weighed somewhere in the neighborhood of one hundred fifty to one hundred sixty pounds. He probably walked somewhat cautiously as he grew older. If Tutankhamen actually had Klippel Feil syndrome, and it was manifesting itself, the disease would have observably affected the pharaoh. Tut would not have been able to rotate his neck in order to look left or right and up or down easily. He would have had to flex his spine further down the body in order to accomplish this simple task that we take for granted. His many walking sticks suggest that the disability may have even progressed to the point of requiring assistance, although we cannot disregard the possibility that the walking sticks may have been ornamental rather than necessary.

Because ancient Egyptian physicians practiced medicine in specialized areas including the circulatory system, the eyes, and internal organs, it is safe to assume that Tutankhamen would have had the very best of care, including specialty care. Since he was considered a national treasure, no shortcuts would have been taken in caring for

317 A 2

One of Tut and Ankhesenamun's stillborn female infants
(copyright: Griffith Institute, Oxford).

the pharaoh, who represented a god, if indeed, he was not considered a god himself. Some local Egyptologists suggested that Tut could have been affected by hearing loss, although we were unable to uncover any evidence to support that claim.

As mentioned earlier, Tutankhamen was married at a young age to his half-sister Ankhesenamun. Both regents had the same father, Akhenaten. Tut's mother was Kiya and Ankhesenamun's mother was the beautiful and famous Nefertiti. Egyptologists generally believe that Tutankhamen and Ankhesenamun married when the young king was between ten and twelve years old and his new queen approximately twelve to fourteen. The couple tried to have children, and at least two children were still-born, leaving the couple childless. Evidence suggests that one of the children suffered from the same cervical spine fusion as Tut. The death of these two fetuses must have been extremely upsetting to the king and queen, and it appears they chose to have their children embalmed and mummified in hopes of preserving them and sharing their lives in the hereafter. The process of embalming a fetus who never "took in the breath of life" went against Egyptian beliefs and may have suggested Tut's innate belief in the monotheism of his father, which was entirely different from the beliefs commonly held by the Egyptian people at that time. Or one must consider the impact that losing the children had on the king and queen. They may have chosen to mummify the fetuses, since their grief was so great. Burying them normally with no chance of eternal life might have been too much to bear. This theory is evidenced by the two small fetuses buried in Tutankhamen's tomb with him, although Dr. Fletcher speculated that the fetuses may have been placed as ritual symbols of rebirth in the afterlife.

It is unknown if Tutankhamen or Ankhesenamun had any relatives living with them since no records discuss this. According to Dr. Fletcher, shortly after the death of Akhenaten, a relative of Tutankhamen, Smenkhkare (possibly either Tut's brother or even Nefertiti) served as pharaoh for a short time and then mysteriously disappeared from history.

Common sense suggests that this nine-year-old boy, who had

lost his father, was faced with monumental decisions in the management of the empire, and his attempts to express his ability to govern might have depicted him as intimidated, scared, and unsure. This period in the young Tut's life must have been frightening and confusing, if in fact relatives and loved ones were dying at the hands of assassins. Until some record of this time and the tombs of these people are discovered, we will remain in the dark about what happened to them.

Tutankhamen would clearly have had only one occupation during his lifetime. His time would have been spent learning the job of pharaoh. Being pharaoh of the most powerful country in the world must have placed a tremendous strain on the young king, who actually was still a boy. He undoubtedly ached over the losses of his father and mother—Kiya seems to have died giving birth to him. Although he may have sensed being manipulated from time to time by Maya, Ay, and Horemheb, Tut was so immature that he dared not question the manner in which they were treating him. Although there is no evidence to support that Tut was not treated as a pharaoh, as a nine-year-old boy led by a seasoned, sixty-year-old vizier, Tut surely was directed in what he did. If he ever asked about the suspicious nature of his father's death, he was likely subjected to incredible pressure and made to feel guilty for suggesting that any of Akhenaten's cabinet would participate in such a crime. (Evidence for Akhenaten's possible murder was found in his police chief's tomb, that of Mahu. Akhenaten abruptly drops out of Egyptian history. For a short time, Smenkhkare leads and then disappears, and Tut is made the pharaoh.)

Tut was probably treated as new members to cults around the world are treated in our time. Incredible support, love, and kindness were expressed when he was doing what his "elders" expected. If he did not do things the way they wanted, Tut would have been given the cold shoulder. A young man needing the love and attention of a fatherlike figure would have been easily manipulated. Idolizing a great military commander like Horemheb would encourage him to "act like a man" and not cry or worry or show weakness.

As Tutankhamen and Ankhesenamun grew together in purpose

and love, Tut probably felt less need for the support and acceptance from his inner circle of advisers. As he counseled more with her and less with them, he may have been able to examine each of them with a clearer understanding of who they really were.

Even though the most powerful man in the world, Tut probably felt very insecure about his safety and position. In fact, he may have felt like a puppet in a world filled with deceitful, dreadful, and dangerous people. He may even have felt powerless to prevent many of the actions that he participated in because as a nine-year-old who had recently lost his father, he lacked the confidence to stand up against his instructors.

King Tut would have received the very best formal education. In addition, he was taught at the feet of the most influential men in Egypt. He probably learned financial matters from Maya, who unquestionably understood the economic impact of major political and religious changes following the Amarna period. Tut would have learned how to tax the population to maintain the state as well as his lavish lifestyle that the pharaohs were accustomed to.

Ay, the consummate politician, would have mentored the young pharaoh in his manner of conduct not only with his people but with the leadership of the other countries he would come in contact with. Ay surely taught Tut about the careful wording of epistles or documents. If there was ever a loophole, Ay would have known about it and probably would have taught the young pharaoh the ways in which he could take advantage of it.

Most certainly, Horemheb would have been a person Tutankhamen idolized, since Horemheb represented everything powerful to him. Like the young men of today, Tut would have been engrossed by the sheer power of the tools of the warrior. Horemheb probably oversaw the training of the king in the ways of the warrior. Tut most likely went into the field to observe troop movement and perhaps even small skirmishes. Several artifacts show Tutankhamen with the armies. While this was a normal activity for a pharaoh in order to try to memorialize such an event on his tomb wall to further prove his greatness, it made sense that the king would have wanted the hands-on experience that could only come from "being there." Furthermore, living such experiences through the tales of the great general would be enhanced by personally experiencing the thrill of high-speed chariot assaults, the firing of the bow, and the thrusting of the sword. The royal privilege would have guaranteed Tut access to anything he desired, and "playing army" in any epoch is very desirous to all future rulers.

In addition, Tutankhamen would have been taught the art of hunting—learning at the feet of one of the very best stalkers in the land. He would have learned of the arts, sciences, and any other discipline he desired. Again, the important thing to remember is that the pharaoh could do anything he or she wanted, whenever, and at anyone's expense.

It would be important at this time to remark on the impact Ankhesenamun would have had on Tutankhamen in this learning process. One can only imagine how self-reliant and confident the daughter of Queen Nefertiti must have been. It seems natural that Nefertiti would have taught her daughter well in all the arts of being a queen and coregent. This young woman was destined to become a queen and would have been a great asset to Tutankhamen as he served as pharaoh of Egypt.

In a normal victimology study, we would interview the family and friends of the deceased. Obviously, that is not possible in this particular case, although we can assume those close to Tut might share the following insights that we gained through personal examinations and the observations of many of the world's most learned Egyptologists, including Dr. Fletcher.

Many of Tut's closest confidants would have been from royal or noble heritage. It doesn't appear that the commoner would have much access to a pharaoh. Those who were close to him would have known him for most of his short life. They may have met because they were cousins, stepbrothers, stepsisters, or the children of other royalty or noblemen serving within the temples and royal courts.

We do not know how functional, or dysfunctional for that matter, the family tree in Tutankhamen's genealogy was. We do know that Tut's father, like many pharaohs before him, had several wives at least, who probably produced many children. Interestingly, we didn't see that phenomenon with Tut, who appeared to be monogamously happy loving Ankhesenamun. Throughout ancient history, there are accounts of royal families intermarrying in order to preserve what they believed was a "chosen" bloodline. Today, medical experts have proven that this "in-breeding" results in poor physical composition and causes many medical problems, perhaps similar to what Tut was experiencing. Maybe the Egyptian royalty recognized this and used this reasoning to further legitimize the taking of multiple wives (or secondary wives) to further their offspring.

Tut's hobbies appear to have centered around hunting, fishing, and riding in his chariot. Tut's hobbies are evident by the number of bows, arrows, spears, and depictions in statues, paintings, and carvings of the pharaoh hunting. One might speculate that these were produced to make the pharaoh appear to be more athletic and able than he really was, which may be true, but this is unknown. We can only theorize based on the data we have before us. It makes us wonder if he hot-rodded in his chariot behind a horse with the same recklessness of today's teenagers in a souped-up car. It would also seem—as we gathered from scenes carved in stone before different audiences—that the young pharaoh enjoyed traveling around Egypt, accepting the cheers and accolades of the citizens and commoners who would gather to catch a glimpse of their god.

Because the people flocked around Tutankhamen wherever he went, it would seem natural that he would travel in the company of security in order to protect him and help him avoid the distraction of people always wanting to touch, talk to, and be near him. Tut would probably be somewhat introverted in public to avoid having to deal with people in one-on-one situations. To the commoner, he would appear even dull or unfriendly, yet confident and rigid. Some might describe him as being quick-tempered, based on the fact that he probably never had to negotiate his feelings. He probably never had to make concessions in order to get what he wanted.

Those who knew Tutankhamen intimately probably felt that the pharaoh was moody, irrational at times, aggressive, quick-tempered, or even reckless. We must keep in mind that this was still a teenager at the time of death. His hormones must have been out of control, and from a very young age he would have recognized that his power over others was unquestioned. He may have even lived in a make-believe world surrounded by yes-men who made sure his wishes became his reality. As mentioned, having his father die must have been troubling for the king, especially if he questioned the reason for the death and who might ultimately be involved. Tut may have felt that the only person he could really trust would be his wife, Ankhesenamun. As they lost child after child, he might have questioned his own ability to be a father and worried about producing an heir. He could have worried about his physical condition and be troubled that his fantasy of being a great warrior would never be realized.

Tutankhamen did appear to love and respect his wife. In turn, the queen appeared to love and respect him. Together, they represented a beautiful union that probably brought more peace and comfort to the young man than everything else combined. In her arms he found comfort. In her presence he felt strength and association and looked forward to their future with positive feelings. To Ankhesenamun, her husband probably appeared concerned for the people in his kingdom, in our view religiously motivated to do good, and compelled to be a leader who would be remembered for his greatness.

In the final analysis, it is probable that King Tut may have recognized his own limitations, physically and emotionally. As we know, being thrust into a position of greatness doesn't make a great leader. Tut may have struggled with "getting too much too soon" and overlooked the opportunity he had to improve the lives of others. Instead, he may have been consumed with his own needs to the point that nothing else mattered. We speculate that he had a spiritual awakening of his own during the dark and lonely times in his life when he faced the loss of a child or the memory of his denouncing his father and his belief system when he really didn't want to. Perhaps Tut recognized that Akhenaten was right and considered changing polytheism back to monotheism. If he voiced this opinion, imagine the thoughts of the Amun priests as they once again faced possible expulsion and even extinction at the hands of a boy.

Was the young pharaoh a happy, hormone-driven teenager like

those around us today? Perhaps. But with all the normal physiological feelings he may have had, he also had power, dominion, and total control. Time has often shown that having power over others does not necessarily bring obedience of one's subjects or personal happiness.

Having established Tutankhamen's victimology as far as possible after all these centuries, we now introduce our approach to investigating his death.

OUR APPROACH TO INVESTIGATIVE ANALYSIS

> "When you eliminate the impossible, whatever remains,
> however improbable, must be the truth."
> A. Conan Doyle's Sherlock Holmes in The Sign of Four

The ultimate aim of an investigation is to solve the mystery, answer the questions, and reveal the truth. Exposing the truth is the primary and critical foundation to resolving any mystery. Without the truth, the indisputable facts, a satisfactory conclusion will never be reached. Otherwise, hasty conclusions may be drawn, and unless they are based on accurate and reliable data the answer remains open to conjecture and false claims.

We felt that we must be committed to the discovery of the truth first, which would then lead to a successful and accurate judgment. Every day, investigators err prematurely by developing a theory before first gathering all the relevant data. This can be compared to a physician who begins to prescribe medication and treatment without first gathering the necessary information to determine an accurate diagnosis of the problem. Imagine a patient who complains of headaches to his doctor. The doctor immediately prescribes a new pair of glasses for impaired vision, only later to discover that the patient is suffering from a brain tumor. There have been a number of accounts of innocent people who have been falsely accused, tried, convicted, and sentenced. When additional evidence was discovered, they were subsequently released after several years of confinement. Often, a careful assessment of all the facts could have prevented such miscarriages of justice.

Among the most serious follies of an investigator is to develop a theory before acquiring sufficient data. Gathering accurate, articulable data and indisputable facts is the keystone to developing a reasonable hypothesis, and we knew that by doing so we would be better able to lead the investigation to a successful, certain, and reliable conclusion. Otherwise, we risked adjusting the facts to satisfy some predetermined conclusion, which can lead to the most serious of consequences, including false accusation and conviction of an innocent person. Although we knew that any person accused in this case could not dispute the facts, we wanted to be accurate and convincing in our argument. We needed to consider that Tut's case, like many others over time, could remain unsolved because of inaccurately diagnosing and prescribing a course of action based on impulse and prejudices.

The noted fictitious detective Sherlock Holmes stated this principle well in *A Scandal in Bohemia*: "I have no data yet. It is a capital mistake to theorize before one has data. Insensibly one begins to twist the facts to suit the theories, instead of the theories to suit the facts."

Scientists employ an exhaustive and comprehensive methodology in the search for truth and an explanation of the natural mysteries of life. Like the dedicated scientist, we were committed to an accurate review of the phenomenon of criminal behavior as it applied to the death of an Egyptian pharaoh. We chose to apply a procedure to ensure the best and most objective effort as we explored the facts in our search for the truth.

A complex investigation such as this is often burdened and overwhelmed by an avalanche of information and investigative leads. The labyrinth of interlocking data reminded us constantly of the need to investigate Tut's possible murder in an orderly and disciplined fashion. A logical, sequential approach is the best way to digest the variety of information, which can be likened to taking a drink of water from a bursting fire hydrant. Order must be achieved or chaos reigns. Chaos never helped to solve a crime, and we needed to overcome all the obstacles we could in order to peer into ancient history in a way that had never been attempted before. The more bizarre or complicated the crime, the more orderly the approach required to find successfully the key that will decipher the puzzle.

We found ourselves asking the most common question involved in solving a crime, "Who did it?" This question always sets the investigative objective and basic direction for an exploratory journey to uncover the truth. If unanswered, we might abandon the case for the lack of that one crucial response. In Tut's case, we had to move forward with a death investigation and not a homicide investigation. We constantly reminded ourselves of the following quote by James Thurber, who wisely reveals the essence of every successful mystery: "It is better to know some of the questions than to know all of the answers."

The key to a truthful answer is found in appropriate and fine-tuned questioning. Appropriate questions are the investigator's tools to conduct the diagnostic examination of a perplexing crime. Unfortunately, misguided questions can leave us staggering for direction, but years of developing our investigative protocols lead us to more effective and diagnostic questions, which steer the investigation in the proper direction. We remind ourselves of the Danish proverb: "Better to ask twice than to lose your way once." And the carpenter's rule: "Measure twice, cut once."

Throughout our investigation of Tut's death, we prepared our questions to probe the primary issues while unraveling the secrets. The timing and sequence of these questions needed to be strategically posed to expose the truth. For us, the primary question was, "Who was Tutankhamen?" In the beginning of this chapter, we conducted a psychological autopsy of the victim to help us better understand Tutankhamen. Our process followed closely the tactics developed by the FBI's Behavioral Science Unit and highlighted in the *Crime Classification Manual*:

> Victimology is often one of the most beneficial investigative tools in classifying and solving a violent crime. It is a crucial part of crime analysis. Through it the investigator tries to evaluate why this particular person was targeted for a violent crime. Very often, just answering this question will lead the investigator to the motive, which will lead to the offender. Victimology is an essential step in arriving at a possible motive. If investigators fail to obtain complete victim histories, they may be overlooking information that could quickly direct their investigations to motives and to suspects.

By thoroughly examining Tutankhamen, his environment, associates, likes, dislikes, bias, physical condition, and many other characteristics, we began to better understand his thoughts, feelings, and emotions. As we analyzed the many different elements of Tut's personality, we began to answer questions related to the interdependent and dynamic relationship between each referenced item, while leading the investigation toward the most probable conclusion.

The next important question became "why?" Why did Tut become a victim of a possible murder? Our experience has shown that often the perpetrator will reveal himself inadvertently through the behavior exhibited during the commission of the crime. We had to better understand and then theorize *why* the victim was selected. *Why* was the likely murder committed in this or that particular manner? *Why* did the offender approach the victim, inflict the wounds, or choose the type of weapon?

As in any investigation, it was necessary to complete an evaluation of Tut's lifestyle and the corresponding risk level to which he was exposed. This evaluation included assessing his general activities in connection with the environmental, situational, and circumstantial factors proximate to the time frame of his death.

First, by looking at his lifestyle and presumed daily activities, we plotted his risk level regarding potential victimization. In other words, we had to make a determination if his daily ritual activities made him particularly vulnerable to this type of crime. Once we formed an opinion based on his lifestyle, the second step was to consider that in light of the situation, circumstances, and environmental factors that existed at the time of his demise.

As we explored the level of risk that Tut was exposed to, we needed to develop an opinion about the nature of his relationships with those he spent the most time with and who had greatest access to him. Of particular interest were those people with whom he probably had the most precrime association and contact. Additional questions related to this line of thinking were: If Tut were a victim of a crime, was he a victim of opportunity, or was he specifically targeted? Or did he perhaps contribute to his own victimization ? If so, was it through ignorance, innocence, or naivete? Or even recklessness, negligence, and disregard for his own safety?

We couldn't stop there. Now we were getting to understand both Tut and the probable relationship that could have existed between Tut and a would-be assassin. In consideration of this option, we also had to consider the criminal elements of preplanning, premeditation, and forethought. Was this a crime of passion, impulse, and spontaneity? What was the level of criminal sophistication? The formulation of answers to these questions began a chain of connected queries relating to possible characteristics of the offender(s). For example, how would we see the offender's emotional age versus chronological age based upon our perception of his sophistication or lack thereof? Was it possible to determine a probable motive of the offender(s) and his thoughts, feelings, and emotions? Furthermore, should we consider the possibility that Tut was an intended victim who may have also symbolized some real or perceived grievance to the offender?

We needed to answer these questions through an understanding of the victim, his lifestyle, and the degree to which he may have contributed to his own victimization. We had to keenly consider Tutankhamen's influence in the crime and most importantly the effect of the current social, economic, political, and religious situation, circumstances, and environment that may have played in the overall equation.

As we carefully examined all of the foregoing elements, we became acutely aware of the dynamics within them. Each factor and its interdependent association led to the formulation of a progressive system to effectively unravel this exciting mystery and direct our investigative steps to a successful conclusion.

We have found in our other assessments that a comprehensive and accurate "victimology," the in-depth study of the victim, and the respective assessment of the victim's risk level will lead the investigator to an educated and credible opinion about the relationship between the victim and the offender. The following principles are derived by incorporating the referenced factors and testing them against numerous examples. The test cases include those worked by us and compared with the findings of police investigators from all over the world. Although these principles generally apply, exceptions are anticipated as we recognize that we are dealing with human behavior and often variable factors. Nevertheless, due to our own personal experience and that of hundreds of colleagues, we are confident that the application of this process generally leads the investigation away from a universe of possibilities and toward a concentrated sampling of probabilities, thereby eliminating a lot of wasted time, energy, and emotion on diversionary boondoggles.

Victimology Continuum Principle 1: The lower the victim's risk level to the associated crime, the higher the probability that there was preassociation between the victim and the offender.

Certainly there are exceptions that are influenced by the situation, the circumstances, and the environment. The filtering process will either validate the principle or explain the exception. In addition, it does not imply necessarily that an intimate knowledge or familiar acquaintance between the victim and the offender exists. The association between the victim and the offender may range from quasi-casual contact up to and including an intimate, formal, social relationship. The low-risk victim can fall prey to a stranger-related interpersonal violent crime, due to the situation, circumstances, and environment that exist at the time of the event. For example, a happily married woman whose life is socially centered around her husband and children and whose activities are limited to domestic associations is generally considered low-risk. However, if she is situationally and circumstantially displaced to an unfamiliar environment, her risk level begins to incrementally advance toward medium and even high risk. If she is alone and driving on a remote and isolated interstate, her risk level is elevated by a number of situational, circumstantial, and environmental factors. Consider her exposure to possible disastrous scenarios if her vehicle breaks down. She may be in unfamiliar territory with no automotive knowledge, without a cell phone, and therefore dependent on assistance from any stranger who happens by. She has progressed from low to medium to high risk, and the consequences are potentially deadly.

The risk level is diffused if a highway patrol officer drives by. But what if a Ted Bundy–type pulls up to assist her? Such are the things of which exceptions or accidents are made. But generally stated, a low-risk victim has had some contact or association with the offender. The contact may be completely innocuous. Moreover, the victim may never have even consciously been aware of the offender at the point of contact, although the offender fixated on the victim. This opens the door to principle number two.

Victimology Continuum Principle 2: The lower the victim's risk level to the associated crime, the higher the consideration given that the victim was targeted by the offender.

Although principle 1 suggests that the low-risk victim is probably associated in some way to the offender, the situation, circumstances, and environment will aid in assessing whether the victim had the misfortune of an unexpected opportunity or was, in fact, specifically identified and targeted by the offender. For example, using the same domesticated housewife scenario, let's change the situation, circumstances, and environment. In this case, social lifestyle is similar, but the filters are different. As usual, at 5:30 A.M. her husband leaves for work. She stays in bed and their nine-month-old baby lies asleep in a crib in an adjoining room. At 5:45 A.M., an intruder breaks in through the basement apartment window. The assailant threatens to injure the child if the victim doesn't comply with his demands. The offender places a pillow on the victim's face and she is raped. The intruder then escapes.

The situation (basement apartment, 5:30 A.M., etc.), circumstances (victim is alone as usual with a baby; the couple has lived at the location for only three months; husband leaves at the same approximate time daily during the week, etc.), and the environment (apartment complex, filled with students and transient tenants, etc.) screen out the possibility of a stranger/opportunity crime. The probability suggests that the victim was "targeted" by the offender, who may or may not have been known by the victim. But certainly the offender was aware of the victim and her domestic lifestyle and availability.

The environment further implies the offender's familiarity with the apartment complex and his prior presence there.

Anubis, god of embalming, guards the secrets of the innermost treasury of Tutankhamen's tomb (copyright: Griffith Institute, Oxford).

Victimology Continuum Principle 3: The higher the victim's risk level is to the associated crime, the higher the probability that the offender is a stranger to the victim.

Typically, high-risk victims, as defined by lifestyle (prostitute, runaway, hitchhiker, drug addict, gang member, etc.), simply place themselves recklessly and without regard to their own personal safety in situations, circumstances, and environments that elevate their risk level. Furthermore, they are willfully exposed to a variety of disreputable characters and unfavorable surroundings; they are consistently vulnerable, by choice and lifestyle, to the criminal element. This creates an atmosphere of predictable victimization, high-risk vulnerabilities, and predators. These victims are often those of serial offenders who wait and watch and even seek for such victims. This leads to the next and final principle:

Victimology Continuum Principle 4: The higher the victim's risk level is to the associated crime, the higher the probability that the victim is one of opportunity.

The consistent high-risk lifestyle of the victim and associated dangerous vulnerabilities invite the notice and attention of the "human predator." This unique criminal is on the hunt constantly—seeking, lurking with stealth and concentration for the opportunity to strike. He often waits, with confidence and patience, for this victim who easily falls prey to his design. The high-risk victim forfeits control over his or her fate while willingly stepping into situations, circumstances, and environments that are within the dominion of the offender. The offender, often appearing harmless, is in fact a wolf in sheep's clothing, who cunningly and inconspicuously lures the victim into his control. This type of criminal is often disguised in a "legitimate" role to the victim (i.e., truck driver, "John," hitchhiker, etc.), and when the situation, circumstances and environment are consistent with the offender's design, the victim may be simply devoured, as in the spider and the fly fable.

Victimology consists of asking the appropriate diagnostic questions, acquiring accurate data, and then assimilating that data through diagnostic filters and principles designed to lead the investigation. By using this approach, the investigator is better equipped to focus his energy and efforts toward reasonable probabilities rather than the mere chance of this or that possibility.

In brief, then, victimology is the key to crime analysis. It is the basis for understanding the crime, the offender, the criminal motive, and the victim. The integration has multidimensional impact and multidisciplinary considerations. By understanding who the victim is, we begin to better understand why he was selected, what the offender's motive was, and what the offender likes and dislikes and his or her strengths and weaknesses.

In addition to all these factors, let us not forget that Tutankhamen was young, nonthreatening, and, of course, very influential. Since he was cared for by those who were closest to him, we don't have any reason to believe he was ever, or would be, at risk. This is probably because he had not come to terms yet with his political beliefs or his religious tenets. How do you threaten older men entrenched with rigid belief systems if you don't have any? And physically, he certainly was nonthreatening. On top of all this, he was nonthreatening from political, social, and economic perspectives. All these elements are significant in terms of where it places him in the activities of the powerful few who surrounded him. The degree to which he is in harm's way at this early point is still in the low-risk category.

Also remember that Tut was considered by almost everyone to be a deity, a national treasure who must be protected at all costs. By being a boy pharaoh he was the choicest commodity the guards in charge of him had to protect. Hence, they were extremely careful about the activities they would allow him to engage in. And of course, being a deity, he was generously provided with the best of supplies, treatment, and so on everywhere he went. In short, it would be reasonable to expect the boy to receive the highest degree of physical protection. Like a current-day president or prime minister, this national treasure would be guarded by the very best security in the world.

Somewhere between the ages of fifteen and seventeen, the young man started to come into his own. He was maturing and for the first time showed signs of developing his own value system of political, social, economic, military, and religious beliefs. And when he did show an independent thought, it inevitably had an impact on all those around him, especially those who had such a powerful influence upon him as a child. A good example is Ay, who had actually been the de facto pharaoh while serving as Tut's personal counselor and adviser, thereby winning the boy's trust for many years. We, of course, wondered whether or not Ay would have been supportive of any new ideas and thoughts Tutankhamen was struggling to articulate. What was Ay's response? We had to find out.

So, as we move the boy along our continuum of questions, we begin to see that exposure to possible danger increases. Conflicts, even those of a minor nature, are inevitable, especially in light of the fact Akhenaten brought about revolutionary religious changes just the decade before. Even though Tut is known for virtually denouncing his father in the Restoration Stela (the complete text of which can be found in the appendixes), it is feasible that he experienced a wide range of emotions after his father's death. We must consider the impact Akhenaten's death may have had on the young boy and his mother Kiya's death in childbirth. We are unsure what happened to Smenkhkare, who may have been a brother to Tut, or even Nefertiti, Tut's stepmother. Regardless, Tut probably experienced a great deal of anger after the loss of those close to him. Ay, Maya, Ankhesenamun, and Horemheb may have been his closest confidants, and at the tender age of nine or ten, he could easily have been swayed to denounce his father, or perhaps he was so terribly hurt at the loss that he acted out of rage.

We concluded early on that because the boy loved his father he was somewhat sympathetic to Akhenaten's religious visions, thereby elevating his risk level with those who had been threatened by Akhenaten's radical concepts. After all, throughout history we have examples of how religious fervor caused criminal actions, including murder, in the name of God. For the perpetrators, what once was considered a felony is now a righteous and timely move that not only is sacred but also must be maintained as a royal secret for the good of the common man.

If the teenage king showed independent religious thinking, is it not reasonable to believe he would also show some management initiative, for example, in the restructuring of some of his government and administration? Wouldn't he, to some degree, advocate certain types of changes in policies, procedures, and future strategies for his reign? As this young pharaoh, buoyed up and supported by his sibling bride, came into his own, wouldn't he innocently question the need for some of his advisers? Also, in a country that was struggling financially after the expensive expansion launched by Akhenaten, Tut may have considered reducing his forces to save money. No doubt this would not sit well with the military and, more specifically, with Horemheb.

And wouldn't those who survived in the old days employing old systems suddenly be faced with a series of minicrises? Previously, they had made all the decisions for the boy of nine, ten, eleven, and twelve. Now they had to face a young man who assumes the right and privilege to do whatever he wants. After all, he is the pharaoh, a god on Earth. He may even have wondered if he needed certain individuals who had previously served him. How do people who have job security and are then reassigned react to their loss of power and prestige?

For a moment, picture the frustration felt by Ay. As Tutankhamen's role increases, the role of the advisers would decrease. And how about the concern of Horemheb, the army leader, when he sees the teenager begin to question military matters and decisions? Although relatively minor issues at this early stage of Tut's growth and development, the boy is nonetheless in growing danger. He is still below the medium-risk level, although as he enters puberty he begins to experience outside factors that raise his risk level considerably.

One of the new factors that enters the equation deals with his lifestyle: the boy is about to get married! And who is the woman he is going to marry? Ankhesenamun, a half-sister. Did he like her? Did he need to marry her so young? What was their interpersonal relationship like? Did he look forward to the marriage? Why did it seem that so many of his closest advisers were pushing him into marriage?

Marriage is an emotional upheaval in anyone's life, regardless of how much love is involved.

As far as we know from our readings, there was an intimate, loving relationship between Tutankhamen and Ankhesenamun—at least in terms of what the murals in Tut's tomb tell us. There is speculation on both sides of the table regarding what Tut's statues, paintings, carvings, and historical accounts may have meant. Many of those accounts show Tut and Ankhesenamun as a close, loving couple, "yoked" as one in purpose. Some current-day Egyptologists, such as Dr. Fletcher, argue that these paintings are just romantic depictions, not reality. Yet as we looked at them, not individually, but in their totality, we felt they painted a truer picture of who the young king was because they were shown even in the intimate settings of Tut's tomb. Although some murals suggest that Tut was a great warrior and leader, while a large number depict him with walking canes, his physical condition may suggest something entirely different. If Tut had Klippel Feil syndrome, as we suspect, this could have dramatically impacted him. The recovery of more than one hundred canes from this tomb leads us to this speculation. In fact, we do not know at what point Tut's physical condition began to change, for better or worse.

Another outside factor revolves around Horemheb. As mentioned, Tut was pharaoh of a kingdom that was not engaged in any wars or troubled by internal conflicts. For one of the few times in ancient Egyptian history, there was peace in the land. Certainly the boy-king would have accompanied his military commander-in-chief on training exercises and, like most boys, would have been fascinated by weapons, troop movements, and mock warfare. Certainly he would have been enamored with the troops themselves. But the peaceful scene was about to change, as it inevitably does for all nations. What role did he expect himself to play in an invasion, for example, by the ever-present threat of rebellion by the Hittites?

As a young man, Tut would have participated in certain types of recreational events, even if modestly so. And these sporting and hunting activities would have meant facing certain dangers. Riding horses and chariots and engaging in mock boating battles only would have increased his risk level of being hurt.

According to Dr. Fletcher and what's commonly known about the traditional duties of the pharaoh, the young king was spending a considerable amount of time traveling around Egypt, since his kingdom was experiencing good trade with neighboring kingdoms. Tut not only wanted to attend the various trade markets but also mingle among the people. Historical records show that he loved to travel with Ankhesenamun. His risk level continues to rise with each outing but then again so does his level of protection, which, of course, reduces his overall risk.

As the sliver of shade grew ever larger and we turned our eyes to the setting sun, we summarized our thoughts and determined that King Tut was probably a low-risk victim during his early reign, but as he developed physically, emotionally, spiritually, and temporally, his level of risk slowly began to creep up because of the circumstances he was living in, the situations he found himself dealing with almost daily, and the ever-changing environment.

With all of this in mind, and this is very important, the theory of victimology teaches us that the lower the level of risk an individual has, the higher the probability that the victim will be a target of an aggressive act toward him, and most importantly, that the perpetrator will be known to the victim.

* * *

As the brilliant white sun drifted below the red skyline, we thought of how the Egyptians believed that the gods had once again gone to sleep, only to wake in the opposite sky. As the dark fell upon us and we traveled back to Cairo, the sounds of the tombs of Saqqara were replaced with the hustle, bustle, and noise produced by twenty-two million Muslims celebrating another Ramadan breakfast. What a pleasure it was to join them that night in good food and fascinating cultural exchange. But above all, how great that bed in the Cairo Sheraton felt. Yet as we drifted off to sleep, the emotionless gaze of the poverty-stricken people of that land burned in our minds' eyes.

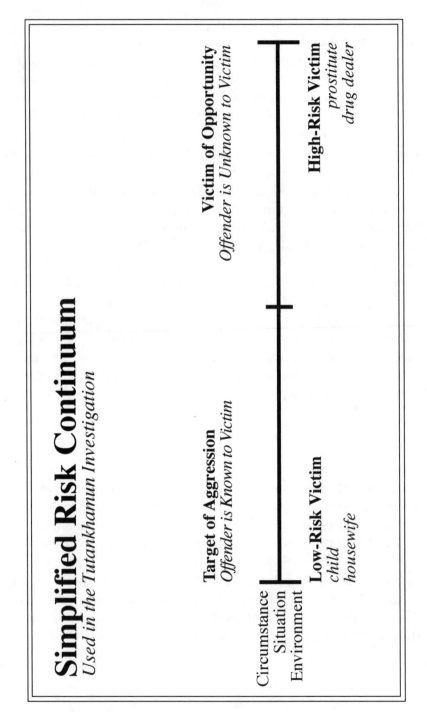

Simplified Risk Continuum
Used in the Tutankhamun Investigation

Target of Aggression
Offender is Known to Victim

Victim of Opportunity
Offender is Unknown to Victim

Circumstance
Situation
Environment

Low-Risk Victim
child
housewife

High-Risk Victim
prostitute
drug dealer

Chapter 6
IT'S MURDER
REASONABLE SUSPICION RULES OUT DEATH BY SUICIDE, NATURAL CAUSES, OR ACCIDENT

Investigating a homicide is both an art and a science, a blend of the practical and the scientific. Without that realization, and that blend which includes a coordinated effort by a team of specialists, the chance of a successful case solution is greatly diminished. I remember having a discussion with a group of homicide detectives in England about the difference between a detective and an investigator. It went like this: All detectives might be called investigators, but not all investigators can be called detectives. Investigators need a trail of investigative factors which might eventually lead to a successful conclusion of their inquiry. If there are no investigative factors to pursue then they are finished. That is where the detective comes in; a person who can paint a landscape he or she had never seen from inside a darkened room, which is actually the crime scene. That's the difference between the craft and the art.

Pierce R. Brooks, Captain (Ret.)
Los Angeles Police Department

Captain Brooks clearly understood the use of profiling in the art and science of criminal investigation. The process of profiling can be defined as the innate sense, the street sense, the ability to see not just what is visible but what isn't visible at a crime scene, to see into the offender's personality, to understand his strengths and weaknesses, and to see what motivates him and gets his motor running.

Whether we're known as detectives or investigators doesn't matter. Some cops even refer to us as "profilers." What we have come to believe is that together we're stronger than alone. We have developed the ability to question and examine each other's opinions and theories. And one thing was clear while in Egypt: while behavior is the same today as it was thirty-three hundred years ago, without our living-day expert, Dr. Joann Fletcher, we would have had a much more difficult time cracking this case.

As we sat outside the oldest coffee shop in Cairo, explaining our thinking thus far to Joann that we might truly be "on" to something, she responded, "Yes, what you are telling me is possible. Listening to the two of you is like walking into a very familiar house through a different door." We sat quietly and watched the Egyptian people across the street walk in and out of the mosque, which was decorated like a home at Christmas time. As different cultures appeared all around us, we realized how very much we were all the same.

Later that evening, after a delicious Egyptian dinner, we gathered not only to film with the Atlantic crew our impressions of the day but also to continue our discussions with Dr. Fletcher. The three of us met in the lobby to discuss what we in law enforcement know as "reasonable suspicion leading to probable cause." We wanted Joann to hear our reasoning as we applied the principle to our investigation into Tut's death.

For a few moments, we clarified both terms for Joann, explaining how they actually work in the law. Many factors contribute to a police officer's level of authority. Varying standards of police proof exist to justify respective levels of police action during citizen contacts. *Reasonable suspicion* (RS) and *probable cause* (PC) are the standards required by the courts to justify any police action that is determined to surpass constitutional protections. Police are given authority to enforce laws, to conduct arrests, and even to apply deadly force; however, such action is always scrutinized and evaluated under the magnifying glasses of RS and PC. They are legal standards that measure the reasonableness of police action, and they further legitimize police authority.

Reasonable suspicion justifies police action when it can be shown that the facts or circumstances observed by the officer would lead a reasonable person to suspect that a *crime* has been, is being, or will be committed. It is a less rigorous standard than that for PC. It justifies an officer's action to take additional investigative steps to further corroborate his suspicion and confirm what he believes. After acquiring additional evidence, the officer is now equipped to continue his or her actions in identifying and arresting a suspect.

The next level of police authority, that is, arrest, is justified by the corresponding level of proof described in probable cause, which is similar to RS. It incorporates the same principles of the belief of a crime being committed but with the added emphasis of *who* committed it. PC exists when the facts or *evidence* would lead a reasonable person to believe that a crime has been, is being, or will be committed, and *the person arrested* is responsible. There is no specific rule or determining factor for what establishes probable cause; the existence of probable cause is ultimately determined by the *trier of fact* from the facts in the record. For example, a judge is considered a "trier of fact" and may have to determine in court if a police officer acted reasonably under the circumstances based upon the facts of the case. Mere suspicion is not sufficient to establish probable cause. There must be some corroborating facts articulated by a police officer to illustrate that he or she had probable cause when detaining or arresting a citizen. The police officer's mere opinion that a crime has been committed is insufficient. The officer must articulate *why* he or she believes a crime took place and show a logical explanation and rationale for this belief based upon observations, experience, education, and training. PC is also a common-sense standard, requiring that the available facts would warrant a man of reasonable caution to draw the same conclusion. It is important to note also that probable cause does not demand proof that such a belief is correct or more likely true than false.

Reasonable suspicion is a term that not only is used to justify an investigation but also allows law enforcement to open up an investigation and answer important questions that help lead to a conclusion, a satisfying conclusion that a death is natural. Probable cause is a higher standard of proof than reasonable suspicion and requires more evidence in order to bring charges against a suspect. In short, reasonable suspicion justifies an investigation to answer general questions; probable cause answers the questions with sufficient evidence to justify actually bringing charges against a person in court.

We began our investigation of the Tutankhamen case on the grounds of reasonable suspicion that the young pharaoh died under suspicious circumstances. But then we needed to develop sufficient data and information that would satisfy our question to determine whether or not his death was due to an accident, natural causes, suicide, or a homicide.

We believed that through a comprehensive evaluation of Tut's death, we could better determine how he died. Reflecting on the fact that we will all die at some point, and that our death will fall into one of these traditional categories, we concurred with Dr. Fletcher and other antiquities experts that there was reasonable suspicion to warrant further examination of the facts that the young King Tut may have met with foul play.

So what were the unanswered questions?

Rather than answer the most difficult question of all first, "Was Tut murdered?" we chose to examine the manner in which he was buried. Our suspicion of homicide was founded on the many indications that suggested that Tut was buried in a manner that was different than other pharaohs of the time. The first indication evaluated was the amount of time taken to mummify Tut. Traditionally, at that time in Egyptian history, we understood that the mummification process took approximately seventy days.

Some experts have theorized that Tut may have been decomposing and the stench was too great for the embalmers to continue the mummification process. Because of the smell and the need to

The wreath, garlands, and linen shroud that covers Tut's second coffin.
The garlands consisted of olive leaves, blue lotus water-lily petals,
cornflowers, and celery leaves (copyright: Griffith Institute, Oxford).

still be around him, it is thought that the problem was overcome by covering the body with unguents and perfumes. This might explain why he was discovered in the condition he was. The unguent/decomposition concept raises some interesting questions. One is "If Tut's mummification followed the outlined protocol for the procedure, wouldn't the removal of the brain (which held no real value in the hereafter) never have happened?" Protocol would have suggested that the internal organs would be the first thing removed so that the lengthy process of preserving and drying them out could be accomplished. Our experience has shown that animals that have died and begun to decompose usually exhibit similar characteristics to humans. Their stomachs first begin to swell and eventually they will burst, releasing horrible gases and smells. In a human, this fleshy, fluid-rich environment is, too, generally the most odorous after death. In Tut's case, it could have stopped the efforts of even the most conscientious embalmer. One can only imagine how terrible the smell would have to be to stop the process that would ensure the pharaoh's ascension into the afterlife.

To further argue this point, we are able to rely on the evidence that supported Tut's mummification extending beyond merely removing his soft internal organs and placing them into canopic jars. The canopic jars were containers specifically set aside for the organs of the mummified pharaoh. It was believed that after death, the organs would go from the jars back into the body of the pharaoh, possibly with help of the spirits of the afterlife. The natron solution is made up of a sodium carbonate. It absorbs water readily, making it an excellent solution for drying the body tissue. Natron was found easily in the Egyptian playa lakes and was much better than salt as a drying agent because it also destroys grease and fat. Since we know that the young king had his organs placed into the canopic jars and that the process of removing the brain and filling the cranium with resins was accomplished in due time, we can only assume that the smell must have not been so bad to prevent completion of the mummification process. The large muscle tissues would have continued to decompose to some extent, but they shouldn't have created smells more horrific than those of the thoracic region. In addition, current evidence of located unidentified bodies in dry, desert climates supports the idea that the bodies themselves appear to self-mummify. Ancient Egypt is nature's best drying region in the world.

Continuing this train of thought, the mummification process first required the removing of the organs and placing them in the natron and other drying agents. It appears that the majority of the odor problem associated with the decomposition would have been removed or greatly lessened with just this process alone.

In considering the four classifications of explaining Tut's death, we first excluded the least probable situations: suicide, death by natural cause, and death by accident.

Suicide?

Suicide seems unlikely for the young pharaoh, who appears to have been enjoying his role and responsibility. Records reflect him as an active king—hunting, chariot racing, training with the army, and learning the duties of leadership. One could speculate that Tut would have fallen victim to depression after the loss of his children to miscarriage. We presume they were mummified and protected by Tut and Ankhesenamun if, in fact, they were the children placed in the tomb. Dr. Richard Boyer at the Utah State Medical Examiner's Office informed us the two fetuses bore similar physical defects of Klippel Feil Syndrome in the cervical discs as Tut.

Other suicide scenarios seem unlikely since Tut had everything at his "beck and call," although some—including us and, at times, Dr. Fletcher and Dr. Hawass—theorize that Tut had everything but happiness. Nonetheless, there is nothing to support this view, and it seems appropriate to disregard suicide as a possible means for the young man's death.

DEATH BY NATURAL CAUSES?

According to all of the experts we interviewed in Egypt, the United Kingdom, and the United States, as well as all the documentation we could get our hands on, it appears less likely that Tut died of a natural event. The mortality rate for the infants and young children of "commoners" was probably very high in 1500 BCE, and perhaps even for those of royalty, but our interviews led us to believe that the royal families had much better living conditions, cleanliness, and medical care than those afforded to everyday Egyptians. In fact, some of the experts we interviewed suggested that once a royal child reached age ten or so, his or her lifespan was significantly longer than most people in the kingdom because of the great care received from attendants and their advantaged lifestyle.

As Tutankhamen developed into a teenager, he probably sought out more adventure and excitement, leading to an increased love for hunting, chariot racing, and learning the art of war. There are several reasons to believe that although he was very active, he probably had some physical disability. First, Dr. Richard Boyer, who examined the x-rays, indicated that Tut's spine appeared to be afflicted with the disease. Second, there were one hundred thirty walking sticks found in Tut's tomb. Third, certain paintings in Tut's tomb showed Tut leaning on a cane with his legs crossed awkwardly underneath him. Fourth, there was a U-shaped headrest found, which scientists believe was for King Tut in order to keep his head and spine in a straight line. Fifth, evidence showed that one of Tut's children that were buried with him also had scoliosis.[1] We can only suppose these renditions are true, since they are consistent with his age, position, and access to challenging activities. If Tut, even though a king, were like most young boys then and today, he probably fantasized about being a great hunter and warrior and would probably be found hanging around Horemheb's army, learning the art of war. As a teenager, it would be important for him to be among the troops in order to be seen as a war leader. Fulfillment of the need for power, dominion, and control was not only sought by Tut, but these were absolutely necessary in order to be esteemed as a leader of the great Egyptian kingdom.

The rushed embalming process is inconsistent with a pharaoh who might have died as a result of natural causes. In fact, even if he had been decomposing to some degree, it seems that the greatest effort would have been made to ensure his ascension into eternal life. At Tut's young age, it is unlikely that he would have suffered any ailment consistent with sudden death. Most illnesses of the Eighteenth Dynasty would have caused the young King to be sick for some time before death, clearly providing leadership ample time to prepare for his burial.

Some theories—including that of Dr. Ernst Rodin—suggest that Tut may have been injured or killed while away from Thebes, and during the course of returning him to the embalmers, the corpse may have begun to decompose. The stench would explain the need for great quantities of unguents placed both in his body and in the sarcophagus. Although the heavy use of unguents was one of the embalming processes practiced during this period, it is not a basis for considering death by suicide or natural causes. While alone this may raise questions, in totality, the burial, record-keeping, and so forth would have been more complete under normal circumstances. One must remember that this was a pharaoh, a god. To simply drop him in a tomb to be forgotten didn't make sense.

In closely examining the x-rays of the skull of King Tutankhamen, Carter discovered that the young pharaoh's entire brain had been removed through the nose. In addition, resins were poured into the skull cavity in several different handlings. It seems unlikely that the embalmers would take such care in clearing out the brain and skull cavity portion of the body, since that area was considered virtually useless. Furthermore, if the purpose of the unguents was to stultify the stench from Tut's decomposed state, it seems less likely that the embalmers would spend time in removing the unimportant (and not stinking) brain, if their goal was to perfume the rotting body and get it buried. This further suggests to us that the embalming process was going normally and then suddenly stopped.

This process of quickly burying Tut also raises questions about the placement of Tut in Ay's tomb. According to most Egyptologists, the construction of a pharaoh's tomb coincides with the beginning of his reign. We learned from our study of the many differing theo-ries on pharaonic tomb preparation that Tut's tomb may have been as much as 80 percent completed at the time of his death. Again, we were reminded that this is the eternal resting place for the pharaoh. More importantly, as we considered the move from Amarna to Thebes, it only made sense that the pharaoh's tomb would take precedence over that of a servant like Ay. Furthermore, it wouldn't make sense that Ay's tomb would progress faster than that of the leader, the god of Egypt, the pharaoh. At 80 percent completed, the burial chamber was already larger than the tomb where he was actu-ally buried. As mentioned, a large portion of the items entombed with the boy-king did not even belong to him. Many artifacts had the original owner's name on them. Other names were etched out.

By Accident?

It is difficult to focus upon or exclude the possibility that Tutankhamen died as the result of an accident. Yes, it's possible he may have crashed while racing his chariot across the desert floor. Or in a violent fall, he could have broken his neck or hit his head on a rock. Or any other number of scenarios are possible. Forensic exam-inations tell us that Tut had several, if not all, of his cervical discs fused together. His lack of motion in the neck may explain the pos-sibility of a high neck fracture or severing of the spinal cord in a vio-lent collision or fall. Other forensics tests suggest that a blow to the nose region of the face may have occurred, dislodging a small piece of bone that is visible in x-rays. Although the origin of this bone fragment is disputed, it must be considered in any theory of death, especially homicide. The sudden frontal attack could cause his head to rock back, snapping the already-brittle neck. Even today, people die from the brain swelling after a blow to the head.

One thing is for sure, though. King Tutankhamen was a national treasure. As such, he was closely guarded. And it seems that he may even have been protected from his own immaturity when it came to safety. It seems that those who were assigned to protect the boy

Tut's six chariots as found in the tomb's antechamber. The broken wheels suggest to some scholars that young Tut died in a racing accident (copyright: Griffith Institute, Oxford).

would have done everything in their power to minimize the risk level in any activity he undertook.

In every scenario we discussed regarding Tut's risk level during his daily activities, he remained on the low end of the risk continuum. The only thing that elevated his risk seems to have been his circumstances and environments as he became more powerful and more closely aligned with Queen Ankhesenamun and perhaps more comfortable in deciding how the Egyptian government should be run. It appears that as Tut's need for Ay's advice and leadership diminished, his risks began to rapidly increase, leading us to conclude that the most probable cause of King Tutankhamen's death was murder!

MURDER?

In evaluating the possibility that King Tutankhamen's death was a homicide, we had to evaluate the stages of Tut's life before, during, and after his demise. The one person who had the ability to remain in a position of power throughout Akhenaten's reign, and even before that during Amenhotep III's leadership at Thebes, was Ay, the perfect politician. Under Amenhotep, Ay learned the art of manipulation, and by the time of Akhenaten's reign, he was in the powerful position of "God's father and fan bearer on the king's right hand" to Akhenaten. In fact, after Akhenaten's spiritual rebirth and move to Amarna, Ay may well have maintained his close association with the Amun priests, who had been stripped of their power and position yet remained a strong force among the Egyptian people. Ay purportedly placed himself as the great mediator between the Amun priests and Akhenaten in his role as the chief high priest of the Amun priesthood and may well have been considered by Akhenaten to be keeping the Amun priests under control.

During this period though, at least one murder plot was hatched against King Akhenaten while living in Akhetan, several years before Tut became pharaoh. This murder plot was portrayed in the tomb of the police chief of Akhetan, Mahu; the wall painting depicted how the plot was foiled and the suspect tried, convicted, and presumably executed. This pictograph provides solid proof of at least one assassination attempt against the pharaoh, and Ay is found prominently in the scene. It is during this reign of Akhenaten that we first learn of Horemheb, a dutiful soldier in the army but clearly not yet a great leader.

Details seem sketchy at this point, but it is clear that Akhenaten chose someone to rule with him for a very short time prior to his death. Dr. Fletcher explained that the coruler was either Smenkhkare (a son of Akhenaten), or perhaps Smenkhkare was the throne name of Nefertiti, the ruler's wife and queen. Nonetheless, the records are vague, and we soon see the end of Akhenaten's reign and the emergence of Tut as king. Perhaps Ay felt he was in a position at this time to take over, since it would seem he may have been surprised by the young boy's appointment to the throne. And, as past vizier, Ay is able to maintain his high position in the Egyptian government as Tut is brought into leadership. Incidentally, Ay often referred to his humble beginnings and ascent to greatness, even though he was just a commoner.

Over time, Ay convinced young Tut that he needed to return to Thebes in order to bring suffering Egypt back together, uniting the peoples of the upper and lower regions. When Akhenaten moved the power seat to Akhetaten, his building effort placed a great financial burden on the entire country. Early in his reign as king, and when he is very unsure of himself and his abilities as a leader, Tut returns to Thebes. He knowingly or unknowingly denounces his father's beliefs and returns the kingdom to the worship of the Amun, signified by the words pronounced in the Restoration Stela.

It is our theory that as Tutankhamen grows and develops and as he and Ankhesenamun assume greater leadership of Egypt, their need for Ay diminishes. As Ay witnesses his power base decreasing and reflects on the difficulties of bringing the kingdom back to the worship of the Amun, he develops a plan to murder Tut, perhaps as he did for Akhenaten.

Some theories suggest General Horemheb was away from the area on assignment by Ay at the time of Tut's death, and Tut was buried before Horemheb could return. If this is true, it focuses our attention even more on Ay.

In the end, it appears that Ay has the greatest motive, means, and opportunity to commit the homicide. We can theorize that Ay was responsible in part for the assassination attempt on Akhenaten. And to this day we don't know what happened to Smenkhkare. At the time of Tut's death, Ay figured prominently, and no one, including the chief of police at Thebes, would dare challenge him in any investigation of Tut's death. With General Horemheb gone, Ay and his conniving Amun priests crown Ay as the new pharaoh. Never again will his words and orders be questioned.

This raises some interesting behavioral questions. If the mummification process generally takes about seventy days to perform, didn't Ay have adequate time to gather his craftsmen and appropriately complete Tut's rightful tomb?

Even if Tut's body had begun to decompose (which seems unlikely,

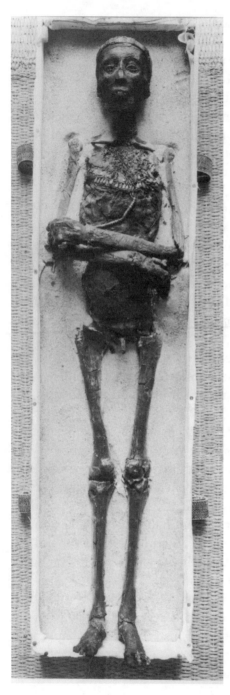

The remains of Tut in 1926. While living, the king stood 5 feet, 5.5 inches, but the postmortem shrinkage of tissues and subsequent mummification reduced his height to 5 feet, 4 inches (copyright: Griffith Institute, Oxford).

since the embalmers were going through the basic steps of mummification when they removed his brain), wouldn't the decaying process have been slowed or stopped by removing the entrails and stuffing and drying the body, thus preserving it for enough time to appropriately bury the king?

Why does Ay promote himself (with the support of the Amun priests who he had ushered back into power with the return of Tut to Thebes and the forsaking of Akhenaten's beliefs) and bury Tut before General Horemheb can return from his travels?

Why does Ay place himself in a position of providing the Opening of the Mouth ceremony and confiscate Tut's tomb while placing the rightful pharaoh in his own, less ornate crypt?

Why is Tut buried with treasures, furniture, and other artifacts that are not his? After ten years as king, it seems that he would have developed a large quantity of personal items and property that would have accompanied him into eternity. Yet he was denied his possessions, leaving them behind with others. Unless his burial was seen as a convenient way of getting rid of anything and everything connected with his hated father, which some Egyptologists think is another explanation.

We wonder if General Horemheb, a true patriot of the Egyptian empire, found himself questioning the deaths of his two great leaders. In his personal and quiet time away from the others, he surely must have questioned why he had been dispatched from the capital prior to the deaths of Akhenaten, Tut, the Hittite king's son, and perhaps even Ankhesenamun.

Had Horemheb thought such things, he probably pushed them to the outer limits of his consciousness since he was a "patriot" and a guardian of the pharaohs of Egypt. Not much different from our military leaders today, he would not speak ill of his boss because it was the office of pharaoh he represented to the people that was most important.

Yet, as Ay's life comes to an end (most sources believe he lived to approximately sixty-five years of age), we wondered whether he may have made a deathbed confession about his role in the death of the pharaohs, and if so, did he confess to Horemheb? In the end, however, Horemheb made the final decision in terms of who was to have power and control throughout the eternities. Did Horemheb finally render just punishment as he ordered the cartouches and eyes, nose, and mouth of Ay's figures to be removed, thus removing him from history and eternity? If indeed Ay had killed young Tut, throwing him into a small, half-finished tomb to be forgotten forever, isn't it ironic that in spite of Ay's wishes, the kid became the most famous pharaoh of all time?

Was Ay the actual assassin or the evil eminence behind the assassination of Tutankhamen? We still didn't know.

NOTE

1. "Discovery Channel: King Tut" [online], dsc.discovery.com/anthology/unsolvedhistory/kingtut/kingtut.html [December 8, 2003].

Chapter 7

ZIGZAGGING
ACROSS EGYPT
SOAKING UP THE SUN,
LISTENING TO THE EXPERTS,
AND COLLECTING CLUES

U p at 5:30 the next morning, we scrambled to catch a
7:00 A.M. flight to Luxor, only to learn a few minutes before
departure that the plane had been delayed for hours. Fortunately,
another was readily available, and we flew uneventfully to Luxor, a
much more social and hospitable city than Cairo. For one thing,
Luxor isn't so crammed. We were surprised to see that most of the
city's citizens were going about their activities on foot. Dressed in
gowns and turbans, and with countless children with no shoes inter-
mingling among them, the vacant-eyed pedestrians showed little or
no emotion or expression. In contrast, the children flashed toothy
smiles and appeared to be warm, friendly, and trusting. Most of the
unfortunate adults live in modest, even primitive, conditions. For
them, life is little more than work, a little rest, and death.

Prior to leaving Utah for the African continent, we had contacted
some local retailers and a friend and owner of SuperSonic Car Wash
to see about obtaining a supply of Olympic memorabilia and lapel

Greg and Mike
pose in front
of the Saqqara
Pyramid
(photo owned
by Mike King).

pins to give to the children we would come across in Egypt. Our friend Mark Goddard made sure that we had a large supply to share with the locals we would encounter. With the state of Utah preparing to host the 2002 Olympic Winter Games, we were certain the pins would be a "hit."

In addition, at the direction of FBI specialists in Washington, DC, who had lived extensively in Egypt, we left at home all information that would point toward our profession as law enforcement officers, especially our badges and credentials. Furthermore, we were instructed to make sure that our passage was listed as tourism rather than research to avoid the inevitable scrutiny that would come.

Once in Egypt, we quickly learned how valuable the Olympic pins were. We were continually approached by children screaming, "Pin! Pin! Please, pin!" We couldn't have been the first to enter the country with pins to trade. But we gladly passed out the expensive collector pins of the Olympic Games to anyone who asked, especially the children. In one case, Mike offered a pin to a teenager who was demanding "Pin! Pin!" But the young man pushed Mike's hand aside and pointed to the pens in upper pockets. We pulled them out and held the pens in front of the teenager—each holding a pen probably worth about twenty-five cents. Our other hand held a collector pin worth over ten dollars. The fellow delightedly grabbed the twenty-five-cent pen and tested its ink on his open hand. Assured that it worked, he clutched it closely to his chest and said, "My name is Mohammed. Thank you." That evening we made sure that we picked up every pen we could find in the hotel, and the following day we purchased a large quantity of pens to hand out in the future.

It wasn't until many months later, back in Utah during the Olympic games, that we found an opportunity to pass out those Olympic pins. Later, we laughed about it all. After all, what would children from a country covered with sand and heat know or care about the Winter Olympics? In fact, the most important thing in most of their lives was just making it through another day.

In Luxor, we checked into a hotel that must have been created as a movie set. It was simply stunning in all its luxury. From our seventh-floor balconies overlooking the Nile, we could see clearly to the west bank opposite Luxor—a plush green land full of life for a short distance, then appearing more like the west side of Utah Lake, barren and destitute, a condition that developed as the Nile receded. No one can doubt that the great river is the aorta that brings life to Egypt's otherwise desolate wasteland.

In the hotel lobby, we met up with the Egyptian guide, Ali, who handled all our travel arrangements. Good friends of Dr. Fletcher's, Ali and his family adopted Joann when she lived with them while studying Egyptology in the area. A warm, generous, and sweet-natured man of forty, he supported himself, his wife, and five children not only by serving as a guide for tourists and foreign dignitaries but also by earning a small commission from selling silver cartouches and other items. These unique memorabilia are indeed something to cherish! They are small charms depicting a person's name in ancient Egyptian symbols. During the dynasty periods, artisans painted or sculpted cartouches on the walls of tombs, crypts, and temples, identifying the names of not only the entombed but also those who participated in the lives and events of the deceased.

Since Joann spoke so highly about these inexpensive little treasures, adding that Ali knew where we could buy them, we immediately asked if he would drive us to the shop of the craftsman. Of course, he was delighted to do so.

Driving through the narrow streets of the downtown area, high rises lining the small passageways like dominoes about to topple, we soon arrived in a neighborhood absent of any commercial activity whatsoever. Entering an artisan's humble home, furnished with only the barest necessities, we met the man and his apprentice son, who showed us a variety of examples to choose from. After making our selections, we were invited to follow the two to the back of the dwelling and into a small cubicle where we sat down and watched them fashion our cartouches.

It was amazing. The craftsman's son pulled out a small wooden box from his drawer and with a small pair of tweezers carefully extricated certain ready-made symbols from among hundreds and carefully placed them on a silver charm. Using the most basic of tools on a rudimentary workbench, the artisan and his son were quickly engrossed in the most minute of all possible craftwork. With the boy intent on observing every move his father made, the artisan slowly and meticulously attached some five or six symbols, each no more than an eighth of an inch in width and length, to the silver charm.

Upon completing this task, the artisan motioned for all of us to follow him through a straw door into his small backyard. Enclosed by the walls of high rises on three sides, the square of pounded old earth couldn't have been more than fifteen feet by fifteen feet. Looking straight up ten stories, we saw nothing but a forest of protruding pipes and windows. In the small backyard was a simple makeshift oven, or kiln, where he soldered his metal elements together. Next to this crude heating apparatus was another homemade device that contained grinding and buffing rotors, propane tanks, and prongs. After fusing the small symbols to the base of the cartouche, which took only a few minutes, he began the process of polishing the charm to his satisfaction. When we asked for one more cartouche, he literally leapt to his feet and repeated the entire process.

Using the crudest of all instruments, as well as the most inexpensive materials, he had created a work of art that rivaled any piece of jewelry in the entire history of ancient Egyptian art. Joann was right. The guy was a genius.

On our drive back to the hotel, thanking Ali all the way for the introduction, we marveled at what could be done by the man if he were provided the latest state-of-the-art jeweler's technology. Not having it, however, did not affect his craftsmanship. He was content believing that he did indeed have all the latest equipment. Each of us was delighted to have a beautiful memento to take home.

From the hotel's pier later that afternoon we boarded a small motorboat and cruised over to the west bank of the Nile. That calm, great blue-green river is obviously the lifeblood of the nation. It teems with life and action. All around we saw the absolute dependency. Without the Nile's precious waters there would be utter desert desolation.

Disembarking, we were suddenly mobbed by children of all ages! And every single one trying to sell us something—anything—everything under the sun! A rock of alabaster, a small basket, a piece of throw-away fruit. You name it, they had it to sell. But what beautiful, charming kids, the likes of whom you have never seen before, all endearing, all innocent! "Look," we exclaimed, "There's Tut at nine. And over there, I see Tut at fourteen!" Hey, for that matter, he could have been any one of these youngsters thrashing around us today. Later, of course, we laughed because we were really the innocent ones. The little rascals had charmed us out of virtually every pen we had. We couldn't figure out why we bought so many alabaster rocks of no consequence. And we had given up our money freely and happily! Who cares, we chuckled, since the joy they gave us in those few moments made us feel good and rich.

Here, on the west bank opposite Luxor, we spent a sunny afternoon visiting crypts, tombs, and temples. First on the agenda were two magnificent statues of Amenhotep III, grandfather of King Tut, and father to Akhenaten, Tut's dad. Chiseled and carved by ancient artists who had removed all the dross to reveal what they visualized was inside, the statues were from monolithic chunks of sandstone, not plaster or some other pliable mold. We had never seen any statues or materials like this.

During that marvelous outing, partially led by our guide Ali, we were filmed and photographed playing our roles for the Discovery Channel. In a way, we weren't really acting but seriously going about our job of sleuthing. For example, the roadway we were traversing to the location where we were to be filmed was an ancient canal used to transport both people and goods to the great Palace of Amenhotep. Tutankhamen would have traveled the same route upon his return to Thebes. Wouldn't he have been awestruck to see what his grandfather had designed and built? Wouldn't it be natural for the young king to want to carry on his legacy? But countering his dream, on the other hand, were sinister people attempting to influence and manipulate the pharaoh to return to the polytheistic ways of the past, rejecting his father's efforts to transform the kingdom into a monotheistic devotion to Aten, the one and true God.

Early that evening, we headed for the ancient foundations of Amenhotep's palace and its rambling eighty-acre site. Joann described the king's own vast apartment with its reception rooms, robing room and en suite bathroom, kitchens, offices and storerooms, the queen's apartments, those of the royal family and royal women, the high officials, and of course the retinue of servants each would require. The palace buildings also housed the royal workshops, a separate temple of Amun and Ra to the north, and a great viewing platform and altar out in the desert, with a causeway running northward, linking the palace to the king's funerary temple.

Like all ancient Egyptian dwellings, the whole complex was built mainly from standard mud-brick, stamped with the royal name, just like modern brick factories mark their products. Fixtures and fittings were made of stone and wood, and the general level of luxury was indicated by the presence of columned halls, bathrooms, and walled gardens complete with pools. The rooms themselves were once sumptuously decorated in varied designs of vivid color, embellished with glazed tiles and gold leaf, and quite comparable to anything from Akhenaten's city at Amarna, to judge from the ten thousand fragments of painted plaster that have been recovered so far.

To sit there in silence as the sun descended in the west and attempt to visualize the grandeur that once enshrouded the legendary facilities was one of the highlights of our Egyptian travels.

After an hour or so, we stopped at a small outdoor café situated directly in front of another huge temple—that of Ramses II. Here, amid the hustle and bustle of ordinary business, socializing, and general chaos of everyday Luxor life, we were filmed sitting in front of the little restaurant, quietly enjoying the Egyptian fare. Unbelievable! We had only seen something like this in the movies. So many people, so many activities, so much noise! Of course, we loved it, as we proceeded to cut our own separate dimension in time and space as far as the investigation was concerned.

The next morning, it was lift-off time, believe it or not, in no less than a Jules Verne *Around the World in Eighty Days*–type balloon, to drift over the Valley of the Kings. As we climbed into our minivan, the multitudes were already beginning to line the streets with their daily goods. With considerable grace and poise, women scurried along, balancing their burdens atop their heads. Men rode in their donkey-driven wooden carts piled high with you-name-it. Some of the carts were even pulled by water buffalo! For the owners, this simple, dependable transportation was life itself—a true gift from God. For a moment, we were again transported thirty-three hundred years back in time. Meanwhile, unfinished row houses lined the streets. Our immediate impression was that the structures resembled in material, composition, and construction those of the Anasazi Indians in the Canyonlands. We learned that these small units of housing didn't just house husband, wife, and children but also aunts, uncles, cousins, and grandparents. Nowhere in the back alleys, or off-streets, was a modern-day vehicle to be found. Every now and then, we would come across a camel or two, their proud owners riding atop with a genuine sense of dignity and pride, if not outright arrogance.

Finally, in contrast to all the congestion we had just driven through was the open, barren desert. There before us was a small group of ordinary laborers employing a gas-powered generator to blow hot air into a large, nylon balloon. We saw that the edges were attached to three-inch- to four-inch-diameter nylon ropes draping down to linkages attached to a very large basket divided into five sections. Each section was separated by waist-high walls also composed of thick, fibrous material. Compartments one through four were reserved for passengers who dared the safety and security of the device. Section five was set aside for the so-called captain, who would fly the air-lifted, air-transported vehicle.

Needless to say, we were both taken aback. And as we came nearer to lift-off, we became downright scared—especially as we considered a failed lift-off or landing on sudden impact. But the thrill of adventure prevailed, and we climbed aboard along with several of our camera crew members. The last one to jump aboard was the self-appointed captain, who, with a friendly and toothless grin, inspired both fear and confidence at once. Just what the doctor ordered! His old, food-stained white shirt with gold "captain" shoulder lapels also added to our increasing depression. After all, wouldn't you, too, be reassured sailing a thousand feet over the low hills and rugged mountains of the Valley of the Kings in a God-only-knows-how-old private, possibly homemade, contraption guided by a man whose only qualification to fly was the fact that he owned the thing? Were we dreaming? Were we seriously going to risk our lives? Was this a scene out of *Dumb and Dumber*? Was the moment pure fantasy or a reality challenging our sanity?

Lift off! The balloon expanded to appropriate capacity as the captain barked orders to his "boys," who were all wearing promotional shirts advertising his flying balloon enterprise. The securing ropes, which were now the only attachment we had left to the earth, were released and we were suddenly airborne. Floating smoothly and peacefully higher and higher, we looked down into the faces of the ground crew, who were chanting some melodious tune we couldn't understand, hoping the score wasn't from the musical production *The Curse of King Tut*. Actually, as we thought about it, most of that crew, and probably the captain, too, believed in a Tut curse. As our land-secure observers waved farewell, and we in turn to them, except more soberly, our feelings were not commensurate with our weak gestures. But suddenly, as we began to look around, we were filled with exhilaration. The vista was overwhelming, a panorama extending as far as the eye could see. The perspective was incredible. Below us we could see the tops of and into the most basic of Egyptian dwellings, the residents pouring out of their homes to wave at us.

Beyond us in the western mountain area were endless ancient trails cutting through the dry, dusty, and rocky terrain, all steep and jagged from side to side. All, of course, were man-made cuts along

An aerial photograph of the Valley of the Kings. The shadow of the hot-air balloon that Greg and Mike rode in can be seen against the hillside (photo by Mike King).

cracked and blistered mountainsides. Heaven only knows how many Tut-type tombs remain undiscovered there, we thought.

In a diary he maintained throughout our visit to Egypt, Greg was so moved by this experience that he wrote the following:

> Human hands bent and twisted at the waist perpendicular to the barren ground. Yielding only to the toil and heaving labor by the chainlinks of men. Moistened exclusively by streams of their perspiration extracted by rays of parching sunlight. Numerous tombs line up like dominoes across the face of the mountain uninterrupted by blank and vacant reflections of emptiness. I see the bird's-eye view of Ramses II Temple and the foundation of what was once the palace and City of Amenhotep. We also see the ancient temple of Medina Net Abu, the notorious location of another Islamic Jihad terrorist attack ending the lives of 63 tourists. The terrorists were hunted down into the mountains where they attempted escape and were executed by the Egyptian police without hesitation. Quick justice—no mercy; immediate

and swift retaliation. Egypt suffered immeasurably subsequent financial losses from the tourist industry. It has taken several years to even begin the financial recovery process and now the September 11th attack had added insult to injury while causing billions of dollars lost in tourism revenue.

It's like economic arterial spray draining the life blood of much of this beautiful country's financial backbone. This is one country that can't afford it. Its people suffer terribly and in a sense bleed to death economically speaking from the irreparable damages caused by these radical militants who will gain nothing but more social and deplorable misery of their own countrymen.

So this magnificent panoramic and spatial scene is more than I can describe. Suffice it to say that it has left an indelible imprint on my psyche that will last indefinitely. A recognition of our need and responsibility to expand our vision, perspective and understanding of other foreign people while acquiring a dimension of personal development and thinking that will remain stagnant otherwise. I guess I feel like it's more of a personal responsibility more than a general responsibility that applies to everyone. Not even a responsibility, really—more of a drive and mission to just experience and grow from.

An hour or so later, as we gradually descended, the captain threw the ground crew the balloon's ropes, and we landed safely. That was the experience of a lifetime, sailing quietly high over the Valley of the Kings. Today, we laugh every time we think about how fearful we were that morning. As we walked around, stretching our feet, we noticed that the desert, like most ancient lands, was strewn with broken pieces of pottery—ancient pottery made and used by people of one of the most progressive civilizations known to man. How far they had descended from their once–pinnacle of glory was beyond us. The now-barren wasteland and scattered remnants of an industrious and productive people were but a prototype of what was to be and has now become. We regrouped and returned to Luxor Temple at Luxor, in ancient times known as Thebes, which translates to the "most choice of all places," the religious center of the kingdoms.

Luxor Temple was awesome. Presently, it is very well preserved and reflects approximately three time periods from front to back. It

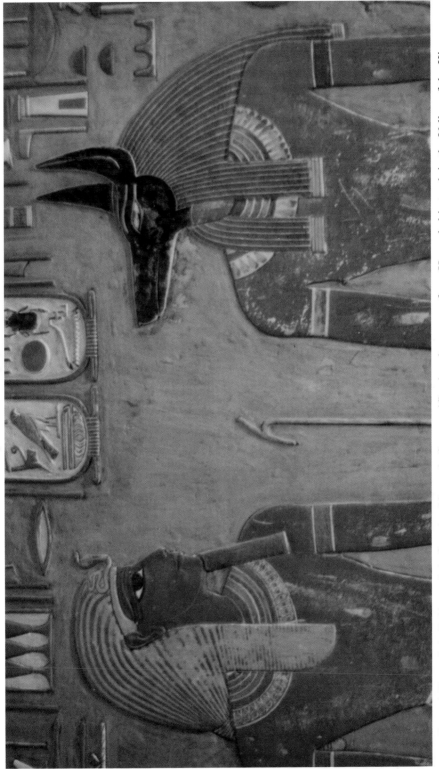

General Horemheb (*left*) stands before Anubis, god of mummification, in a scene from Horemheb's tomb in the Valley of the Kings.

Tut as depicted in a pictograph in his burial chamber.

Ay performs the Opening of the Mouth ceremony in the same pictograph.

Tut (*center*), followed by his soul (ka), embrace the god of resurrection, Osiris (*left*).

Two views of Tut's death mask found in the second coffin.

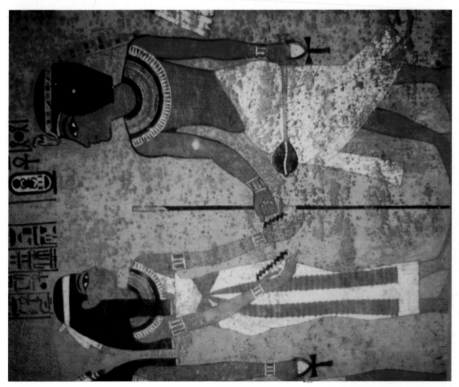

Tut stands before Nut (*left*), goddess of the sky.

The reconstruction of Tut's head. (*Image © by Atlantic Productions/ Atlantic Digital for Discovery Channel/ Granada*)

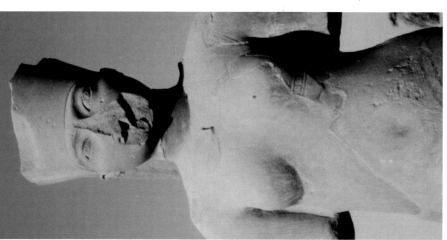

Statue of Ankhesenamun at Karnak.

Originally at the Karnak temple, the sculpture of Akhenaten is now housed in the Cairo Museum.

Ay as depicted in his Amarna tomb.

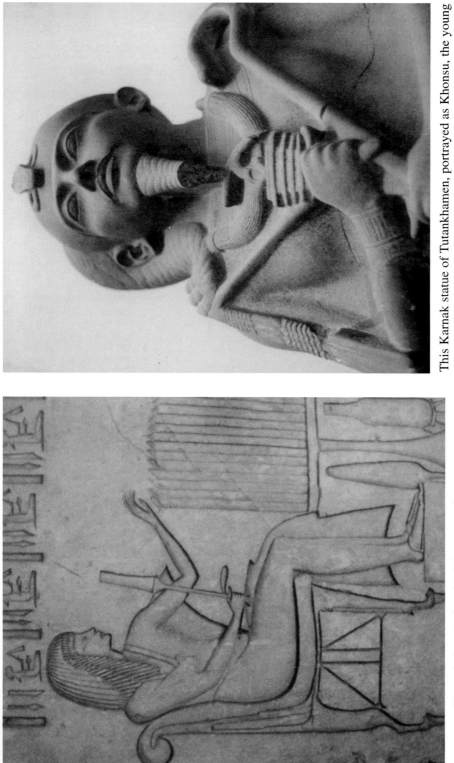

This Karnak statue of Tutankhamen, portrayed as Khonsu, the young moon god, now sits in the Cairo Museum.

Horemheb as depicted in his tomb at Saqqara.

Detail from a small gold shrine of Tutankhamen that shows Tut and his wife, Ankhesenamun, hunting wild birds.

was originally built around 1500 BCE and at the entrance is the obelisk and one or two magnificent stone carvings of Ramses II. The obelisk is symbolic of the light rod for knowledge as a conduit of the revelation or divine information granted or awarded from the gods. The high point or cap suggests the contact point where the conduit diffuses the light and knowledge from the heavens. Ramses is depicted on it and so is a chronicle of all his military victories or at least those he claimed!

Further into the temple was the colonnade hall of Amenhotep III, its walls finished off in the reign of his grandson King Tut. Here was a representation of the Opet Festival Tut celebrated after his return to Thebes upon leaving Amarna shortly after his father Akhenaten's death. This return represents a restoration of the old order of polytheism, and it was not only an observance by the people and ruling monarchy but also a resumption of the old belief system, the longest-enduring in Egyptian history. It was the same system that Amenhotep and his forefathers worshiped and sustained for a thousand-plus years.

For centuries the people annually celebrated the Opet Festival, in which the pharaoh united with the god Amun and partook of his divine essence in a secret ceremony in the temple's inner sanctum. The ritual only involved the pharaoh and the god's statue, with the high priest on hand for other parts. The high priest was the king's representative in the temple and presided over all the other priests on the king's behalf. Also participating in the festival were certain high governmental officials appointed by the pharaoh to administer the business, civic, and diplomatic affairs of the kingdom. Opet was dramatically orchestrated in a public setting so that all could witness the pivotal event. The apex, or crescendo, of the ceremony occurred following the pharaoh's exit from the Holy of Holies, that is, representing the transformation of the pharaoh into the elevated status of a god. At that moment in the ritual, the pharaoh joined in and was "accepted" into the society of the gods. He was now rejuvenated with the powers of a deity. Each year he would recharge his divine batteries at the Opet and remain a divine pharaoh, the son of the gods.

As we walked through the Luxor Temple site, we reflected upon the first day of the Opet Festival and the jubilant crowds as they celebrated the two most significant events in decades at that time. First was young Tut's public coronation. Second, there was the public renunciation of his father's apostate form of monotheistic religion. Simultaneously was the return of a secure tradition and the archaic temple worship of polytheism for the public. Remember that for years Akhenaten had closed down the polytheistic-centered temples as he attempted to force the kingdom to worship only one god— Aten. His restricting of temple devotion to the public at large meant the people suddenly lost their cultural tradition. Their only form of collective religious worship and social solidarity must have been difficult at best. Remember that the temple outbuildings had always been a civic, social, and industrial center for the commoners. In addition, a very powerful subset of the ruling class, the priesthood, had been displaced, putting the priests into the unemployment lines. Many of the priests had never been trained to do anything more than apply a craft to some god or another. They had been the elite. Now, they were in Akhenaten's line of fire.

And who do we find somehow maintaining his stature during this chaotic, possibly dangerous time of religious, even political, upheaval? Ay! As mentioned, he not only served as one of Akhenaten's closest advisers but also was highly influential among the Amun priests. Imagine for a moment the raucous public reaction when Tutankhamen exits the Holy of Holies. There is an absolute riotous approbation by the crowd. This kid, who is not only dependent but also easy to manipulate, dominated and influenced by those he believes love him, must have relished the hour. And who is presiding over the festival? Ay! Who remains at Tut's side as Opet concludes and the celebrations begin? Ay! Ay, who had endured a recent isolation from the general populace while serving Akhenaten in Amarna. Ay! Ay, continuing to maintain his chameleon role.

Nonetheless, Ay could have been faithful to both Akhenaten and Tut for a whole lot of reasons, probably the most important being that a high priest had at times more power than the pharaoh himself. Furthermore, if he was so ambitious, why didn't he assassinate Tut when he was much younger, much more vulnerable?

There was no question about it. We were having fun as we considered that this case had all the elements of political intrigue and usurpation of power. But by whom?

The Opet Festival, Tut's coronation, his return to traditional ways, and the new pharaoh's building phase were all etched in the walls surrounding us. Immediately to the right were the elegant statues of a young, smiling Tut accompanied by and sitting next to his wife, Ankhesenamun, who has her right arm supportively placed around his back. Ali explains that their identities are also a transfiguration of the gods Amun (Tut) and his wife, Mut (Ankhesenamun). They are equal in size, and the transfigured statues suggest a sense of equality in stature, purpose, and ultimate destiny. We commented that this must have played a significant role as Tut and Ankhesenamun began to assume their responsibilities and appropriate roles, which, in their case, were probably not too well received. The ancient Egyptian philosophy revolved around attaining *maat*—balance. The concept focused upon everything having a counterpart, a balancing, complementary element. Maintaining balance in life and the universe was paramount. In a way, this principle is found in most of the world's religions and philosophies.

From these Luxor Temple pictographs, we proceeded deeper into the temple, approaching the Holy of Holies. It was absolutely amazing! All around us were wall scenes depicting "the journey," all ending in front of an altar supporting a smaller version of the god Amun, the ultimate destination of the final journey.

After continuous filming of the two of us interviewing Joann, and our uttering of an endless stream of "gollies" as the paintings and pictographs were explained, we were driven to Karnak Temple, five miles from Luxor. In Tut's time, the roadway, lined with sphinxes, was a straight arrow between the two temples. Some are still present, resting peacefully in front of the Luxor Temple. Again, incredible! It was late in the evening, and we were ready to collapse from sheer exhaustion, but we nonetheless attended a light show in the temple that was simply stunning. Although we were so tired that we kept bobbing in and out of consciousness, we refused to leave before it was over. There was so much to take in! We were glad for the nature of the unconscious. In each of our minds, we would assimilate all we were hearing and seeing, and it would be on call whenever needed. For us, the entire day of zigzagging across Egypt by car and balloon was like drinking from a fire hydrant.

Chapter 8

TWO COPS IN A CRYPT

TRACKING FOUR MAIN SUSPECTS

Affter a short but sound sleep, we were up early the next morning to make a 7:00 jump-off with the film crew to cross the Nile for our most important crypt visits yet. As we stood by the rail of our little cabin cruiser, again deeply touched by the quiet flowing beauty of a river unlike any in the world, we reminded ourselves to focus on the task at hand. After all, the Atlantic Productions crew was monitoring our every movement, our every facial expression. Today, we were going to visit the burial chamber we needed to survey the most—Ay's. On the walls might be an important, long-overlooked, perhaps even undeciphered, tale-telling clue. Although a prime suspect, if indeed Tut was murdered, Ay was presumed innocent until we could uncover more solid evidence to indict. No court can convict on hunches or intuition.

An hour later, in the Valley of the Monkeys, the western branch of the Valley of the Kings where Amenhotep III's tomb is located, and where a mile or so down the road Tut's crypt was originally intended to be, the film crew photographed us in a jeep traversing up and down the desert, imitating Indiana Jones detectives on the case of the lost tombs.

With the jeep scenes completed, we were driven to Ay's burial chamber. Along the way, however, we stopped to visit Amenhotep's tomb. Unfortunately for us, the Japanese were undertaking restoration for the Egyptian government, and, therefore, we were denied access. Although disappointed, we were pleased by the unusual combination of a relatively wealthy Far Eastern nation collaborating with a relatively poor Middle Eastern country to restore a treasure that in essence belongs to the whole world.

As we approached Ay's burial place, we recalled that after Tutankhamen was deified a living god, he returned to Thebes (Luxor) and, as was typical of a pharaoh, he immediately ordered the design and construction of his own tomb in the Valley of the Monkeys in order to be buried near his beloved grandfather. So far, only two complete tombs have been discovered in the Valley of the Monkeys, Amenhotep's and what was supposed to be Tut's. Surprisingly, Tut's burial chamber was confiscated by Ay upon the young man's death. As mentioned previously, Tutankhamen's tomb was originally designed for his nobleman and prime minister, Ay. Upon Tut's death, Ay apparently used his position to amend the final resting place of the young pharaoh by proclaiming that Tutankhamen would be buried in his, Ay's, intended tomb, meant for a nobleman of little consequence. Ay must have justified this move by proclaiming that since Tut's tomb was only partly complete, and that time was of the essence, the switch of tombs was needed. In fact, Tut's tomb, although only partly complete, was maybe still larger than Ay's and could easily have been modified for use.

The name Valley of the Kings was not designated for the area until modern times. Ironically, no other pharaoh, or for that matter anyone significant, was buried in the region where Ay was entombed. Horemheb, who became pharaoh after Ay's death, and who ruled for almost thirty years, was buried in the same vicinity as Tut in the Valley of the Kings.

A short while later, we descended into Ay's thirty-three-hundred-

Mike and Greg pause before reentering Ay's final burial tomb (photo owned by Mike King).

year-old crypt. Like most in the Valley of the Kings, the entrance in the side of a mountain opened into a long, narrow stairwell leading almost straight down four floors. It was extremely hot. We thought that since we were so far underground the temperature would be cool. Sweating and rather uncomfortable due to the excessive heat, we were filmed several times approaching, entering, and descending the stairwell into the tomb. The first room originally contained the conspicuously placed sarcophagus, a monstrous six-foot-high by four-foot-wide hollowed-out rock, which had once held Ay's mummified remains.

As we commented how interesting it would be to be able to interview Ay, we also reflected upon the peril that such a basic investigative response would have had on our early Egyptian comrade detectives. They, too, probably felt the need to investigate Tut's mysterious death further, but like the wise morticians who kept their mouths shut while they busied their hands in the preparation of their pharaoh's body, they were careful because Ay's police were probably all around watching every movement, listening to every comment.

As we looked around the tomb though, we quickly began to analyze the personality traits of Ay and felt we truly could hear his words, feel his emotions, and even recognize his strengths, weaknesses, and motivations. In fact, the great vizier who would become pharaoh began to speak very clearly to us. In many of today's homicides, detectives aren't so lucky. At least in Tut's case, we still had a body, and autopsies had been performed on it. Sometimes inspectors don't even have a body to work with. A corpse can yield a lot of evidence if you know what to look for and how to interpret it in the context of the investigation. Again, this is where our experience as investigators rather than Egyptologists was helping us—we were able to see the big picture and not get bogged down in the minutiae. No offense to Egyptologists! Of course, minutiae are important. But sometimes the big picture is equally, if not more, important.

Remember, this is a pharaoh we're talking about. The corpse is like that of an assassinated president. Egypt was a country dominated by tradition. You can see it everywhere you look—in the monuments, statues, and temples. And suddenly someone rocks that carefully crafted status quo of this deeply religious society. Someone has assassinated the pharaoh! Well, they've killed a god, no less, the ramifications of which are huge. And yet the history books (i.e., the wall carvings, etc.) make no mention of it, in typical ancient Egyptian style. That's one heck of a cover-up!

The walls of the crypt were packed with painted scenes and inscriptions that reflected a variety of images of Ay, including certain scenes from his life. What surprised us were the scenes depicting him hunting, an image only found in nonroyal tombs and not consistent with the tomb scenes of other pharaohs. In the cases, the wall paintings simply show a king's progression toward and worship of, to say nothing of final acceptance by, the gods of eternal life, including the living godhood. But Ay seems to be making a point to show his common beginnings as one of the people. He was, therefore, not born to high rank by progenity, but rather he had ingratiated, perhaps even fought his way to the top. We suspected that Ay wanted to make this very clear to the gods. He did it by what he considered merit. And for this he wanted the gods' acceptance. In fact, the scenes could even have been a plea for consideration, or mercy, for all his good works in order to compensate for some unstated, undisclosed contravention. We had the impression that although he may have been appealing to the gods, he nonetheless secretly harbored a deep resentment, perhaps even arrogance, of his right to assume the throne and all its power. It surely must have been a dismal feeling, possibly similar to the frustration of an egotistic claim of privilege that was neither recognized or acknowledged. In the final analysis, Ay knew he wasn't justified to be pharaoh and that fact must have agitated him. How agonizing it must have been for this great manipulator to realize that he probably would only have the respect of men upon the earth and not in the afterlife. This was evident to us in the several ways in which he tried to alter and adjust his ascension.

Even had he been a stone-cold personality, he would have been bothered by the fact that he had betrayed a pharaoh and his son, each of whom had in fact been responsible for his appointments and succession to power. At best, he would have felt a certain weeping, wailing, and gnashing of teeth.

What also surprised us was the obvious and intentional marring and defacing of several of his images. Of particular interest was one depicting the ultimate reward and the acceptance of the gods. Ay's face had been chiseled away in order to remove his identity! Several of his cartouches, the ovals surrounding royal names, had been intentionally blemished. In effect, these destructive acts were intended to remove his name, identity, and even existence from eternity. Not only was his ultimate status removed, but the fact he even lived was blotted out. Who would have ordered such erasures? For what purpose? Who cared enough to do all this vandalism? Not looters, even if they did gain access to the burial chamber. Their only interest was the treasure they could cart away and sell. We concluded that such serious defacing of a former pharaoh's face could only have been ordered by Horemheb. And he probably issued the command to prevent any historical embarrassment or shameful legacy that could be memorialized forever. And the reason behind this must have been something he discovered during Ay's reign or shortly after his death. Of course, this is all speculation on our part. But there had to be some solid reason or motivation to relocate the burial sites to the Valley of the Kings. Horemheb seems to abandon the area and has his tomb placed near that of Tut.

Back at the hotel late that afternoon, and just before dinner, we sat down in the lounge to sum up everything we knew regarding the differences between Ay's and Tut's tombs. First of all, it was apparent that the quality of rock chiseling and cutting in Tut's tomb was significantly diminished. The tool marks were not only much larger and less refined but also indicative of less care and less time taken in preparation. In stark contrast, Ay's tomb was complete and seemed to possess the finesse of a completed phase of care and devotion. Why? Not because of any great respect for Ay, but rather because it was originally Tut's tomb. Joann reminded us that Tut was actually interred in what was thought to have been originally intended for Ay. It was evident to us that the quality of construction, size, and space, as well as the final touches of the wall paintings, were completed with much greater care than was for Tut's. Tut's tomb was obviously incomplete. The walls, adjoining rooms, and ceilings seemed unfinished, and the room containing the young pharaoh's sarcophagus was approximately half the size of Ay's. The murals were beautifully preserved and the colors still bright. The images of Tut were larger in size but depicted no life scenarios. Interestingly, Tut is shown at the culmination of his funeral service receiving the Opening of the Mouth ceremony, the conferring of eternal life as a deity in the society of the gods. Guess who is administering the rite? Ay! Ay is depicted not only granting Tut the final reward but also authorizing it. The presence of this vivid illustration indicates that Ay had somehow already assumed the throne following Tut's death and before his final burial. We understood that Ay was Tut's vizier and certainly would have continued to administer the affairs of the kingdom during the interim between Tut's death and burial. And although Ay may have been ultimately crowned, it seems a bit presumptuous and premature to present himself in an illustration as not only succeeding pharaoh but also having attained the authoritative status to administer the rights of godhood. It assumes Ay had achieved the same status before his own death and particularly a supreme or elevated ranking to Tut.

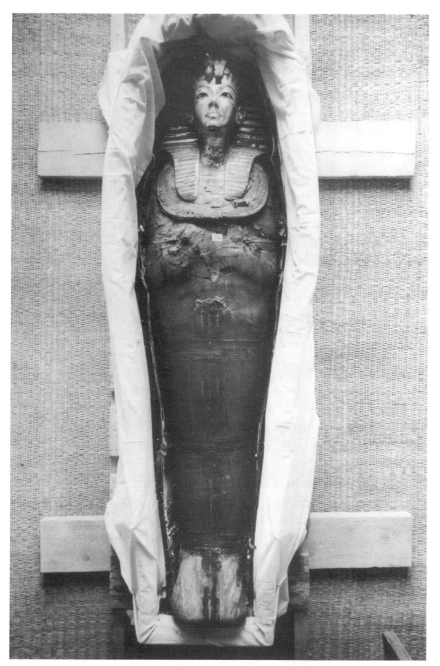

King Tut's mummy with the gold death mask over the head
(copyright: Griffith Institute, Oxford).

Needless to say, we were full of discussion all that afternoon and evening. Mystery and discussion, discussion and mystery. We loved every moment of it.

As mentioned, most good homicide detectives place their victims in either low-, medium-, or high-risk categories. Briefly, high-risk usually means being involved with, or near, the criminal element, while low-risk includes those who are not or are either protected or cushioned from threats or dangers. High-risk violent death victims are usually killed by strangers. When low-risks are murdered, the crime is typically committed by someone familiar to the victim.

Since it was becoming increasingly clear that Tutankhamen was assassinated, we needed to focus upon who was most likely to gain from his demise. And, when you ask such a question, you need to search immediately for a motive. Suspicion of any crime, especially homicide, involves three issues: (1) motive—what's the predator going to gain from the death? (2) opportunity—is the victim accessible and by whom? and (3) means—does the killer have a good weapon and the ability to use it? Known by the acronym MOM, motive, opportunity, and means are the first areas of investigation we always turn to. Now, based upon our visits to the various tombs, and the endless discussions between ourselves and experts like Joann, to say nothing of all the widely contradicting reading we had done, we could match our suspects against MOM. We narrowed all the possible suspects down to four: Ankhesenamun, Maya, Horemheb, and Ay.

Enough discussion, enough mystery for one day. We headed for our respective rooms and beds for a good night's sleep. The next morning, we faced a four-hour train ride to Minya, an outback hot spot known for its ties and sympathies to the Islamic Jihad.

Chapter 9

AMARNA AND MINYA

Early up, then a mad dash to the train station, where we trudged down the platform with all of our baggage and film equipment. People were everywhere as we approached the boarding area to wait for our train. Here, we had the chance to observe the locals. For a few moments, in our time-machine fantasy, we reverted a century. Trains coming and going were packed full of dark people with smudged faces. All around us were vacant stares and despairing expressions. Although the people seemed to have some kind of sense that there is a better life out there, to be gained with a bit of luck and hard work, no one seemed to believe he or she could actually achieve it. Perhaps they knew that rarely, very rarely, someone does break out of his centuries-old condition and attain it. But by their facial expressions and body language, we concluded that most seemed to accept their hard lives as fate. For the most part, they have become simple observers watching others, especially foreigners like ourselves. Just as we wondered about them, mystified, they must have wondered about us, mystified. Finally, we boarded the train— a comic-strip locomotive and passenger train, if there ever was one. In fact, it looked as if it were straight out of the movie *Return of the Mummy*. Bathrooms on board? You've got to be kidding. There was no plumbing—just a straight shot to the tracks below.

More than four hours later, we arrived in Minya and Amarna. Talk about wild! There was an entourage of heavily armed police awaiting us—our guard. We were escorted through the train station and literally swept into a waiting van. A vehicle was positioned in front of our van and one behind us, each containing several armed Egyptian police with automatic machine guns. They escorted us at high speeds through the crammed streets. Cars, buses, pedestrians, donkeys with carts—all moving out of our path like a swath was being laid out before us. We arrived at the Nefertiti Hotel, across the street from the Nile. This is a posh high-rise out in Egypt's boonies. It is really unfair to compare the splendid hotel to anything in the United States, although we have to admit the Sheraton in Cairo is definitely on par with U.S. quality. After being assigned rooms in small bungalows in the inner yard of the hotel, we both hit the sack and lapsed into much-needed naps. At 7:00 P.M., we all met for dinner in the hotel restaurant for more baked Egyptian chicken. By now we were both sick and tired of Egyptian chicken, but we dared not try any other foods. We ate no vegetables or fruit because they were all rinsed in local water. All this time, we had only drunk bottled water. What a tiring but memorable marathon this had all been so far.

AMARNA

For both of us, one of the most dramatic moments of our entire trip came when we were driven to what is known today as Amarna. It is the place where Tut was born. And it is really in the middle of nowhere in Middle Egypt. You have to remember that we went out there just after 9/11, and this part of Egypt is always tense, even in the best of times. We had armed guards with us, as well as a military convoy. But the people were really quite wonderful. We didn't have any problems—in fact, it was a great time to go there.

Amarna is a wasteland, a very evocative place with extraordinary tombs built into the surrounding cliffs. The art in them is amazing, a living testimony to the ancient Egyptians, their achievements, and their losses.

It was important to visit Amarna in order to begin piecing together our victimology. One night as we were sitting in the hotel lobby, talking to Emad Abd-el Hamid, inspector at Amarna, he casually mentioned that he believed there was a tomb nearby that showed an assassination attempt on Tut's father, Akhenaten. For some reason, he was nervous about showing it to us, but after working on him, he reluctantly agreed to take us to it.

The inspector's interpretation of the tomb scenes is quite revolutionary; he believes the wall paintings show the torturing of would-be assassins. But what was most interesting to us was that they apparently also showed Ay. Now, since Ay was one of our main suspects, it was hugely significant to see him there.

The following morning we again met with the inspector. We asked him a question he didn't seem too comfortable answering. Point blank, we asked, "Is there any record of attempts to assassinate Tut's father, King Akhenaten?" "Oh, oh," was his immediate response, and then he tried to change the subject. Seeing we wouldn't dismiss the question, he reluctantly said, "Well, actually there is and it is inscribed on a tomb that belonged to Mahu in Amarna. Chief of Police Mahu is shown in the mural as honored by Akhenaten for having uncovered an assassination plot and preventing it from having been carried out."

This was no surprise to us because it made perfect sense. Furthermore, it established a possible pattern of such plots in Tut's family. To add to the intrigue was the mystery of what happened to Tutankhamen's stepmother Nefertiti or the rest of Akhenaten's five daughters other than Tut's wife. Neither of us was suggesting that a serial killer was at work, but there were certainly a lot of missing people and unexplained deaths. To add to the suspicion, Ankhese-namun, Tut's wife, seemed to have disappeared after she was possibly required to marry Ay following Tut's premature death. All these facts suggested any number of plausible, if not probable, scenarios.

Throughout the rest of the day, neither of us felt very vigorous, thinking we were either coming down with the flu, food poisoning, or Tut's curse. Nonetheless, we kept reflecting on Ay's original tomb—the one he had built while he was serving in Akhenaten's administration and relocated to Amarna. The detail and colors were simply amazing. The tomb was incomplete due to the relocation to Thebes (Luxor) after Akhenaten's death. Incredibly, there were still very detailed blueprints on the wall. The artists were very precise in their planning and drafting. They had to be, since it was pretty difficult to make corrections from chiseled rock and very permanent paint. But as mentioned, the hieroglyphic inscriptions were pompous enough. Ay certainly was quite favorable to himself on his intended tomb walls. But the discontinuation of the cutting of the columns, etchings, carvings, and paintings indicated almost an abrupt halt. Apparently a decision was made to move back, and that decision was disseminated very thoroughly. And, as we know, it was at least two to three years before they returned.

For the next few days, we were both pretty sick—Greg first, Mike second—each of us honestly believing that our entire cell structures had been reengineered. We wouldn't touch any particle of food whatsoever, and we barely sipped water in fear of new purgings.

After two nights and one day of total regeneration, we finally drove out to Mahu's tomb. Another incredible burial chamber! The inspector accompanied us, explaining the depictions on the tomb walls, which illustrated Akhenaten's recognition of Mahu for preventing the attempt on his life. Of course, for two old cops like ourselves, we felt great respect for the thirty-three-hundred-year-old police chief, Mahu. Before our raising the question with the inspector, no one had ever suggested a possible plot. Why the inspector was concerned by it, we couldn't guess. But again, our attention drifted back to Ay. What was his role, if any, in that assassination attempt on the pharaoh? If he had been involved, it certainly was well concealed. Ah, but not to worry, mystery fans, Tut buffs, historians, excavators, archaeologists, and Egyptologists, to say nothing of ordinary readers—two top-flight detectives were hard at work on the case and would have answers soon, including the solution to that riddle.

Impressed with our previous investigation of Horemheb's tomb, we were privileged to learn at the feet of the director of Egypt's Supreme Council of Antiquities, Zahi Hawass himself, about Tut and Ankhesenamun. And, fortunately for us, the director led us on a tour of the tombs and the surrounding area. If ever there were a living-day witness to ancient history, it is this Egyptologist. We marveled at his understanding, insight, and deep love for anything and everything to do with his beloved Egypt. We shared with him our impressions about Tut and Ankhesenamun, and he agreed that the couple were deeply in love. He added that in his opinion, Ankhesenamun would never have participated in a plot, or acted alone, to kill Tut. What surprised us a bit was his feeling that General Horemheb might have been the murderer. We explained that for a

Mike and Greg pose with Dr. Zahi Hawass in the tomb of Horemheb, located near Saqqara (photo by Mike King).

while we, too, were leaning toward him as the perpetrator. But now we weren't so sure.

That night, after returning to Cairo, we joined Joann at one of the oldest coffeehouses in Egypt in the Khan El-Kalili, with us drinking our bottled water and her sipping a very strong Turkish coffee. Located in the heart of the city, the Khan El-Kalili was thriving with customers. We arrived quite early and noticed that many of the people were preparing their Ramadan breakfast. Soon, the café was overfilled with Egyptians drinking their tarlike teas and coffees and smoking from pots that reminded us of marijuana bongs found in America's drug houses. We filmed more of our remarks for the Discovery Channel there, surrounded by hundreds of Egyptian men and women. Later, as we walked through the crowds back to our van, they called out to us, "My American friends," believing we were famous American actors.

That night, we again stayed at the Gezierah Sheraton Hotel. And as we sat high up on our decks overlooking the Nile River, we both commented about what another incredible day it had been. We wondered if the rest of our stay would hold a candle to what we had just experienced.

Chapter 10

RADIOGRAPHS DON'T LIE
MYTHS AND THEORIES ABOUT TUTANKHAMEN'S DEMISE

T oo few facts, premises, proofs, and corroborations to solve the thirty-three-hundred-year-old murder of a pharaoh?
Hardly.

Even in many homicides today, a detective finds scant evidence. As already mentioned, in Tut's case, we were actually quite fortunate. At least there were still a skull and some bones to work with. Nowadays, you often can't find the victim. In his situation, we had a recent autopsy report to work with.

Any crime scene can yield quite a lot more evidence than one might expect—that is, if you know what to look for and how to interpret it in the context of an investigation. This is where our solid experience as detectives helped us out. It is so easy to get tunnel vision during an investigation of this magnitude because whether you are a police officer who is trained to observe, an Egyptologist who has spent a career examining artifacts, or the lay person who is approaching this from a fresh perspective, it is easy to concentrate too fully on one single piece of extraordinary evidence and miss a variety of important nuggets of fact. During the famed gold rush of the 1800s in California, the gold miner would first sift the dirt of riverbeds and streambeds for the small slivers of gold. When he found them, he would progressively move upstream, carefully examining each tributary, inching closer and closer to the fruitful cache of large nuggets that lie in a mountainside high above where those first important bits of gold were discovered. Like the early mountain man who panned for gold in hopes of finding Eureka, we too found ourselves carefully examining each sliver, each nugget, trying not to be overcome too early with all our wealth. Often, we reflected on Sir Arthur Conan Doyle's remark about twisting fact to suit theory rather than examining fact and then developing theory.

For us, the big picture was Egypt—the people today, the geography, the history, the heat, and the desert, the tombs, and, above all, the wall paintings. All of this was one immense crime scene, and it was absolutely essential that we move around in it. We had not only to see firsthand the world Tutankhamen lived and ruled in but also to feel it. By being in that great land we obtained a feeling for its scale—and not just architecturally. We tried to feel both as ancient commoners and leaders. After all, we were dealing with the possible killing of a pharaoh. To the chagrin of the gods, someone rocked the carefully crafted status quo. This ancient Egypt bred a deeply religious society that did not look kindly upon someone killing a revered king. So the ramifications for such a dastardly act were huge. Yet, surprisingly, there is virtually no mention of it! A young pharaoh is suddenly dead, and there is no mention of it? Something was terribly, terribly wrong here.

Recently, a number of Egyptologists and historians have tackled Tutankhamen's strange death, more or less agreeing with each other that "yes, maybe he was murdered." But on the other hand, there is no definite proof to that effect. Several have even come up with the same conclusions and evidence that we did. But our skills are so different. Our approach to arrive at the conclusions we did is based upon several crime investigative factors: the ability to interpret evidence from a criminal's perspective; the ability to get inside the victim's head, to say nothing of the head of the suspect; and a thorough understanding of behavioral analysis, a technique that we employ almost on a daily basis.

The two of us brought over forty years of law enforcement and investigative experience to the table as we embarked on this incredible journey. In addition, during our collegiate experiences in undergraduate and graduate studies of criminal justice, we benefited from the experience of others as we read about, evaluated, and discussed hundreds of the most disturbing cases in history. In addition, we had the opportunity of interviewing serial offenders in prisons from the historic walls of San Quentin prison in California to the eastern seaboard of the United States. As we listened to serial offender after serial offender explain the manner and method of his crimes, we gained valuable insight into the psyche of the criminal, and we soon discovered that it didn't matter whether that criminal roamed the earth in 1300 BCE or in the twenty-first century.

But the most important fact of all is that we had new evidence to work with—evidence that we are familiar with and know how to interpret: the x-rays of Tutankhamen, fresh insights about his Klippel Feil affliction, and a reconstruction of his face. This combined new evidence was never before made available to Egyptologists or historians. On top of all this, we were able to access the second batch of x-rays taken of Tut in the mid-1960s. This included the x-rays of the head that first sparked all the rumors of possible homicide. At that time, Prof. R. G. Harrison of Liverpool University claimed, after examining several x-rays he had taken of the pharaoh's skull, that an area of density at the base of the head meant Tut could have died from a severe blow. Most historians and Egyptologists had access to positive prints, or photos, of the x-rays. Anyone who deals with radiographs knows how much more can be seen if you actually can analyze the original x-rays themselves. For us, this was a fantastic opportunity.

Back in Salt Lake City a few weeks before our departure to Egypt, we had quite a group of medical experts drive over to the medical examiner's office to inspect the original x-rays. They pointed out some incredible things hitherto unnoticed. For us gawkers, the new information provided the turning point in the investigation, something that radically altered our perception of how and why Tut died so young. We were absolutely convinced that the conclusions of these experts would change the world's view of the boy-king as well. More about all of this later.

For decades, Egyptologists have discussed the possibility that Tutankhamen suffered from painful physical disabilities. From the paintings in the tombs and temples we learned more of his physical condition. Being able to gaze into the physical condition of Tut through his x-rays taught us more, even suggesting the possibility of Klippel Feil syndrome. Klippel Feil would have affected Tut in the same manner as it does sufferers today. This alone could have made him an easier target than we previously thought.

We had to consider that Tut, being crippled in part by this disease, may have appeared as weak, placing him high on the risk continuum for both enemy outsiders and those from within. In some cases of Klippel Feil, the affected person may lose some hearing or become completely deaf. Being unable to hear would have increased Tut's risk of ambush. This disease also meant that Tut's head could have been likened to a bowling ball sitting on top of a pool cue. Any rapid forward, backward, or side-to-side motion could have snapped the young king's neck at the base of the skull. In a great example of understatement, Dr. Richard Boyer, forensic radiologist for the University of Utah Hospital in Salt Lake City, said, "This type of action is not compatible with life."

As we began our investigation, scientists in the United States were carefully recreating a perfect reconstruction of Tutankhamen's skull. Exacting measurements of the skull were taken and cast in a one-of-a-kind model. Once completed, the skull was shipped to Dr. Robin Richards in the United Kingdom. Dr. Richards carefully undertook the process of examining over fifty Egyptian males to determine their precise skin colors, fat content of their faces, hair, and other facial details. From all that, with great precision and artistry, he began to recreate the face of the famous pharaoh.

In order to appreciate the findings from these 1968 x-rays, we need to consider the Egyptian mummification process, including how the royal body was preserved. First, the physicians of the pharaoh in charge of preparing the corpse for the afterlife inserted a trocar or some other instrument through the nose to reach inside the head to the brain. Since the brain is soft tissue, they wanted to remove it so that it wouldn't decay. This was achieved by quite literally whisking it, then draining it down through the nose. The physicians then employed an interesting process where they poured hot resin inside the head in order to seal and preserve the interior skull and facial features for eternity. Since the resin was liquid, it was going to settle in the deepest part of the skull. The different angles of the head x-ray show a dense area, the resin, and a dark area, which is the air inside the skull sitting above the resin. The ancient physicians, who certainly knew their craft, would allow the head with the hot resin to sit long enough for the resin to solidify, maybe even cauterizing the inside of the skull so that if any residual brain tissue remained it would simply burn away, sealing off the inside of the head. But since the resin did not cover the entire inside of the skull, the physicians hung Tut's head off the end of a table so that he was in something of a head-back position. They would then pour more resin in, after the first lot had set up, in order to obtain another horizontal level with the density at the bottom in the dependent portion and the air on top. And that's why the x-rays revealed a curious configuration of density around the skull.

To explain the unusual density, we asked for help from Dr. Richard Boyer, who, after analyzing the radiograms of Tutankhamen sent him by Atlantic Productions, called us into his office to discuss the x-rays. We were all aware that during the past eighty years, various myths have arisen over the radiographs of Tut's skull and other remains. And those myths have spawned innumerable theories about the mechanism of injury leading to Tut's tragic and untimely death.

"The first one," Dr. Boyer began, "centers on the bone fragment I'm pointing to now. Remember that the dark part here is air and the brighter part is resin. You can also see this area of intermediate density structure, which is a piece of bone. If you look very carefully,

The remains of Tut's head and face in 1926 (copyright: Griffith Institute, Oxford).

there's actually a second piece that projects near to it. If you move over to this next radiograph on the right, this is a view that's a little bit harder for people to relate to. What we're doing is actually looking up from the feet, looking up at the head from the bottom to the top, and so here is the left side of the head, here's the right. The teeth are out in front and the back of the skull where the resin is deposited in the back."

Actually, there were two fragments of bone. The longer fragment sat a little off to the left and a smaller piece just a bit behind that. Most experts believe these bone fragments suggest a skull fracture resulting from some type of trauma to the back of the head or front of the face induced by mechanical force. But not Dr. Boyer.

"Well," continued Dr. Boyer, "having explained how the hot liquid resin was placed in Tut's brain helps us to understand that this really couldn't be the case. If these bone fragments had come from the time when he died, or before he died, at the time the embalmers (the preservers) poured the resin into the head, the bone fragments would be sitting right back there at the back of the skull. Obviously, gravity alone would have carried them back there. Then, the resin would be poured in on top of them. In that case, we wouldn't see them at all. They would have been embedded in the resin, which is actually more dense to the x-ray than they are. They would have disappeared inside of the resin on both of the radiographs we see here."

Boyer's contention was that these bone fragments came about much later when other investigators inserted some object through the nose, dislodging them. On one side of the skull was an area of irregular light at the back of the nose. "In order to orient ourselves," Dr. Boyer continued, "these are the teeth; this is the sinus; these are where the eyes live and so the nose goes right up between the eyes and right to the back. There's a bone called the Vulmer bone, part of what's called the ethmoid complex, which is part of one's sinus group. It is a bone that's sort of porous. It has holes in it where the sinuses are, and that bone could be easily dislodged. This piece of bone sitting up here looks like a portion of the middle of the ethmoid bone called the vertical plate of the ethmoid or the Vulmer bone."

Boyer continued. He thought that if an instrument had been inserted like a pointer up through the nose, it would be very easy to dislodge the bone, especially thirty-three hundred years later, when the bone was brittle. He argued that a little jabbing motion would knock off the fragment, which would then come to rest in the position it did. "Now why it sits out there as if it's suspended in air, I don't really know. I can only guess that there probably are some actually little adhesions or membranes or little veil-like structures that live inside of this air that are not dense enough for the radiography to pick up," he said.

We then asked if he could explain to us what it was on the x-rays that suggested to a number of Egyptologists that Tutankhamen might have suffered a blow to the back of the head.

He smiled. "Well, that's the second myth I'd like to discuss with you. Again, going back to this lateral view of the skull, this side view, people have focused on this area, so let's just orient ourselves again. This is the front of the head, the nose, the teeth, the eyes, and the spine coming up and the back of the head here. Well, there's a sort of shelf of bone called the occipital bone that supports the back part of the brain. The back part of the brain is called the cerebellum, which lives in this region, and some people who have viewed the radiographs say they notice different layers of density."

Pointing to what he referred to as a curved linear density that paralleled the outside of the skull, Dr. Boyer said that those who noticed different layers of density felt this abnormal calcification was probably caused by a blow to the back of the head or underneath the back of the head by some sort of instrument. It's even possible, they speculate, that the calcification could have been caused by Tut falling backward or hitting his head violently against a shelf or something firm. Hence, the interior bleeding calcified. Physicians today refer to the calcification, or forming of a bone or the calcium around it, as a subdural hematoma.

He continued, "I have to say it's very rare in this part of the skull, OK? It occurs much more commonly in the upper parts of the skull convexities. In fact, in all the scans that I have done, I don't think I have ever seen a calcified subdural hematoma in that part of the skull back there. But again, understanding the resin and looking at where it is tells us that's not the case. So let's go back over again to this view looking from Tut's feet up. At the back bottom of his skull, the resin goes from the inside of the skull clear across to the other inside of the skull.

"If any of these lines that we can see I'm pointing at, which account for those densities that people have talked about, if any of those were membrane, calcified membrane, the resin would stop there. It would act like a dam.

"And the resin would only get over as far as that calcified membrane on this side and then would stop. Then there would be no resin between there and the inside of the skull because there's a calcified subdural hematoma. Well, the resin goes all the way from side to side. There is no calcified subdural hematoma in the posterior forceps. People have wondered about the thinness of the bone here and the fact that there are a number of layers. Well, there's an easy explanation for those findings."

Boyer further explained that since the head is tilted, we couldn't see straight from the side. We were looking a little bit up or a little bit down. "So," he continued, "here's the socket for one of the eyes. But here's the top of the socket that tells us the head is tilted. We call this parallax. This is because the x-ray beam projects one higher than the other because of the tilt. Well, the same parallax phenomenon is going on here in the posterior part of the skull. Since it's a little bit more accentuated, it's probably tilted and rotated so that it's accentuated in the back half. We're just seeing part of the back half of the skull here and another part there. The reason this is thin is because the cerebellum sits right on the thin part of the skull. It is in two halves and kind of thins out the skull where it rests, and that's a normal phenomenon."

We then discussed at what angle and distance the x-ray was taken, the relative unimportance of the skull measurements, and how, if necessary, we could use photo magnification to make the skull look as big as we wanted. Boyer then wanted to discuss his most important observation of all—the spaces between Tut's cervical spine, which was disarticulated from the rest of his body.

Pointing to the lateral view x-rays of Tut's body, he said, "Look at these spaces between the vertebral bodies. We can see a space here and a space there. And here you can barely see a space. Then, there are no spaces for the course of about four vertebral body lengths both at back and the front. So, this tells us that the vertebral bodies are fused together. Now, that's not a normal finding. Tutankhamen, this young man, should have a nice, healthy-looking cervical spine. What you see here is not.

"Now, there are two possibilities for this. The first is that in the developmental process of his cervical spine, these vertebrae fused together. This congenital malformation is known as Klippel Feil syndrome.

"The other possibility is that Tut had arthritis as a young man—juvenile rheumatoid arthritis. One of the known consequences of this type of arthritis is fusion of the cervical spine. When others over the years had the chance to examine and radiograph his extremities, there's been no mention of arthritis showing up in his hands or feet or hips or knees. This would lead us to believe that the young pharaoh didn't have JRA. Yet looking at these radiographs, we clearly see that he has a congenital abnormality of his cervical spine. Now, why is the fact that Tut had Klippel Feil fusion important to your investigation today?"

Boyer explained that instead of having a supple, easily movable spine that allowed his head to move forward and back, and to turn from left to right, Tut's head was, if you will, stuck on a broomstick or a poker. "Where was the fulcrum?" he asked, more to himself than to us. "Where was his motion? Well," he continued, "if the boy-king fused up to the base of his skull, then all the motion for the movement of his head had to be at the base of his skull." That would put great abnormal stress on the joints that are at that level. But what would happen if Tutankhamen accidentally fell backward? Whether he slipped or someone hit or pushed him down, the result would be a blow to some spot on the back of the head, Boyer pointed out. "The translational force of his going forward or backward would occur at one level, injuring his spinal cord at that point. A serious spinal cord injury at that level may not be compatible with life."

Boyer's interpretations of the radiograms told us that the bone fragments and subdural hematoma were not as important to the clues of mechanism of death as the discovery of the abnormal cervical spine. We now knew for certain that Tut was less agile than the average teenager of his time, therefore predisposing him to have an accidental fall. And, generally, if a young adult has juvenile rheumatoid arthritis bad enough to make his cervical spine look as bad as this one, he would have other joints involved. "He would be usually quite severely impaired or crippled, and that's why I say it might not be the case—especially if that's not been mentioned by any of those who have had a chance to look at the radiographs or actually examine what's left of his long bones and his joints. I believe it would be most unusual to have juvenile rheumatoid arthritis show up in the cervical spine this bad and not show up elsewhere in the body," he explained.

We then asked him if Tut's gait would have been impaired by the arthritis. He said that he believed the young pharaoh may have had more than one injury. "I have seen radiographs of Tutankhamen's thoracic spine and chest areas, and he does have some scoliosis on one radiograph. Now, unfortunately, we don't know for sure how his body was positioned when that radiograph was taken, so he may have had other skeletal problems as well. Those infant mummies that were found with Tut also apparently had congenital malformations of the kind that is similar to what we are proposing here, and so it's possible if they were related that there may be some inherited tendency in his family for this kind of a congenital malformation in the spine."

Dr. Ernst Rodin, an Austrian-born medical doctor with specific training in neurology psychiatry and clinical neurophysiology, was invited by the Atlantic crew to view the same x-rays. This was our first and only meeting with Dr. Rodin, who spoke with a thick accent and who was fascinated by the Tutankhamen mystery.

Rodin was convinced that Tut probably died as a result of an insect or snake bite, or something comparable, and he is one of those great professionals who struggles with thoughts that are not in concert with his own. He refused to consider that Tut could have been murdered. Rodin stood firmly on his beliefs until we confronted him with the most troubling fact that we thus far had dealt with—how the two resin pours in the skull occurred if, in fact, Tut was decomposing and stinking up the place. It made no sense at all for the early embalmers to spend time on the brain when it had zero religious or afterlife meaning to the Egyptians. For a moment in time, as we shared the better part of three hours with him, that fact alone caused him to quietly reflect on an issue that he had never addressed and couldn't satisfactorily respond to. We thought to ourselves how sad it was that someone so incredibly brilliant couldn't look beyond his own rigid belief as additional facts were presented.

One of our great memories of this investigation and Dr. Rodin's participation was when he finally had the opportunity to gaze upon the x-rays of King Tut. As he tearfully examined every inch of film, he commented that he had pursued the x-rays for nearly two decades and was never, until now, granted permission to see them. It was a wonderful hour for him and one for which he thanked Atlantic, Discovery, and particularly Kate Botting.

The first thing Rodin wanted to explain to us was what really happened during the first medical examination of Tutankhamen, carried out by Dr. Derry in the presence of Howard Carter in 1922. Rodin said:

> Now we must remember that Howard Carter's prime interest as an archaeologist was the artifacts and not any medical examination. After he found the sarcophagus he opened it, found the first coffin, opened that, and from there extracted the second coffin. But it was then, when he opened the second coffin, he found that the bottom of the second coffin and its sides were glued with resin that had hardened over the millennia. He could not extract the second coffin from the real gold coffin. In addition, the mummy was solidly glued to the bottom of the third coffin. And the famous funerary mask was also solidly glued to the back of the coffin and to the chest of Tutankhamen.
>
> So he had a horrendous task on his hands. How do you get the body out? At first he thought that, since this is resin, he would melt it since that is the only way you can do it. So he took the second coffin with the third coffin inside and put it outside into the

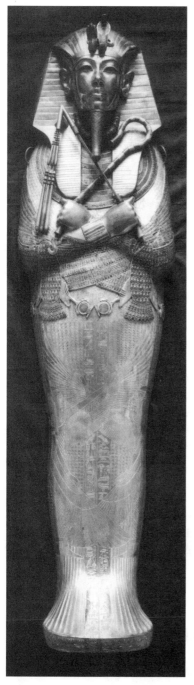

The crook and flail, emblems of Osiris, god of the dead, rest in the hands of Tut's image on a solid gold coffin (copyright: Griffith Institute, Oxford).

Egyptian heat, in the sun, and allowed it to sit there in hopes the resin would melt. Nothing happened. So then he decided that since there was no other way to get the body out, he would have to literally chisel it out. So in the process of literally chiseling Tut's body out, he had to dismember the corpse. And this was not reported by Carter. It came to light as a result of Professor Harrison's x-rays and examination because when they reopened the tomb in 1968 it was obvious that Tut was a disarticulated body.

The legs had been transected at the pelvis and they were separate. The arms were separate. The head was separated. When he separated the limbs to get to the pectoral in order to remove the mask, it's possible that the rib cage and the bones were so brittle that the rib cage also was damaged. It's a good possibility that Carter's post mortem event produced the damage we attribute to murder. Now I'm not accusing him of any malpractice of anatomy. He had no choice, but modern-day instruments were introduced into the mummy at that time and no one knows for sure the enormous damage that was done.

Three theories have been proposed why the body of Tutankhamen was in such bad condition when Carter found it. One is that the embalmers did a sloppy job. The second is proposed by Bikay, who says the exposure of Tutankhamen in the coffin to the Egyptian sun led to spontaneous combustion and carbonization of the body. The third theory is offered by Carter and is the one most widely subscribed to. His belief was that the unguents which had been poured as a religious ceremony over the body and the coffin led over the millennia to spontaneous combustion and thereby skeltonised the remains of the king.

There is yet another possibility; namely, it is that maybe the body was already in a state of decomposition before it reached the house of embalming. How could this happen? Let's assume he was hunting or fishing. All the wall paintings, as well as the events described in the books, to say nothing of his funerary equipment, suggest there was an accident and that this accident occurred far from his residence. Forbes' suggestion is that Tut was run over by his carriage. If this happened while he was hunting in the eastern desert, it does not take long in the heat of the Egyptian sun for the body to start to decompose. In addition, anyone who has been to Egypt knows that the flies are abundant. And if you have a body that cannot move, the flies will settle and you will get maggots. Under those circumstances, it becomes impossible for practical purposes to dessicate a corpse properly. That may have been the problem the embalmers were confronted with.

There are several other aspects to this. One is Dr. Derry, who was with Carter, who saw that there was a lesion on Tut's cheek on the left side. Now he had never seen a 3,400-year-old lesion. He thought it was just a scab that seemed to have healed. It's conceivable then that (a) if Tut fell on the left side, he may have had an abrasion which healed; or (b) it is also possible that with the insects that were around then, there was an insect bite and as a result of the insect bite he [Tut] might have developed sepsis, which is precisely what Lord Carnarvon died from. He had an insect bite, he developed sepsis, and in a few weeks he was dead. In those days there were no antibiotics, even for Carnarvon. Once a body is septic, it becomes very difficult to embalm.

Finally, the Egyptian embalmers were experts. They knew what they were doing. They must have known how much embalming unguents would harm a body. According to Carter, there were at least two bucketfuls of unguents poured over the mummy and another two bucketfuls over the coffin. Why in all the world would one do that? So you ask yourself if you have seen the decomposing bodies which I have as a result of World War II. Not only can you not mummify a decomposing body, but the body also smells. It is quite possible that they used this tremendous, unusual amount of unguent in order to mask the smell. This is an assumption and it may not be unreasonable.

The original autopsy of Dr. Derry did not provide any cause of death. Although he could not provide a cause of death, Derry offered a very peculiar piece of information that puzzled everyone. He mentioned that although the head was clean-shaven, there was a waxy film over it which immediately raised the question of adipolsia. This is a technical term for a drowning victim. But it's not only drowning that can produce this effect. It can also be produced by humidity. But did Tut drown or didn't he?

There is a problem with the canopic jars where his viscera were placed. If the lungs were available after three thousand years they would be of interest to examine to see if anything could be discerned. The problem is that Dr. Bikay tried to find the canopic jars but couldn't. The canopic jars do exist, but I don't know if the viscera are in them. If there are viscera inside, are they really of Tutankhamen? If so, have they, too, been subsequently mishandled?

In the final analysis of Tutankhamen's x-ray, Dr. Todd Gray, chief medical examiner for the state of Utah, was unable to find evidence of a fracture at the base of his skull as has been suggested from previous examinations of the x-rays. He believes that it is the angle the x-rays were taken from that may have misled people to believe there was a fracture. Nonetheless, that small chip of bone in the x-ray does raise interesting questions. This has been dismissed as a post-mortem artifact and is considered a red herring in establishing that Tutankhamen may have died from a blow to the back of the head. Yet it is still interesting. Because it appears outside the unguents, it is likely to have been broken free when Dr. Douglas Derry inserted a sharp object into Tutankhamen's brain to check if there was any-thing in the cranial cavity. But why did it break free? Is it because Tutankhamen's skull was already weakened, possibly because of the evidence that he may have suffered Klippel Feil syndrome and could have fallen over and cracked his head, nonfatally, before? Is it fair to say that although they cannot be seen on the x-ray, there may be small multiple fractures on the skull, hence the easy dislodging of the bone fragment?

It has also been suggested that Tutankhamen may have suffered a subdural hematoma. Dr. Gray could find no evidence for this. If there were a subdural hematoma, it would have been caused by the blow to the back of the head and wouldn't have necessarily meant that Tutankhamen died instantly. He could have lingered over a short period of time, allowing a blood clot to develop. If Tutankh-amen had suffered from the Klippel Feil syndrome, what sort of force would be needed to deal him a fatal blow, and where would the blow have to be struck? How would Tutankhamen have to fall or be struck for the impact to be fatal? And would that impact result in the contracoup phenomenon?

Chapter 11

THE UNUSUAL SUSPECTS

As the investigation heightened, our efforts to examine closely the risk level of Tutankhamen began to pay off. We determined that although the king may have suffered from Klippel Feil, and he may have been slight in frame and less than impressive as a military leader in inner circles, the people of Egypt probably loved and revered him. In fact, Tut was a national treasure and because of his stately role alone demanded close protection and all the other benefits of royalty. There was nothing to suggest that the people of Thebes, or Egypt for that matter, didn't consider him a great leader. Even the Amun priests would have been forced to portray him as a insightful and spiritual leader because he returned the power base back to them. In the quiet rooms in which they planned, though, it seems possible that they conspired for his demise.

As we evaluated the many possible suspects in this case, some of whom popular opinion points to while others are not on the radar screen, we began to narrow the possible suspects down to four people: Maya, the treasurer of the kingdom's money; Ankhese-namun, Tut's child bride; Ay, the vizier and prime minister; and finally, Horemheb, the highly regarded army general.

In all criminal investigations, time is the enemy. And while every passing day pushes the likelihood of solving the crime further away, we had to rely on every possibility yet focus on the greatest probability. Our discussions, preparation, and study prior to arriving in Egypt had caused us both to begin to look closely at Horemheb as the primary suspect. Because of this, we planned our first "impromptu" interview to occur in the unfinished tomb of the army general.

DISCOVERY OF HOREMHEB'S TOMB

General Horemheb grew and matured as a military leader under the reign of King Akhenaten, the heretic father of King Tut. Remember, it was Akhenaten who stripped the Amun priests of their power and transplanted the powerful government seat in Thebes to Amarna. Horemheb probably looked upon Akhenaten with a great deal of respect because it appears that he was a very young soldier at the time and probably didn't have many opportunities to be near the pharaoh.

We were unable to learn much of Horemheb's progression during the time of Akhenaten, but it was apparent that he must have been a "rising-star" because shortly after Akhenaten's death, Horemheb became the commander of the new pharaoh (Tut's) armies. It is also possible that he felt complete disgust for Akhenaten. But because of his patriotism and commitment to his allegiance as a warrior, he quietly continued to serve in a manner that won him the attention of the young Tutankhamen, or perhaps more importantly at the time, the vizier to Akhenaten, Ay.

In considering Horemheb's possible status as a suspect in this mystery, we first evaluated the historical importance of the military in political overthrows. Regardless of the type of culture, the era in time, and the makeup of the people, the military, generally led by the commander, often orchestrated such political disruptions. With all of this in mind, one of our first stops had to be the tomb of

Horemheb. That quest took us to Saqqara, where we hiked through the desert past the Step Pyramid, across the burial site of hundreds of noblemen, and to the entrance of Horemheb's tomb. As Atlantic Production's crew entered first in order to film the looks on our faces as we scanned the tomb, we quite humbly looked into the distance at the three pyramids at Giza. With an strange sense of wonder, intrigue, and excitement we quietly entered the tomb. Dr. Fletcher shared the deep meaning of each carving, cartouche, and stela in the tomb. The wind slowly changed intensity and direction, adding to the eerie sensations we were experiencing. At one point the film's sound director, Simon, placed his index finger to his lips, indicating that he wanted us to be very quiet while he recorded the sounds. As we listened, we hoped that the sounds from the graves of Horemheb's warriors could somehow be heard and understood. How we wanted to hear from those early soldiers what they must have been thinking during this most important time in history.

As we learned more of Horemheb, we realized how easy it could have been for him to commit such a crime, either quietly or in conjunction with other perpetrators. Either way, Horemheb could have easily been our suspect, and as Dr. Zahi Hawass entered the tomb to meet with us, we couldn't wait to ask him who he thought killed King Tut.

In fact, during our first hour with Zahi Hawass in Saqqara, he informed us that he believed that Horemheb killed King Tut. How could we argue with such a great scholar who lived and knew ancient Egypt better than anyone on earth? Meeting with Dr. Hawass was such a thrill. Many times we had seen him in action on our televisions from the other side of the world. His English was impeccable and the added dialect from his Egyptian tongue made us hang on every word. After the initial pleasantries, we discussed not only our native Utah home but also the impact that Brigham Young University's ancient studies program had on both Hawass and the country of Egypt. In turn, Hawass asked a number of questions about Utah. Obviously very curious, he finally asked if we were Mormons! After our enthusiastic response of yes, it was time to get to work.

Dr. Hawass explained that he believed that Tut was murdered by

Horemheb. He said that Tut was probably struck with a blunt weapon of some sort, and he felt that Horemheb was either deeply involved or solely responsible. He described Horemheb as being a powerful general both in war tactics and control of his men and resources around him. At the conclusion of our discussion, Hawass casually mentioned that he had just discovered a new tomb nearby and he and his archaeological team were going to open it in a few hours. But with a wink, he denied our pleas to accompany him on that historic find. Later, we learned who was found in the tomb. But because of our fear of the "mummy's curse," we will not reveal the person in this or any other publication until the renowned Dr. Hawass releases what is truly his to release.

As we bid our goodbyes to Hawass, we cautioned each other to not get too excited over his find. We still had an entire country to cross and three additional suspects to either exclude or focus our attention on.

But we could not ignore the many reasons that Horemheb may have had to want the young pharaoh dead. As a great military leader, Horemheb may have felt that he needed to kill Tut to protect Egypt. There is plenty of speculation that the teenage king was less than a model pharaoh. The many walking sticks in his tomb suggest that he possibly had the need for a cane as he moved around. Many of the murals portray Tut as a great commander, which appears consistent with other leaders even though they may not have been. More often than not, the pharaoh would go into battle in order to bolster the moral of the troops and then be whisked away before the conflict began to threaten him.

Perhaps Horemheb viewed Tut's physical condition as a projection of weakness, or the lack of strength of the armies he commanded, and feared his pharaoh would become more frail and physically challenged as time went on. Tut's frailty could be perceived as a dangerous detriment that could be exploited by Egypt's enemies.

Horemheb may have acted in a conspiratory manner with others to maintain his power and position. It is possible that the general owed a great debt to the powerful advisers who trained the nine-year-old, newly appointed king. He may even have been under devious orders to kill the boy or may have been involved with the powerful Amun priests to diminish the power and dominion of the royalty. By murdering Tut, the priests may have argued, Horemheb would be revered as one who "understood" the gods.

It is also possible, Hawass theorized, that if Horemheb learned of Tut's assassination, he may have decided it was in his best interest to cover it up. After all, he may have decided his patriotic duty was to the kingdom, not the king. As mentioned, Horemheb, by all accounts, was not near the pharaoh when he died. We do not know if this is because his name was recorded erroneously on some military documentation at the time or if the general was really present or nearby at the moment of murder. We did learn of one account that stated that Horemheb was away on a military campaign at the time. He may have learned of the death of the king soon after or much later after the burial had taken place. To us, the general appears to have been the type of patriot who would have made sure that the pharaoh was properly and ceremoniously buried, which, of course, didn't happen.

But, then again, Horemheb may have conspired with Ay to allow Ay to serve as pharaoh for a short time until the general assumed the pharaohship. Horemheb may have made a deal with Ay to help orchestrate the removal of Tut. If that happened, it is possible that Horemheb was actually sent away by "presidential" decree when his real mission was to lie in wait for the king to be executed. Thus, he would have an alibi. Again, speculation. Our responsibility was to examine the facts before developing a theory, and we wondered whether we were considering theories ahead of fact. With Dr. Hawass's revelation of who he thought was responsible, we now looked upon the great army general with jaded eyes.

MAYA

In the beginning I was good. In the end I was great!
Inscription over the doorway to Maya's tomb

Near the Step Pyramid at Saqqara rests the tomb of Maya, the chief of the treasury and close personal aide to Pharaoh Tutankhamen. Maya's tomb was first discovered in 1843 by Richard Lepsius, who also found what he described as the "looted remains" of five other tombs buried beneath the sand dunes near the Saqqara Step Pyramid. Lepsius recorded some information while at the site, and, within a short time after that, the tomb of Maya was once again hidden under the blowing sands of Egypt for more than a hundred years.

Meanwhile, several statues of Maya and his wife, Merit, were found. In addition to their own statues in which they are shown separately, the two were also memorialized in a particularly beautiful dyad or "couple" statue, and all three figures soon found their way to the National Museum of Antiquities in Leiden. Maya and Merit are portrayed in the statue wearing beautifully styled wigs and fine linen robes typical of the late Eighteenth Dynasty. Merit is resting her arm around her husband's waist, depicting the closeness the two shared, or at least the manner in which they wished the world to remember them.

In 1975, a team of British and Dutch archaeologists led by Geoffrey Martin began working at Saqqara. Not only did they find the tomb of Horemheb, which we had visited with Zahi Hawass and Joann, they also continued to work at the site and in 1986 rediscovered the tomb of Maya, the treasurer of Tutankhamen and keeper of the king's money.

While he may have served under Akhenaten, Maya certainly served as treasurer to Tutankhamen and his two successors, Ay and Horemheb, his title given as either treasurer, director of the treasury, or even the minister of finance. In addition to his responsibilities for the kingdom's finances, it is believed that Maya had supervisory responsibility over all of the country's construction projects, including the building and maintaining of the pharaoh's tomb. This privilege allowed Maya the opportunity to access this most special of all places at will.

Interestingly, Maya's tomb is located very close to Horemheb's tomb at Saqqara. It took the discoverers over five years to expose the underground tomb that was cut from rock. "On the last day of our campaign in 1986," says Maarten Raven, field director for the National Museum of Antiquities, "Geoffrey Martin and philologist Jaap van Dijk discovered something strange in a recently uncovered tomb of army officer Ramose. It was a very deep, odd-looking shaft, which had probably been dug out by looters a few thousand years ago. They threw a rope ladder down the dark hole and began to descend." At that point, after a more than a decade of careful archeology, Maya was reintroduced to the world.

After Akhenaten's death, it appears that the safest thing for the new nine-year-old pharaoh to do was to keep in place the established and proven leaders that served under his father. Thus, we see that Horemheb, Ay, and Maya continued to serve in their respective positions, with Horemheb apparently being promoted to the position of commander of the army.

Egypt was in deep financial trouble because of Akhenaten. Whether the decision to move the capital and build a new one was based on proper religious and political reasoning did not change the fact that Egypt was already financially strapped. A great deal of responsibility must have been placed on Maya, who surely assisted in the planning and taxation of the citizens of the kingdom. As Maya helped the country recover from the economic damage that occurred during Akhenaten's reign, he also faced continuing deficits caused by the return to Thebes. One can only surmise the disrepair the temples and cities near Thebes must have fallen into during the time that Amarna was being built. It must have been an exciting day, not only for the Amun priests who regained power when Tut returned but also for the people who could once again plan on the financial support, job markets, and benefits of having a pharaoh once again living among them.

This incredible debt, plus the difficult decisions that were being made by Tut (or his advisers, depending on how active he really was in the process), must have placed a great deal of pressure on Maya, who may have been involved in some of the overspending that occurred in Amarna.

Another consideration was the possibility that Maya may have been "skimming" funds from the treasury for his own use and gain. If this were the case, and Tut had become aware of the thefts, or perhaps mentioned that he would like an audit of the treasury, Maya may have devised a plan to remove the king, thus refocusing the kingdom's attention on the loss of a king rather than an investigation into the management of the money and financial affairs of the treasury.

Finally, we had to consider the very real possibility that Maya could have conspired with the other leaders of the country to overthrow the pharaoh. The reasons for a conspiracy are numerous, for example, the country's finances, Horemheb's fear of Tut's inability to lead, and so forth. We did not uncover any affiliation of Maya with the Amun priests, but it could be assumed that he was involved in the religious affairs of the country and therefore was likely to associate closely with them in one way or another. Above all, this fact was certain: Maya, because of his position of power and trust, would have worked closely with Ay, who may have had a stranglehold on him.

ANKHESENAMUN

In virtually all unsolved homicide investigations, particularly those involving an individual of medium to low risk, it is incumbent upon the inspector to examine those people who are within the inner circle of association with the victim. Without question, the spouse of the victim must be immediately examined and either excluded or focused upon more deeply. To us, Ankhesenamun was no exception. She was the stepsister to Tutankhamen and the daughter of the famed Nefertiti. The third oldest of Akhenaten's children, Ankhesenamun must have not only had a great deal of pride but also exuded confidence in all that she did. By all accounts, she was several years older than Tutankhamen and probably much more mature, if ancient boys and girls are similar in psychological development to those of today. Surely, following in the footsteps of her mother, Nefertiti, who may have even served as pharaoh for a short time under the name of Smenkhkare, Ankhesenamun felt comfortable in her role as co-regent with Tut. Together, relying on their advisers, of course, they began to make decisions on their own, particularly as they grew in stature and years.

Our investigation uncovered that Ankhesenamun and Tutankh-amen attempted to have children and that, indeed, two children were conceived, although they never made it full term. The couple must have been under a great deal of stress as they attempted to conceive children, only to have the fetuses abort each time. It's possible Ankhesenamun could have become more consumed with her need to produce an heir to the throne than with her apparent love of the pharaoh. With that in mind, one could theorize that she may have wanted Tut dead so that she could marry a king who would sire healthy children.

In addition, Ankhesenamun could have recognized that her physically handicapped husband was getting progressively worse. As pointed out, a large number of walking sticks were recovered from Tut's tomb, indicating a need for assistance as he became progressively more handicapped. Because of her concern for her husband's growing weakness, Ankhesenamun may have wanted Tut dead so that she could start fresh.

Finally, it's possible that Ankhesenamun could have conspired with others in the kingdom in hopes that she might either get a husband who could sire children or serve as pharaoh herself, maintaining all the power solely. As a daughter of royalty, and because she and Tut together would never produce a son to continue the family bloodline and position of power, Ankhesenamun could have planned and carried out Tut's murder either with the help of a close confidant or by herself. She certainly had the strength to wield a blunt instrument to the back of the king's head.

AY, "THE GREAT MANIPULATOR"

From day one of our involvement in the case, Ay, the close adviser to Akhenaten, presumably Smenkhkare, and prime minister to Tutankhamen, was and remains our prime suspect. There are numerous reasons for this. First, Ay served as the religious functionary with the title "god's father" during Akhenaten's reign. He was present when Akhenaten had the spiritual awakening that caused him to move both the power seat of the Egyptian empire and the polytheistic worship of the Amun from Thebes to the backlands of Amarna where he established the monotheistic worship of the Aten. Ay, representing the incredible power base of the Amun priesthood, second only to the authority and power of the pharaoh himself, must have been furious to see his role and authority diminish. Nonetheless, Ay recognized that his role as vizier allowed him to remain in limited power and still have some impact on Akhenaten's decisions. Once Ay became the vizier for Tutankhamen after the death of Akhenaten, he may well have orchestrated both the return of the government and the Amun priesthood to Thebes by having Tut denounce his father and proclaim that Egypt would return to the ways of his grandfather, Amenhotep III. It appeared to us that as Tutankhamen and Ankhesenamun matured and assumed more active roles in the decision-making process, the couple began to question whether the return to the polytheistic form of worship was the right decision. In fact, they may have even questioned the return to Thebes as well as the overwhelming reempowerment of the Amun priests. As Ay witnessed what may have been a repeat performance of Akhenaten, he could have considered homicide as his only way to protect the religious powers that Amun now held. The threat of losing the power that one has conspired to attain makes a perfect motive for murder.

In addition, it is conceivable that Ay may have sincerely believed he should have become the pharaoh at Akhenaten's death. He was approximately fifty years old when Tut assumed the throne. If he were ever going to have a shot at becoming king, it would have had to be then. He may have convinced himself that he deserved the pharaohship and that the royal courts would never allow a nine-year-old boy to be put in that position with that particular power. The appointment of Tut as pharaoh meant essentially that Ay would never live long enough to enjoy the puissance and prestige that came only to the king. The life expectancy of royalty in the fourteenth century BCE could easily reach the age of sixty. A nine-year-old boy could have as many as five decades to serve. Ay, realistically, had one, maybe two, left in his lifespan. Maybe angered by having the throne "stolen" from his grasp, he could have begun planning the young pharaoh's death from the onset of Tut's ascendancy.

Perhaps Ay fully supported Tutankhamen's accession to the throne, recognizing that Tut's childlike abilities would be no match for Ay's seasoned manipulations and charismatic techniques. The vizier would be in a perfect position to convince the boy to return the priesthood to the Amun, effectively restoring the power of the priests he served. Offering a kid the accolades of the kingdom by returning to Thebes could be likened to President Franklin D. Roosevelt declaring, "Happy days are here again," as the United States recovered from the Great Depression. But, as fate may have it, and as the young pharaoh grew in stature and maturity, it is conceivable that Tut also began to make decisions for himself. Perhaps he may have even suggested to Ay that he didn't care about his opinion in certain areas, causing Ay to question whether he would be able to continue to serve as the vizier or even as an Amun high priest. Confronted with the possibility of never becoming pharaoh, and more immediately, not continuing in his present position of power, Ay could have devised a plan to kill the young king.

As unusual as it may seem, thirty-three hundred years have taught one of many things about the nature of homicide, including how statistically the inner circle of trust invariably contains the "usual suspects."

Chapter 12
WHY AY?
PRESENTING THE INDICTMENT

One by one, as each suspect is carefully examined and excluded, the pool of possible offenders is sifted, and one individual rises to the surface as the most probable offender. In the final analysis, we cannot rule out the possibility of a conspiracy, specifically one involving General Horemheb. To us, though, his participation in the assassination of a pharaoh was highly unlikely. A great patriot, Horemheb would have served Tutankhamen faithfully, because that's what soldiers did, continue to do, and will always do.

Let's quickly look at why we chose to exclude a few of our "usual suspects." Maya would have had many opportunities to kill the king if he wanted to. But we don't think he was bent that way. Maya, we are told by the wall paintings, protected the identity of Tut's tomb long after the boy's death. Maya probably didn't have the personality to be a murderer. Such a character flaw didn't appear to be in his makeup.

All the accounts of Maya present him as a gentle although arrogant man. One of the primary reasons we exclude Maya is because of the small wooden figurine he had inscribed and placed in the tomb to help in the rebirth of the king's soul in the afterlife. Part of Maya's job was to ensure the safety of the tomb, and we believe that he loved his young king too much to have plotted his death or killed him himself.

Next, we considered Ankhesenamun. Yes, it's true that spouses develop reasons for anger at their companions. Interestingly, though, Ankhesenamun clearly understood her royal bloodline and role as queen. It appears to us that Tut thought of her as an equal. While some may argue that the paintings, inscriptions, and statues are misleading and romanticized, we feel they are very symbolic of the close and loving relationship the two shared. We remember with fondness the impressive and passionate mental picture Dr. Hawass painted for us of their love for one another.

We also believe that the couple deeply grieved the loss of their two stillborn children, and, although the children "never existed" under the religious beliefs of the Egyptians at that time, the couple still chose to have their children mummified. Ankhesenamun undoubtedly saw to it that they were entombed with Tutankhamen, thus keeping the feeling of eternal closeness ringing true in our ears and minds. This painful memory was restated by a royal woman we believe was Ankhesenamun in her letter and plea to the Hittite king as she prayed for a child to continue the royal bloodline. Could she have wanted Tut dead so that she could take on another husband to have children? It's possible. But not probable. If that had been the case, she would never have pled to her mortal enemy to provide a son suitable to be a king over Egypt. She would have had that piece of the puzzle solved long before she concocted a plan of murder. It didn't seem probable, and we didn't believe it happened. No, Ankhesenamun was not a murderess. At the time of Tut's burial, the grieving Ankhesenamun would have entered the tomb, perhaps leaving the bouquet of flowers that Carter found during the excavation.

Finally, as she may well have written to the Hittite king, pleading to marry one of his sons, she remarked that she would never settle for a "servant" as a husband. The son who was sent by the king to marry her was murdered on the way, and Ankhesenamun seems to have been forced to marry Ay, Tut's successor. Sometime later, Ankhesenamun herself mysteriously disappeared from history.

Meanwhile, Horemheb, the great warrior, surely must have watched in horror as his young king, stricken by illness and physical handicaps, was perceived weak by the enemies of the kingdom. First and foremost a patriot, the general could be driven to murder, believing that the gods and country were behind him. Horemheb could easily have orchestrated an accident or an ambush, even though there is no evidence to suggest that he was around at the time of Tut's death. In fact, he was far from home, probably dispatched by the prime minister, Ay. Tut was most likely already buried, or near burial, at the time of Horemheb's return. By then, Ay had been confirmed as the new pharaoh.

When Horemheb's opportunity to reign as pharaoh came several years after Tut's death, he immediately ordered the defacing of Ay's tomb and any remembrance of him. In addition, he ensured that the monotheistic beliefs of Akhenaten were not revisited. It's possible that all of this was done upon learning of Ay's actions, but it doesn't seem likely that Horemheb killed Tut.

This leaves us with our final suspect in this intriguing mystery. As our final specks of evidence fall to the ground, and as the sifting completes, one character remains in the forefront—Ay.

Ay may well have known about the assassination attempts on King Akhenaten as recorded on the tomb walls of Akhenaten's police chief, Mahu. Ay was one of the leading officials to the heretic Akhenaten, who stripped the Amun priests of their power and relocated the government to Amarna. Could Ay have been secretly playing both sides of the fence? Did he promise allegiance to Akhenaten and promise to keep the Amun priests "at bay" while secretly conspiring with those same priests to kill Akhenaten and return the Amun priesthood to power?

Shortly after Akhenaten's death, Ay was prime minister. During this time (where very little information is recovered), it appears that the mysterious pharaoh Smenkhkare disappears from history. Who was left at the time? Ay.

After Smenkhkare's departure, Ay might have demanded that the country should place the experienced high official into power as pharaoh. But luck didn't swing his way. Instead, probably to his anger, the nine-year-old son of Akhenaten was crowned the pharaoh. Wisely, Ay convinced the young king to keep him on as vizier. Thus, the conniving Ay maintained his power and control over Tut for many years, convincing him to denounce his father and his father's religion. He sold the kid on the idea he'd get a huge reception, plus accolades, if he denounced his father and returned the kingdom seat to Thebes. Ay probably orchestrated the overwhelming Opet Festival, the return of the pharaoh to Thebes, and the return and restoration of the Amun priesthood.

It can only be surmised how Tut died. But it appears likely that as he reached his seventeenth to twentieth year he became quite confident in his own abilities to lead. Perhaps there was discussion between Tut and his queen that together they could make better decisions than the elderly, "old-fashioned," Ay. We even theorize Tut may have put Ay in his place, explaining something to the effect, "No, Ay, we won't do it your way. I am the pharaoh, and you are just a servant." Imagine the anger a comment like that, or even such a perceived belief, would have raised in the man.

Nonetheless, either at the hands of murderers or by accident, Tut died. It appears from the way that Ankhesenamun reacted that the death was due to murder because she immediately writes the Hittite king regarding concerns of marrying a "servant."

A tried and tested statement we've used repeatedly in our work reminds us, "Past behavior predicts future behavior." For a moment, consider the following:

When Akhenaten dies, Ay is there!

When Smenkhkare dies, Ay is there!

When Nefertiti (Ankhesenamun's mother and Tutankhamen's stepmother and potential heir to the throne after Akhenaten's death) dies, Ay is there!

When Tutankhamen dies, Ay is there!

When the Hittite king's son sent to marry Ankhesenamun is murdered, Ay is there!

When Ankhesenamun disappears from history, Ay is there!

And when Ay dies, the mysterious deaths seem to stop.

The manipulative master of deceit, Ay is present at every stage of mystery and death. He secretly planned and coveted the throne of pharaoh. He spent his entire life in pursuit of the position, and like most psychopathic personalities, figured, "I want it. They have it. I deserve it. I'll take it." He then spent the remainder of his time as pharaoh trying to convince himself and the gods that he was a commoner who rose to the greatness of pharaoh. In reality, he was a murderer who crushed anyone in his way.

We reflected on Daniel Troyer, a serial killer of eight elderly women. He once explained to us, "Let's put it this way. Let's say that I hate my brother-in-law. In fact, I hate him so badly that I decide I want to kill him. The problem is my mother loves my brother-in-law. I, in turn, love my mother, and I wouldn't do anything to hurt her. Nonetheless, I hate my brother-in-law, and I want to kill him. The answer is easy. I must first kill my mother because I would never do anything to make her feel bad. Once she is dead, I can kill my brother-in-law without the fear of hurting mother."

Ay lived for power, dominion, and control. He was no different than any other murderous psychopath who roams the streets today. The only solace in solving this thirty-three-centuries-old murder is the knowledge that the eternities do continue. Howard Carter, the Egyptologist who brought King Tutankhamen into the light and made him the most famous of all pharaohs, brought Tut the gift of fame. We look forward to one day meeting the pharaoh knowing we brought him the gift of justice. Now, perhaps, King Tut can rest in peace in the Valley of the Kings.

High Court of the Pharaoh of Egypt
for the Central District of Thebes

EGYPT,	)	CR 03-881
	)	
Plaintiff,	)	I N D I C T M E N T
	)	
v.	)	[Criminal Homicide]
	)	[Breach of Fiduciary
AY, PRIME MINISTER AND VIZIER	)	Responsibility]
TO TUTANKHAMEN,	)	[Ethics Violations]
Criminal Homicide;	)	18 E.C.C. § 1330
BCE(a)(5):		

The Grand Jury charges:

COUNT ONE

[18 E.C. §§ 1343, 2a, 2b]

INTRODUCTION

1. Beginning in or around the reign of King Akhenaten of the 18th
   Dynasty (1352–1336 BCE) and continuing until the concluding
   days of the reign of King Tutankhamen (1336–1327 BCE)
   defendant PRIME MINISTER AND VIZIER AY carried out a
   scheme to remove Tutankhamen from the role of pharaoh for
   all of Egypt by means of false pretenses, representation and
   promises, by: (a) misleading Tutankhamen's father, Akhenaten,
   into believing he represented the best interests of the kingdom
   of Egypt while conspiring with the Amun priests to restore
   power to the priests, having first been stripped from them by the
   monotheistic beliefs of Pharaoh Akhenaten during the hereafter
   referred to period of Amarna, and (b) by continuing a secret
   relationship with the Amun priests who had been removed

from power, and (c) secretly conspiring with the Amun priests to regain their power through murderous acts.

2. Furthermore, Ay participated in part or whole in at least one assassination attempt on the life of Pharaoh Akhenaten and later in the defamation of the late Akhenaten by coercing the young Tutankhamen into publishing the Restoration Stela, which proclaimed a return to the polytheistic belief system.

3. Finally, Ay, in concert or alone, plotted and arranged for the untimely death of King Tutankhamen in a successful attempt to become pharaoh and prevent the return of the kingdom of Egypt to a monotheistic belief system.

4. Tutankhaten, Tutankhamun, Tutankhamen, or King Tut as he is informally known, is an Egyptian male, age seventeen to twenty. At the time of his death, he was the reigning pharaoh for the country of Egypt following the untimely and unexplained death of his father, King Akhenaten. Tutankhamen and his child bride and half-sister, Ankhesenamun, ruled over the country of Egypt in the District of Thebes. Tut mysteriously died, and local law enforcement was prevented from examining the case in detail.

5. During the time relevant to this indictment, the defendant Ay was serving as the close adviser to the honorable Akhenaten and as prime minister (vizier) to Tutankhamen. The remainder of this affidavit will deal only with the death of the latter victim, Tutankhamen, and the relationship placing the defendant under scrutiny.

6. Ay, having managed the affairs of the late Akhenaten, became the surrogate father to the late king's son, Tutankhaten. Ay assisted the young nine-year-old prodigy in the art of leadership.

7. During this important time in Tut's life, Ay manipulated the young pharaoh and convinced him that if he truly wanted to win the hearts of his countrymen, and restore wealth and prosperity to the land, he must abandon the city his father built and return to Thebes, where the disempowered Amun priests resided.

8. Ay orchestrated the construction of the Restoration Stela, effectively declaring to the world the rejection Tut had for his father's monotheistic belief system. The Restoration Stela, which still exists today, over thirty-three hundred years later, publicly denounces all that Akhenaten believed in and caused his people to live under.

9. In order to circumvent the established belief system that made Ay powerless politically, Ay then orchestrated Tutankhamen's triumphant return to Thebes and the restoration of the worship of Amun, thereby returning the powerful Amun priests to office. This defiant act against his previous employer Akhenaten was recorded in the great Opet Festival in which Tut entered the sacred temples to meet with the gods.

10. Defendant Ay, aided and abetted by other actors, both known and unknown to the grand jury, obtained confidential government information regarding strategies, weaknesses, and strengths and used them for personal gain by further strengthening his position in the kingdom.

11. Defendant Ay posed as a confidant to the young king and his queen while secretly planning to take over the kingdom by using his powerful position with the priests of Amun.

12. Often, defendant Ay questioned the pharaoh about the future direction of the kingdom in order to ascertain his position and stability in the leadership.

13. As the king and queen assumed greater responsibility and began making more decisions on their own, the royal partnership leaned less on Defendant Ay and his abilities and may have even remarked that his services were not needed as often, causing said Defendant to be concerned for his own future.

14. To conceal his murderous plot, Defendant Ay sent the pharaoh's commander and leader of the army away on a military campaign. This act ensured said Defendant the appropriate amount of time to assume the crown after the death of Tutankhamen.

15. Defendant Ay, aided and abetted by others known and unknown to the grand jury, planned the execution of Tut, or took advantage of the accidental death of the pharaoh in order to obtain the throne. Said individuals participated in part or whole with the cover story and orchestrated the quick burial proceedings.

16. Defendant Ay then ordered that the dead pharaoh be buried in his own tomb, claiming that the pharaoh's tomb was not complete enough for a proper burial. While the embalmers were rushing the mummification process in one-half the normal timeframe, Ay demanded that his own tomb be used to entomb the king.

17. Victim Tutankhamen's intended tomb, although partially complete, represented approximately 165 square meters of floor space. When finished, the tomb, presently held by Defendant Ay, was over 222 square meters, or twice the size of that in which Tut was interred (Defendant Ay's original tomb).

18. The completed tomb of Ay, which became the final resting place for Tutankhamen, was only 110 square meters of finished floor space, nearly 40 percent smaller than the tomb he placed Tutankhamen in.

19. The final resting place, hereafter referred to as Tutankhamen's tomb, was filled with artifacts belonging to people other than Tutankhamen. Evidence supports that over 80 percent of the artifacts in Tutankhamen's tomb belonged to someone else.

20. Before Tutankhamen was interred, Defendant Ay instructed craftsman to hastily finish the tomb of Tut with paint. Craftsman were prevented from cleaning up spilled paint and smears on the walls or repairing poor craftsmanship. This is evident by the large dripping and running stains down the interior walls and on the floor. Tut's sarcophagus was not his own and had the previous owner's name scratched out and his own carved over it.

21. Defendant Ay proclaimed himself pharaoh before Tutankhamen was even interred. This is evident by the painting inside

Tut's tomb of Ay performing the Opening of the Mouth ceremony while wearing the robes of a funerary priest.

22. Shortly after Tutankhamen's burial, Ankhesenamun was forced
    to marry the elderly Ay, further legitimizing his role as pharaoh.
    In a tragically worded letter to the Hittite king, Ankhesenamun
    pled with the mortal enemy of the Egyptians to send one of his
    sons to marry her and rule Egypt. She is quoted as saying that
    she will not marry a "servant," referring to Defendant Ay.

23. According to ancient history, the Hittite king feared that her
    request was a trap and sent his servants to inspect. Upon their
    return and notification that this was truly the wish of the wid-
    owed queen, the Hittite king sent one of his sons to marry
    Ankhesenamun. En route to the Egyptian empire, the son of the
    Hittite king was murdered.

24. Evidence shows that Ay then forced Ankhesenamun to marry
    him, legitimizing his role as the pharaoh. This is evident by the
    ring bearing the name of Ay and Ankhesenamun that was discov-
    ered in 1970 and now sits in evidence in the museum in Berlin.

25. According to the Hittites, the letter said, "My husband is dead
    and a son I have not. But of thee, they say thy sons are many. If
    thou wouldst give me son of thine, he would become my hus-
    band. I am loathe to take a servant of mine and make him my
    husband. . . . I am afraid!"

26. The dead pharaoh's young wife clearly sensed something was
    wrong and that Ay was to blame. The queen's testimony (in letter)
    would place blame on Defendant Ay for Tutankhamen's death.

27. Defendant Ay used unauthorized control and political power to:
    (a) circumvent investigative responsibilities of local law
        enforcement and prevent adequate investigation into the
        untimely death of the pharaoh;
    (b) force the rushed mummification of the victim, Tutankh-
        amen, by demanding that the embalmers cover him with
        unguents and seal his sarcophagus without completely and

properly mummifying the body, as evidenced by the completion of the laborious resin poured into the insignificant cranial cavity;

(c) manipulated the burial chambers in order to keep the larger, more quality tomb for himself while placing the intended owner and king into a tomb built for only a nobleman, not a pharaoh;

(d) assigned the only leader capable of stopping his criminal plan, Horemheb, to military duties away from the capitol of Thebes;

(e) used his political position as prime minister and his religious power as chief Amun priest to appoint himself as the successor to Tutankhamen; and

(f) forced Tut's wife, Ankhesenamun, to marry him against her wishes, further legitimizing his position as pharaoh.

Conclusion

THE CURSE
OF THE MUMMY TUT

Meanwhile, as we prepare to go to press with our effort, we learn of more ancient tombs being found in Egypt. Apparently, French archaeologists unearthed a huge necropolis filled with rock-hewn tombs more than four thousand years old. Located near the pyramids of Saqqara, the necropolis dates back to and even earlier than the Old Kingdom, which lasted from 2400 BCE to 2100 BCE. Writings on one of the tombs identified it as belonging to Hau-Nefer, a priest who served in the mortuary temple of King Pepi I. When Ay assassinated Tut, Hau-Nefer's mummy was already a thousand-plus years old. Not only was the tomb decorated with colored scenes that featured Hau-Nefer in different poses with preferred deities and family members, but also it yielded an amazingly well-preserved colored limestone relief depicting the priest with his wife, Khuti, and their thirteen children. To Zahi Hawass, Egypt's chief of antiquities, the discovery of the barely excavated necropolis may soon yield mummies and treasures equal in importance to those of Tutankhamen.

Will they be as blessed or cursed as his?

For well over eighty years, there has been considerable speculation and mystery about the "curse" that fell upon anyone who
entered the sacred tomb of Tutankhamen and became ill or died. We
studied with great interest the hype and history of those who sup-
posedly had been plagued by the mummy's curse. As we reflected
upon the many stories that we had heard or read about, and as we
considered the prospect of entering the tomb ourselves, the same
tomb that those early explorers discovered and entered, fear of the
curse entered our minds, too. We could not escape the impressions
made by current-day Hollywood blockbuster hits about the tombs,
catacombs, and chambers of the ancient pharaohs and noblemen
without feeling twinges of concern.

Each of us recalled our own experience swimming in the Pacific
Ocean back in the mid-1970s when the feature films *Jaws* and *Jaws II*
portrayed killer sharks consuming swimmers, divers, and anyone
unfortunate enough to be sailing or wading within the reaches of
these giant predators. The "duh-dum, duh-dum, duh-dum" echo of
the theme song rang in our ears with each step we took into the
waves. Needless to say, we found ourselves scanning the crashing
surf and didn't remain too long in the tide.

Similar to those fears we felt entering the ocean years earlier, we
found ourselves affected by the movies of mummies—mummies
who come alive, reach through the sand, and grab the legs of unsus-
pecting explorers like ourselves. We imagined the flinging darts and
arrows that protected the way from trespassers. We thought of the
ferocious sandstorms that carried thousands-of-years-old deceased
criminals to different locations in order to continue their evil work
of destruction.

As we approached the tomb of Mahu in particular, we felt a
twinge of concern as the inspector informed us that there was no
electricity in the tomb and that we would have to rely upon our
cheap pocket flashlights and the infrared capability of the camera.
As we slowly made our way into the tomb that had remained sealed
for thousands of years prior to its discovery in 1883, and that had
been undisturbed much of the time since its discovery because it was

Photo of the temple near Tut's home during his reign (photo by Mike King).

only the tomb of a nobleman, the chief of police for Akhenaten, our nervousness began to consume us. When a small sliver of light crept in from the outside entrance to the tomb, we thought about how few times during the past three thousand years the sun had graced the inside of this pitch-black burial spot. After exploring the foyer-type areas, we discovered a stairwell in the back portion of the tomb. With the inspector's permission, we carefully walked down five flights of stairs to the bottom of the tomb. The scene was eerie, only made visible by the infrared camera and the small flashlights. With each step, the dust that had lain on the stairs for thousands of years swirled around our feet. On camera, it appeared as though we were scuba diving and had disturbed the sandy sediment of the ocean floor. With each step taken lower into the tomb, sweat drained from our foreheads. The thought of what lay below the next dark step in the abyss actually propelled us forward and deeper into the earth as if drawn by an ancient magnet.

At the bottom of the stairwell we found the skeletal remains of an early citizen. It also appeared that the early craftsmen had suddenly been recalled from their work, leaving behind piles of rock and rubble from their excavation. To us, this was a subtle reminder of Tut's abandonment of Amarna and more specifically Akhenaten's ways. We recalled the words of the Restoration Stela (whose complete, fully translated text is found in the appendixes).

Throughout this investigation, like all our previous investigations, there were times when we thought our efforts were being cursed. There were equally as many times when we sincerely believed that our investigative work was really being rewarded with small victories. We had heard about the terrible bouts of sickness the directors, producers, and film crew of various movie companies had endured on their trips to the tombs. Was the mummy's curse a real possibility? Clearly, as Greg became ill in the middle of the trip, and as Mike fell victim to dysentery on the last day of filming, common sense caused us to rethink our disbelief of the tale.

A few months after our return to Utah, we learned of the Atlantic film crew's follow-up trip to Egypt and how the producer became violently ill and had to return home to London in a wheelchair. Thankfully, she recovered some time later. Could the "curse" be only the result of the crew's long days and sleepless nights of filming demanded by the company, which tried to make the wisest use of its production dollars? Possibly. Another possibility was that dehydration took its toll not only upon the early explorers but also upon us as we spent days and much of the nights in the dry desert air, working without adequate rest. Although we tried to drink plenty of liquids, we may have exhausted our reservoirs of the needed fluid.

More than a year passed before we again reflected on the mummy's curse. In fact, we felt we had been the recipients of the mummy's blessings, not the curse, since we received the highest ratings in our world premiere of the film. We were advised that our two-hour documentary, "The Assassination of King Tut," was among the top ten shows of all-time for the Discovery Channel. In fact, during the nine months that followed the original October 2002 showing, some twenty-two million Americans, in eighteen repeat performances, viewed the production. Ratings worldwide were just as high, if not higher. In Mexico, Brazil, Argentina, Chile, and Spain, "The Assassination of King Tut" ranked number one among cable households, among adults twenty-five to fifty-four years of age. In Spain, the rating was the highest during the past four years for all pay-TV networks. Needless to say, we were very, very proud and pleased.

The 2002 Winter Olympic Games started within a few weeks of our return home, and we were drawn immediately back into our individual assignments. We both had full-time assignments in the public safety of the games. When off duty, needless to say, we watched the competitions with a great deal of pride.

Since that time, we ended our careers with our respective employers and moved on to other projects. The invitations to speak, train, and consult have been rewarding, and we continue to work, Greg with the security of our nation's airports and Mike as intelligence supervisor within the Department of Homeland Security. In retrospect, the mummy's curse may have nipped at our heels, but it appears, at least for the time being, that we survived. Perhaps, there really is no curse intended for us. In fact, if we truly did solve the murder of Tutankhamen, we may be enjoying the rewards of bringing justice to the fallen young man.

In retrospect, we cannot blame anything on the early investigators of Tutankhamen's death. In an imperfect world, we nonetheless hope that all investigators have the integrity and fortitude to blaze forward in solving crime. We recognize that our early predecessors probably faced retribution from Ay's political leadership if they wondered aloud how the young pharaoh died. In fact, we can imagine the frustration that the investigators, the family of Tutankhamen, those political advisers who truly cared for Tut, to say nothing of the people of Egypt, must have felt as rumors of assassination trickled throughout the kingdom. We believe it would have been similar to the rumors and frustrations that are faced by people today as they evaluate the nature of prosecution, the criminal justice system, the effectiveness and fairness of police, and the courts. We cannot help but reflect on the many unsolved homicides across the United States and abroad. We think often of the e-mails and letters that we have received from sad and confused family members of those who are missing, have been murdered, or have been victimized by the predators who roam our streets.

We have made some attempts to assist them to one degree or another, but without greater financial resources, adequate assistance is only a hope. Nonetheless, their concerns, frustrations, and hopes for resolution push us forward in the belief of one day developing a unit of experts who can travel the country helping in cases of unsolved homicide, missing persons, unidentified bodies, and serial crimes of violence.

Traveling to Egypt and meeting King Tut was an incredible journey. From our first opportunity to look into this ancient mystery, our hope was to formulate and share some additional insight into what has been a dark and confusing scene. We thought often about our teachers in both elementary and high school who tried to convey an appreciation for venerable civilizations of the past. How we wished we had paid more attention! Now, of course, we value the incredible vision of organizations like the Discovery Channel that dramatize history in a way that bridges the span of time. What an exciting journey it was for us to delve into old books, magazines, Egyptology reports, and films dealing with the ancient Egyptians and more particularly the pharaohs who led them.

We will never forget the distant look in the faces of our fellow human beings whom we passed along the streets of Cairo, Luxor, Minya, and the other communities in the backlands. We will always cherish the beautiful smiles of the children and the charismatic way in which they tried to sell us their goods. The awful and the sweet smells of a city of twenty-two million will remain in our memories for many years to come. We will forever remember our feelings of concern as we left American airspace shortly after the destructive forces of evil collapsed the Twin Towers of New York City and our nation's powerful command center in the Pentagon.

In addition, we'll always retain the memories of our work terribly late at night, only to be shattered by terribly early morning departures; the incredible work ethic of the film crew, partly motivated by the skyrocketing costs of filming such a production; the sheer dedication of that wonderful crew to their art; the sun rising above the desert floor as we watched an old Egyptian, high atop his donkey, riding from one horizon to the other; and the stirring sunsets, beauty matched only by the humble Muslim kneeling before his maker in earnest prayer.

We will remember the excitement of sifting through the sand and discovering pottery that is thousands of years old and the personal satisfaction of carefully returning it to the sand that would protect it for many more millennia; the heavy exhaust as it rises from the engine of the boats transporting us along the Nile; the oxen lounging in the water next to a young Egyptian woman washing her family's clothing; the dust in the air as Egyptian children played soccer in a nearby field; and a simple farmer huddled next to a small twig fire, preparing his dinner.

Although our memories of Egypt and her people will fade over time, we hope that the impressions they've left upon us will be indelibly etched in our personalities, our appreciation, and our gratitude. We will not soon forget the humble circumstances of our Thanksgiving meal away from America. Recollections of the hard dirt floor and the labor-strained faces of the loving mother who welcomed her son's American friends will be revived each Thanksgiving season.

Finally, our thoughts and fantasies turn to Tut. We look forward to that great reunion that occurs for each of us when we pass from this earthly life into eternal existence.

Like the pharaohs of old, we believe in a life after this. We believe that we existed before we came to this earth. We believe that a loving Father in Heaven placed us upon this earth to become a better, more capable, more compassionate people and that He loves us so much that He prepared a way for us to return and live with Him forever.

When that time comes for us, we hope that we meet our friend Tutankhamen. We hope that he is standing arm-in-arm with the love of his life, Ankhesenamun. We hope that their children are close by and that he will sit with us for a moment in time and share the true story of his death. We hope that we were correct in our theory and that he whispers the words, "You two were right," and "thank you."

Today, we often think of the pressure that must have been on

General Horemheb. We will always view him as a great patriot who would have done anything for his country and pharaoh. We cannot believe that such a patriot would kill his king. We do not believe it was in his makeup. A true patriot would have died in the service of the pharaoh and felt honor in that above power.

Our personal hope is that Horemheb questioned the timely actions of Ay from Akhenaten's death through the mysterious disappearance of Smenkhkare, the mysterious death of King Tut, the mysterious murder of the son of the Hittite king, through the conclusion of those murderous acts when Ay appointed himself to the throne. He must have wondered why Ankhesenamun mysteriously disappeared from history shortly after her marriage to Ay. We also hope that as the great patriot Horemheb served Pharaoh Ay, he continued to wonder about Ay's ascension to the throne. Surely, bit by bit, he realized the nature of Ay's psychopathic behavior and was privileged to hear from the murderer a deathbed confession of all his evilness.

Finally, as pharaoh himself, powerful General Horemheb delivered the most significant justice of his reign: the defacement and removal of Ay's name from the cartouches. As workmen scratched Ay's eyes from the statues and carvings and removed his nose and lips, they essentially struck Ay's existence from the eternities.

How sad Horemheb's final years must have been as he reflected on whether he could have saved Tutankhamen from sure death had he only recognized the monster who served within the pharaoh's closest circle of aides.

In the final summation, if our analysis is correct, Ay will receive the justice he deserves from the most just of all: the Creator of earth, heaven and flesh. Our greatest hope is that we have the opportunity to present our evidence and testify in that eternal and final court that we are convinced exists.

BIBLIOGRAPHY

Aldred, C. 1972. *Tutankhamun's Egypt.* London: BBC Publications.

————. 1988. *Akhenaten, King of Egypt.* London: Thames and Hudson.

Bennet, J. 1939. "The Restoration Inscription of Tut'ankhamun," *Journal of Egyptian Archaeology* 25: 8–15.

Blackwood, Algernon. 1923. "The Literary Traveler in Egypt," *Literary Digest International Book Review* (June).

Brackman, A. C. 1976. *The Search for the Gold of Tutankhamen.* New York: Mason/Charter.

Brier, B. 1998. *The Murder of Tutankhamen: A 3,000-Year-Old Murder Mystery.* London: Weidenfeld and Nicholson.

Carter, H. 1927. *The Tomb of Tutankhamen II.* London: Cassell.

————. 1933. *The Tomb of Tutankhamen III.* London: Cassell.

Carter, H., and A. Mace. 1923. *The Tomb of Tutankhamen I.* London: Cassell.

Conolly, R., et al. 1976. "Serological Evidence of Tutankhamen and Smenkhkare," *Journal of Egyptian Archaeology* 62: 184–86.

Davies, N. de G., and A. H. Gardiner. 1926. *The Tomb of Huy, Viceroy of Nubia in the Reign of Tutankhamen.* London: Egypt Exploration Society.

Davis, T. M. 1912. *The Tombs of Harmhabi and Touatankhamanou.* Repr. London: Duckworth, 2001.

Derry, D. 1922. "Report Upon the Examination of Tutankhamen's Mummy." In *The Tomb of Tutankhamen I*. London: Cassell, pp. 143–61.

Desroches-Noblecourt, C. 1963. *Tutankhamen: Life and Death of a Pharaoh*. London: Penguin.

Edwards, I. E. S. 1972. *The Treasures of Tutankhamen*. London: British Museum Press.

Filce Leek, F. 1972. *The Human Remains from the Tomb of Tut'ankhamun*. Oxford: Oxford University Press.

———. 1977. "How Old Was Tut'ankhamun?" *Journal of Egyptian Archaeology* 63: 112–15.

Fletcher, J. 2000. *Chronicle of a Pharaoh: The Intimate Life of Amenhotep III*. New York: Oxford University Press.

Fletcher, J., and D. Montserrat. 1998. "The Human Hair in the Tomb of Tutankhamun: A Re-evaluation." In C. Eyre, ed., *Proceedings of the Seventh International Congress of Egyptologists*. Leuven: n.p., pp. 401–407.

Fox, P. 1951. *Tutankhamen's Treasure*. London: Oxford University Press.

Frayling, C. 1992. *The Face of Tutankhamen*. London: Faber & Faber.

Freed, R., Y. J. Markowitz, and S. D'Auria, eds. 1999. *Pharaohs of the Sun: Akhenaten, Nefertiti, Tutankhamen*. Boston: Bullfinch Press.

Harris, J. E., and K. R. Weeks. 1973. *X-Raying the Pharaohs*. New York: Scribner's.

Harris, J. E., and E. F. Wente, eds. 1980. *An X-Ray Atlas of the Royal Mummies*. Chicago: University of Chicago Press.

Harrison, R. G., and A. B. Abdalla. 1972. "The Remains of Tutankhamen." *Antiquity* 46: 8–18.

Hepper, F. N. 1990. *Pharaoh's Flowers: The Botanical Treasures of Tutankhamun*. London: HMSO.

Hoving, T. 1978. *Tutankhamun: The Untold Story*. New York: Simon & Schuster.

Hornung, E. 1990. *Valley of the Kings: Horizon of Eternity*. New York: n.p.

Hunter, J., et al. 1996. *Studies in Crime: An Introduction to Forensic Archaeology*. London: n.p.

James, T. G. H. 1992. *Howard Carter: The Path to Tutankhamun*. London: British Museum Press.

Lewis, F. 1929. "Egypt the Incredible." *Woman's Home Companion* (January).

MacQuitty, W. 1978. *Tutankhamen's Last Journey*. New York: Crown.

Martin, G. T. 1991. *The Hidden Tombs of Memphis*. London: Thames & Hudson.

Murray, H., and M. A. Nuttal. 1963. *A Handlist to Howard Carter's Catalogue of Objects in Tut'ankhamun's Tomb*. Oxford: Oxford University Press.

Newberry, P. E. 1927. "Report on the Floral Wreaths Found in the Coffins of Tutankhamen." In H. Carter and A. C. Mace, eds., *The Tomb of Tutankhamen II*, pp. 189–96.

Ray, J. 2002. *Reflections of Osiris: Lives from Ancient Egypt.* London: Profile.

Redford, D. 1984. *Akhenaten the Heretic King.* Princeton, NJ: Princeton University Press.

Reeves, C. N. 1990. *The Complete Tutankhamun.* London: Thames & Hudson.

———. 1990. *Valley of the Kings: The Decline of a Royal Necropolis.* London: n.p.

Reeves, C. N., and J. H. Taylor. 1992. *Howard Carter Before Tutankhamun.* London: British Museum Press.

Reeves, N., and R. H. Wilkinson. 1996. *The Complete Valley of the Kings: Tombs and Treasures of Egypt's Greatest Pharaohs.* London: Thames & Hudson.

Romer, J. 1981. *Valley of the Kings.* New York: Morrow.

Saleh, M., and H. Sourouzian. 1987. *Official Catalogue of the Egyptian Museum Cairo.* Mainz: von Zabern.

Schaden, O. 1984. "Clearance of the Tomb of King Ay (WV. 23)." *Journal of the American Research Center in Egypt* 21: 39–64.

———. 1992. "The God's Father Ay." In *Amarna Letters: Essays on Ancient Egypt ca. 1390–1310 BCE.* Vol. 2. San Francisco, KMT Communications, pp. 92–115.

Seele, K. 1955. "King Ay and the Close of the Amarna Age." *Journal of Near Eastern Studies* 14: 168–80.

Shaw, I., and P. Nicholson. 1995. *British Museum Dictionary of Ancient Egypt.* London: British Museum Press.

Smith, G. E. 1912. *The Royal Mummies.* London: Duckworth.

Taylor, J. H. 2001. *Death and the Afterlife in Ancient Egypt.* London: British Museum Press.

van Dijk, J. 2000. "The Amarna Period and the Later New Kingdom." In I. Shaw, ed., *The Oxford History of Ancient Egypt.* Oxford: Oxford University Press, pp. 272–313.

Vogelsang-Eastwood, G. 1999. *Tutankhamun's Wardrobe.* Leiden: n.p.

Watterson, B. 1999. *Amarna: Ancient Egypt's Age of Revolution.* Stroud: Tempus Publishing.

Wente, E., et al. 1976. *Treasures of Tutankhamen.* New York: Metropolitan Museum of Art.

Winlock, H. E. 1941. *Materials Used at the Embalming of King Tut'-ankhamun.* New York: Metropolitan Museum of Art.

Winstone, H. V. F. 1993. *Howard Carter and the Discovery of the Tomb of Tutankhamun*. London: Constable.

Wynne, B. 1972. *Behind the Mask of Tutankhamen*. London: Corgi.

APPENDIXES

Appendix 1

MAPS AND CHARTS

ANCIENT EGYPTIAN TEMPLES AND TOMBS

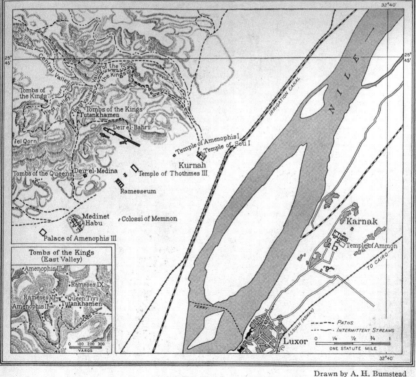

Drawn by A. H. Bumstead

These 1923 maps of the Valley of the Kings show the known temples and tombs
at the time of Tut's discovery. (From "At the Tomb of Tutankhamen,"
National Geographic 43, no. 5 [1923]: 467. Courtesy of National Geographic.)

THE VALLEY OF THE NILE

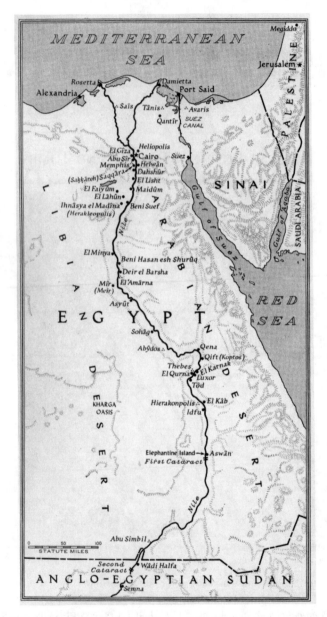

This 1921 map depicts about thirteen millennia of Egyptian history, archaeology, and treasure "digs." (From "Daily Life in Ancient Egypt," *National Geoghraphic* 80, no. 4 [1941]: 426. Courtesy of National Geographic.)

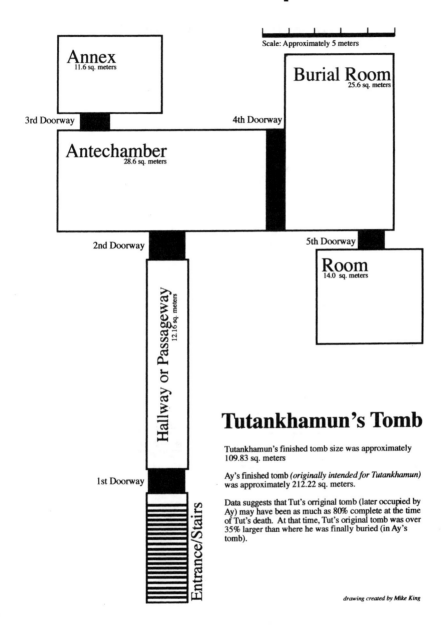

Scale: Approximately 5 meters

Annex
11.6 sq. meters

Burial Room
25.6 sq. meters

3rd Doorway

4th Doorway

Antechamber
28.6 sq. meters

2nd Doorway

5th Doorway

Room
14.0 sq. meters

Hallway or Passageway
12.16 sq. meters

Tutankhamun's Tomb

Tutankhamun's finished tomb size was approximately 109.83 sq. meters

Ay's finished tomb *(originally intended for Tutankhamun)* was approximately 212.22 sq. meters.

Data suggests that Tut's original tomb (later occupied by Ay) may have been as much as 80% complete at the time of Tut's death. At that time, Tut's original tomb was over 35% larger than where he was finally buried (in Ay's tomb).

1st Doorway

Entrance/Stairs

drawing created by Mike King

Tutankhamen's Family Tree*

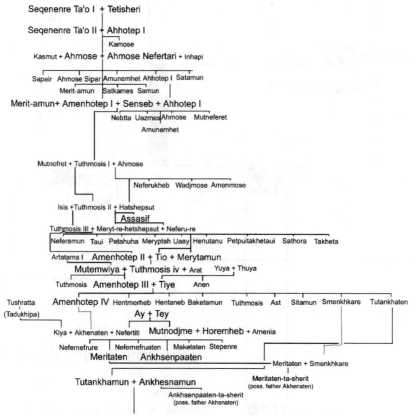

Seqenenre Ta'o I + Tetisheri

Seqenenre Ta'o II + Ahhotep I
　　　　　　　　　Kamose
Kasmut + Ahmose + Ahmose Nefertari + Inhapi

Sapair Ahmose Sipar Amunemhet Ahhotep I Satamun
　　Merit-amun　Satkames Samun
Merit-amun+ Amenhotep I + Senseb + Ahhotep I
　　　　　　　　Nebtta Uazmes Ahmose Mutneferet
　　　　　　　　　Amunemhet

Mutnofret + Tuthmosis I + Ahmose
　　　　　　　　Neferukheb Wadjmose Amenmose

Isis +Tuthmosis II + Hatshepsut
　　　Assasif
Tuthmosis III + Meryt-re-hetshepsut + Neferu-re
Neferamun Taui Petahuha Meryptah Uaay Henutanu Petpuitakhetaui Sathora Takheta
Artatama I Amenhotep II + Tio + Merytamun
　Mutemwiya + Tuthmosis iv + Arat Yuya + Thuya
Tuthmosis Amenhotep III + Tiye Anen

Tushratta Amenhotep IV Hentmerheb Hentaneb Baketamun Tuthmosis Ast Sitamun Smenkhkare Tutankhaten
(Tadukhipa)　　　　　　　Ay + Tey
　　Kiya + Akhenaten + Nefertiti Mutnodjme + Horemheb + Amenia
Nefernefrure Nefernefruaten Maketaten Stepenre
　　Meritaten　　Ankhsenpaaten
　　　　　　　　　　　　　　　Meritaten + Smenkhkare
Tutankhamun + Ankhesnamun　　　Meritaten-ta-sherit
　　　　　　　　　　　　　　(poss. father Akhenaten)
　　　　　Ankhsenpaaten-ta-sherit
　　　　　(poss. father Akhenaten)

End of Line

*From Ian Bolton, "Family Tree of the 18th Dynasty" [online], members.tripod.com/~ib205/18th_dynasty_tree.html [December 8, 2003].

SOME OF THE KINGS AND DYNASTIES OF ANCIENT EGYPT*

NEW KINGDOM: CA. 1539–1075 BCE

Dynasty 18   *Dynasty 20*

Ahmose	Sethnakhte
Amenhotep I	Ramses III
Thutmose I	Ramses IV
Thutmose II	Ramses V
Queen Hatshepsut	Ramses VI
Thutmose III	Ramses VII
Amenhotep II	Ramses VIII
Thutmose IV	Ramses IX
Amenhotep III	Ramses X
Akhenaten (Amenhotep IV)	Ramses XI
Smenkhkare	
Queen Ankhetkheprure	
Tutankhamen	
Ay	
Horemheb	

Dynasty 19

Ramses I
Seti I
Ramses II
Merneptah
Seti II/Amenmesse
Siptah
Queen Tawosret

---

*From "Great Peoples of the Past: Ancient Egypt," *National Geographic* supplement (April 2001). Copyright © 2001 by the National Geographic Society. Reprinted by permission of the National Geographic Society.

CHRONOLOGY OF MAIN EVENTS

1922   4 November: the first stone step is removed.
       5 November: the steps are cleared.
       23 November: Carnarvon arrives in Luxor.
       26 November: first view of wonderful things.
       29 November: official opening of the antechamber and inner room or annex.
       30 November: first press report in the *Times*.
       18 December: assembly of an excavation team with help from the Metropolitan Museum in New York.
       27 December: the first object, a painted wooden casket, is removed from the tomb.

1923   30 January: Harry Burton's photographs of the interior tomb published.
       17 February: official opening of the tomb.
       25 February: controversy in the American press about who owns the name of Tut.
       6 March: Carnarvon bitten by a mosquito.
       5 April: death of Carnarvon.

1925   28 October: first view of the mummy of Tut.
       11 November: postmortem of mummy commences.

1930   10 November: the last artifacts are taken out of the tomb.

1939   2 March: Carter dies in South Kensington.

1969   Harrison from Liverpool University reenters the tomb. Tut is sawed in half and x-rayed.

1979   Dr. James Harris, professor of orthodontics at the University of Michigan, enters the tomb and takes another x-ray.

2001   Japanese enter to take a DNA sample and are stopped by authorities.

Appendix 2

THE GREAT RESTORATION STELA OF TUT-ANKH-AMUN*

1) [. . .] Fourth month of the inundation season, day 19, under the Majesty of Horus, "Strong bull," "Beautiful of Birth," Two Ladies [Goodly of Laws, he who pacifies the Two Lands, Horus of Gold, "Exalted of Crowns," Who placates the Gods, "King of Upper and Lower Egypt," Nebkheperure, "Son of Re," Tutankhamun, Ruler of Hermonthis," Given Life like Re, Forever]

2) Beloved of [Amun-Ra] Lord of the Thrones of the Two Lands, Chief of Ipet-Sut; Atum, Lord of the Two lands and Iunu; Re-Harakhte; Ptah, South of his Wall, Lord of [Ankhtawy] and Thoth, Lord of the Gods speech; He who ap[pears on] The Horus [Throne of the liv]ing like his father Re, everyday;

3) The Good [God], Son of Amun; image of Kamphis, Glorious Seed, [Splendid offspring], Scion of Amun Himself; [Father of

---

*From Ian Alex Blease, "The Great Restoration Stela of Tut-Ankh-Amun" [online], trans. John Bennett, www.geocities.com/debunkinglc/Stela.html [December 8, 2003]. Text within parentheses indicates the translator's additions.

the Two Lands] who moulds his moulder, who fashions his fashioner;

4) For whom the Souls of Iunu assembled, in order that he might be fashioned to act as King of Eternity, as the everlasting Horus; The Good God who does things beneficial to his father and all the Gods,

5) He has made that which was in ruins to flourish as a monument of Eternal age; he has suppressed wrongdoing throughout the Two Lands; truth is established, she (Maat) causes falsehood to be the abomination of the Land, as in its First Time.

6) The Temples of the Gods and Goddesses, beginning from Elephantine [down] to the marshes of the delta, [their —— had] fallen into neglect

7) Their shrines had fallen into desolation and become tracts overgrown with k[3t?]-plants, their sanctuaries were as if they had never been. Their halls were a trodden path.

8) The land was in confusion, the Gods forsook this land.

9) If an [army] was sent to Djahy to widen the frontiers of Egypt, it met with no success at all; if one prayed to a God to ask things of him [in no sense] did he come. If one made supplication to a Goddess in like manner, in no sense did she come.

10) Their hearts were weak of themselves (with anger). They destroyed what had been done. After some days had passed by this [his Majesty app]eared on the throne of his father; He ruled the countries of Horus, The Black Land and the Red Land were under his

11) dominion and every Land was in obeisance to his might; Behold his Majesty was in his palace which is in the estate of "Ankheperkare" like Re in the heavens and his Majesty was administering this land and making daily governance of the Two-River banks,

12) then his Majesty took council with his heart, searching out every excellent occasion, seeking what was beneficial to his father Amun for fashioning his August image of real fine-gold. He has added to what was done in former times,

13) He has fashioned [an image of] his father Amun upon Thirteen

carrying poles, his Holy image being of fine gold, lapis lazuli and every rare and costly stone,

14) whereas formerly, the Majesty of the August God had been upon Eleven carrying poles. He has fashioned [an image of] Ptah, South of his Wall, Lord of Ankhtawe, his August image being of fine gold [upon eleven carryi]ng poles, his holy image being of fine gold, lapis lazuli, turquoise and every rare and costly stone.

15) Where as formerly the Majesty of this August God had been upon [six?] carrying poles and his Majesty has made monuments for the Gods [fashioning] their statues of real fine gold, the best of foreign lands,

16) Building anew their sanctuaries as monuments of eternal age, they being endowed with property forever, establishing for them divine gifts as a lasting daily sacrifice and supplying them with food-offerings upon earth.

17) He has added to what was done since the time of the ancestors; he has inducted priests and prophets, children of the notables of their towns, each the son of a noted man and one whose name is known;

18) He has multiplied their [wealth?] with gold, silver, bronze and copper without limit of [all things?]; He has filled their storehouses with slaves, men and women, the fruits of his Majesty's plundering.

19) All the [possessions?] of the Temples are doubled, trebled and quadrupled with silver, gold, lapis lazuli, turquoise, all rare and costly stones; royal linen; white cloth; fine linen; olive oil; gum; fat [. . .],

20) incense, ihmt incense and myrrh without limit of all good things. His Majesty (may he live, prosper and be in health) has hewn their barques which are on the

21) river of fresh cedar, the best of the hill slope, the pick of Negau, worked with fine gold, the best of foreign lands; and they illume the river. His Majesty (may he live, prosper and be in health) has consecrated men and women slaves,

22) singers and dancers who are servants in the house of the King; and their wages are to the [. . .] palace of the Lord of the Two Lands.

23) I cause them to be protected and preserved for my fathers, the Gods, in the desire to placate them by doing what which their Ka's love so that they may protect [Ta-meny] The Gods and Goddesses who are in this land, their hearts are joyful,

24) The possessors of shrines are glad, lands are in a state of jubilation and merry making, exaltation is throughout [the whole land]; a goodly state has come to pass. The Ennead of Gods who are in the Temple their arms are raised up in adoration,

25) Their hands are full of jubilees [of] eternity and everlastingness, all Life and Prosperity with them [are placed] to the nose of Horus who is born again, beloved son [of his father, Amun-Re, Lord of the Thrones of the Two Lands-] He (Amun) has fashioned him that he (himself) may be fashioned, King of Upper and Lower Egypt, Nebkhperure, Beloved of Amun.

26) His Beloved, real Eldest Son, who protects the Father who fashioned him that he may exercise the Kingship over K[ings in all Lands], Son of Re, Tut-Ankh-Amun, Ruler of Hermonthis, a Son who is profitable to him who fashioned him, wealthy in monuments, Rich in Wonders,

27) Who makes monuments in righteousness of heart for his Father, Amun; Beautiful of Birth, Sovereign [who assumed the Crowns in Chemmis]. On this day, one was in the goodly palace, which is in the estate of Ankhkheperkare, Justified;

28) Behold, [his Majesty] was rejuvenated, he who seizes (?) hastened of himself, Khnum has moulded him[. . . .] He is Mighty of Arm, Great of Strength, One distinguished more than the mighty, vast of strength like the son of [Nut].

29) Mighty of Arm like Horus, there exists no equal to him among the mighty ones of all lands together; He who knows like Re, who [. . . is] like Ptah, who understands like Thoth, who ordains excellent laws, who commands[. . . .],

30) Excellent of Utterance; King of Upper and Lower Egypt, Lord of the Two Lands, Lord of Rites, Lord of the Strong Arm, Nebkheperure, He who placates the Gods, beloved Son of Re of his Body, Lord of every Foreign Land, Lord of Crowns, Tut-Ankh-Amun, Ruler of Hermonthis, Given Life, Stability and Prosperity like Re [for all time].

Appendix 3

THE SKULL AND CERVICAL SPINE RADIOGRAPHS OF TUTANKHAMEN
A CRITICAL APPRAISAL*

*Richard S. Boyer, Ernst A. Rodin,
Todd C. Grey, and R. C. Connolly*

THE SKULL AND CERVICAL SPINE RADIOGRAPHS
OF TUTANKHAMEN: A CRITICAL APPRAISAL*

BACKGROUND AND PURPOSE: Tutankhamen, the last pharaoh of the Eighteenth Dynasty, died unexpectedly at approximately age 18 years. A cause of death has never been established, but theories that the young king was murdered by a blow to the head have been proposed based on skull radiographs obtained by a team from the University of Liverpool in 1968. We recently had the opportunity to evaluate the skull and cervical spine radiographs of Tutankhamen. The purpose of this study was to report our critical appraisal of the radiographs of Tutankhamen regarding the findings alleged to indicate traumatic death.

---

*From *American Journal of Neuroradiology* 24 (June/July 2003): 1142–47. Copyright © 2003 by the American Society of Neuroradiology. Reprinted by permission of the American Society of Neuroradiology.

METHODS: Copies of lateral, anteroposterior, and submental vertex skull radiographs of Tutankhamen were reviewed with special attention to the claims of a depressed skull fracture, intracranial bone fragments, and calcified membrane of a posterior fossa subdural hematoma. A phantom skull was radiographed to reproduce the appearance of the floor of the posterior fossa in the lateral projection.

RESULTS: The skull radiographs of Tutankhamen show only postmortem artifacts that are explainable by an understanding of the methods of mummy preservation used at the time of his death. Some findings also relate to trauma inflicted by an autopsy performed in 1925. The alleged calcified membrane of a posterior fossa subdural hematoma is easily reproduced with a skull phantom.

CONCLUSION: Our critical review of the skull and cervical spine radiographs of Tutankhamen does not support proposed theories of a traumatic or homicidal death.

It is generally agreed that Tutankhamen, the last pharaoh of the Eighteenth Dynasty, died unexpectedly at approximately age 18 years. The cause of his death has never been conclusively established. It has been alleged that a blow to the head murdered the young pharaoh. Skull radiographs obtained in 1968 by a team from the University of Liverpool headed by Professor R. G. Harrison have been used as supportive evidence of this allegation (1). A video documentary of the conditions under which the radiographs were obtained and Harrison's conclusions about the radiographic findings was shown on British television in 1969 (2). The radiographs were never published in the medical literature, but an article by Harrison (3)—"Post Mortem on Two Pharaohs: Was Tutankhamen's Skull Fractured?"—was published in the December 1971 issue of *Buried History*. Harrison stated, "While examining X-ray pictures of Tutankhamen's skull, I discovered a small piece of bone in the left side of the skull cavity. This could be part of the ethmoid bone, which had become dislodged from the top of the nose when an instrument was passed up the nose into the cranial cavity during the embalming process. On the other hand, the X-rays also suggest that this piece of bone is fused with the overlying skull and this could be consistent with a depressed fracture, which had healed. This could mean that Tutankhamen died from a brain hemorrhage caused by a blow to his skull from a blunt instrument."

This evidence, taken together with the knowledge that the pharaoh was only 18 years old when he died and considered against the troubled times during which he lived, poses an intriguing question. Was Tutankhamen murdered?

A second article by Harrison (and coauthor Abdalla) (4)—"The Remains of Tutankhamun"—was published in *Antiquity*. In that publication, Harrison's team reported that Tutankhamen's body had been dismembered during the first autopsy, which had been performed by Carter and Derry in 1925 (5). This process was necessary because the mummy was glued to the innermost coffin by an excessive use of unguents and had to be literally chiseled out to unwrap the body and retrieve the artifacts, which are now in the possession of several museums and have been displayed around the world. In the process, the head and cervical spine were severed from the remainder of the spinal column below the seventh cervical vertebra. Harrison (4) described the radiographic findings as follows: "The most prominent feature, however, is the presence of two attenuated shadows, the first along the vertex of the skull, and the second occupying the back (posterior) region of the skull. Each of these shadows possesses a fluid level, suggesting that radio-paque [sic] fluid was introduced into the cranial cavity with the skull lying vertex downwards, and then with the body lying horizontally, so that the posterior region of the skull was most dependent. In addition a small fragment of bone is seen in both lateral and frontal views of the skull, lying in the posterior aspect of the left parietal region of the skull. This, at first sight, looked like a piece of bone from the thin bony roof of the nasal cavity (the cribriform plate of the ethmoid bone), and perusal of the frontal X-ray of the skull confirms that this bone has disappeared from both sides of the floor of the skull. This would be very understandable, and could fit in well with known theories of the practice of mummification. It is a generally accepted view that an instrument is passed through the nostril, up into the nasal cavity to perforate or remove this bone, allowing extraction of the brain, and the introduction of any preservation fluid into the cranial cavity. On closer analysis, however, after further X-rays were developed and became available for study, several main objections to this theory were apparent and an alternative explanation suggested itself. This additional analysis will be discussed in a future publication."

No further publication was produced. However, on the previously mentioned BBC videotape in which the events surrounding the second autopsy as performed by Harrison's team are shown, the radiographic findings are explained by Harrison (2). As recorded on this tape, he regarded the bone splinter as a postmortem artifact. However, in the same video documentary, Harrison raised a question about the appearance of the posterior fossa of Tutankhamen on the lateral radiograph. Pointing to the floor of the posterior fossa, which he called "eggshell thinning" of the occipital bone, he said: "This is within normal limits. But in fact, it could have been caused by a hemorrhage under the membranes overlying the brain in this region, and this could have been caused by a blow to the back of the head, and this in turn could have been responsible for death."

These sentences have since been taken to indicate that the pharaoh had, in fact, been murdered. However, we propose that all findings alleged to indicate a traumatic death are explainable by an understanding of normal anatomy and the process of Egyptian mummification in practice at the time of Tutankhamen's death. Some artifacts are also due to an entry into the cranial vault at the time of the autopsy performed by Carter and Derry in 1925.

METHODS

Personal Investigations, Obtaining the Radiographs

One of the authors (E. A. Rodin) has had a longstanding interest in Egyptology. When he read in a German language publication regarding Tutankhamen (6) that radiographic evidence had revealed a skull defect, he pursued the matter further with R. C. Connolly in Liverpool, who was a member of the British investigative team led by Professor Harrison, which radiographed the remains of Tutankhamen in the pharaoh's tomb in 1968. An attempt was made to obtain copies of the radiographs, but this was not successful until Kate Botting contacted Rodin in August 2001 for an interview in anticipation of a Discovery Channel production, which aired in 2002 (7). Rodin agreed to the interview under the condition that Botting would obtain copies of the radiographs for our review from Connolly at the University of Liverpool. Copies of the radiographs were subsequently produced in Liverpool and, along with a copy of the videotape of Harrison's 1969 BBC presentation, were made available to Rodin and coauthors R. S. Boyer and T. C. Grey in September 2001 on the day of videotaping the Discovery Channel production.

Review of the Radiographs

Three radiographic copies of the skull and cervical spine of Tutankhamen were provided for our review. The copies were in good condition and had satisfactory resolution and contrast to critically examine the skull and its opaque contents as well as the cervical spine. The radiographs were in our possession for only a few hours before filming, and there was no opportunity for us to exchange views before the taped interviews. They were subsequently examined in greater detail by authors Boyer (a pediatric neuroradiologist) and by Grey (a forensic pathologist) in the company of Rodin (a neurologist and epileptologist). The digital images were stored in electronic file format and are available to the interested reader (contact Boyer by e-mail at pcrboyer@ihc.com).

Phantom Study

A skull phantom was radiographed in the lateral projection resting on a sponge ring to simulate the process by which the skull radiographs of Tutankhamen were produced during the 1968 expedition. Slight tilt of the head was created to show the appearance of the posterior fossa when the head is tilted. Images were acquired with a computed radiography system and were archived in an electronic imaging network for review on a workstation.

Video Documentary

The time allotted was insufficient for a detailed examination of the radiographs before the videotaping of the Discovery Channel documentary. This led to the initial assumption by Boyer and Grey that Tutankhamen may have suffered from Klippel-Feil syndrome (7). However, after the videotaping was concluded, subsequent analysis of the radiographs excluded this diagnosis as an acceptable possibility. Most of the authors' observations and conclusions regarding the radiographs were not included in the final video production but are presented herein.

RESULTS

Analysis of the Radiographs

Lateral, anteroposterior, and submental vertex radiographs of the disarticulated skull and cervical spine of Tutankhamen were reviewed. The radiographic images were of sufficient quality to allow a critical appraisal of the skull, spine, and intracranial contents. A digitized print of the lateral view radiograph with contrast reversed (black on white) showed the two intracranial bone fragments more clearly than did the traditional white on black images.

The cranial-facial proportion appeared appropriate for a young adult male. The calvaria appeared to be intact. No skull fracture was identified. However, as discussed by Harrison (2, 4), two fluid levels were present, which resulted from the resin introduced at the time of embalming. The resin deposits in the vertex and occipital regions of the cranial vault were well seen on the lateral view radiograph. The resin in the vertex was seen on the frontal view radiograph. The sub-mental vertex view showed the resin in the occipital region. The presence of this hardened, opaque resin was actually helpful in understanding and refuting the commonly held theories of skull fracture and subdural hematoma.

Careful inspection of the radiographs showed that there are, in fact, two intracranial bone fragments, which are in the right parietal/occipital area, not on the left, as suggested by Harrison. These fragments are separate from the attenuated shadows of the intracranial resin. No other bone fragments or abnormal intracranial contents were detected. The nasal-ethmoid-cribriform plate region appeared to be intact. No fracture or missing parts were noted, in distinction from Harrison's observations. Radio-attenuated material was also seen in both nasal passages. These plugs were placed in the nasal passages to seal the intracranial vault after the embalmers had removed the brain and cauterized the inside of the skull with hot resin, presumably to prevent leakage of resin or liquefied brain. Careful inspection of the bone fragments shown on all three images indicated that the larger of the bone fragments appeared to be a portion of the posterior arch of the first cervical vertebra.

No calcified membrane was seen in the posterior fossa. Two parallel linear opacities in the posterior fossa represented the lateral aspects of the floor of the posterior fossa on which rested the cerebellar hemispheres. Mild tilt of the head on the lateral view radiographs projected the contour of the floor of one side of the posterior fossa above that of the other. A lateral view radiograph of a skull phantom showed that the parallel lines of the right and left sides of the floor of the posterior fossa project one cephalad to the other when the head was tilted. The appearance of the lateral view radiograph of the phantom was very similar to the appearance of the lateral view radiograph of Tutankhamen, confirming our impression that there was no calcified membrane, as suggested by Brier's consultant (1), but only normal posterior fossa anatomy (except for the resin, as discussed above).

Most of the posterior elements of the upper cervical spine were missing. In addition, there was a continuous beaded-appearing line posterior to the cervical vertebral bodies and disk spaces visible in the lateral view radiograph. The disk spaces were poorly visible, especially in the lateral projection. The cranial-cervical alignment appeared normal. No evidence of platybasia, basilar invagination, cranial-cervical dislocation, cervical spine fracture, or subluxation was observed. No congenital abnormality of the cervical vertebrae or scoliosis was detectable.

DISCUSSION

Intracranial Bone Fragments

Reeves (8) and Brier (1) previously published in the lay literature a photograph of the lateral view radiograph of Tutankhamen showing the bone fragment(s). However, the complete set of three radiographs of Tutankhamen's skull and cervical spine has not been previously published or made available to the scientific community for review. Two bone fragments were noted within the calvaria, a finding not mentioned by other observers. It is not clear why Harrison reported that the fragments were on the left side, when they were clearly on the right. Connolly, a member of the Harrison expedition, confirmed that the markings on the radiographs were correct and that the fragments were thus on the right. If these had been dislodged from the calvaria by a blow causing a skull fracture before death, the fragments would have been imbedded in the resin, which was instilled after death, and hence the fragments would not be visible on the radiographs. Alternatively, it has been suggested that the fragments may have been dislodged in the embalming process, but similar logic applies. Had the embalmers dislodged the fragments, they would have been buried in the resin, which was poured in after the intracranial contents were evacuated. Furthermore, there is no visible donor site in the cribriform plate region, as suggested by Harrison, to suggest a fracture in this region. The nasal plugs placed after instilling the resin were observed to be intact. It is most likely that the fragments were dislodged, not at the time of embalming but at the time of the autopsy performed by Derry and his associates in 1925. This assumption is supported by a set of radiographs obtained in 1978 by J. E. Harris of the University of Michigan (personal communication). These images showed that the bone fragments were no longer in the superior parietal region but near the base of the skull. The mobility of the fragments within the cranial vault indicated that they were not fixed to the skull or resin but were freely moveable, consistent with postmummification trauma.

The process of mummification of Tutankhamen is typical of that applied by the royal embalmers during the time of the pharaohs. Harris and Weeks (9) and Harris and Wente (10) documented, in two books, the process of extracting the brain from the calvarial vault and partially filling it with a radiopaque resinous material. Several of the royal mummies that they radiographed showed intracranial densities with fluid levels, similar to those seen on the radiographs of Tutankhamen. None of these radiographs showed intracranial bone fragments, consistent with our conclusion that the bone fragments were produced long after the mummification process was complete and the resin was hardened. Likewise, none of the mummies published in these references showed absence of the posterior arch of C1, also consistent with our conclusion that the royal embalmers entered the cranial cavity via a nasal approach, but the approach used by Derry et al. was through the foramen magnum, probably introducing fragments of the upper cervical spine into the cranial vault in the process in 1925 (5).

Leek (11), who was also a member of Harrison's team, published additional information regarding Derry's autopsy, which is not available in Carter's book. Leek wrote, "Toward the end of the report, Derry makes two terse observations: first the skull was empty except for some resinous material which was introduced through the nose, and second that the third molar teeth had just erupted the gum."

It is our opinion that because Derry did not have radiographs available, he must have entered the skull with the use of unspecified instruments, creating a sufficiently large window to observe the intracranial vault. This could be more easily achieved through the foramen magnum than through the nose. If the entry was through the foramen magnum, it may well have produced fractures of portions of the upper cervical spine, whereas an entry through the nose could have produced fractures of parts of the nasal, ethmoid, and/or sphenoid bones. This is unlikely, however, because the mentioned plugs in the nasal passages appeared to be undisturbed. Our review of the radiographs indicated that the larger of the bone fragments appeared very similar to the posterior arch of the atlas (C1), which was missing on the radiographs. In our opinion, this observation supports the conclusion that Derry entered the cranial cavity through the foramen magnum, dislodging the posterior arch of C1 in so doing, with the bone fragments then remaining inside the cranial vault where they were radiographed by Harrison's team. This conclusion is consistent with the report presented by Harrison and Abdalla (4), in which they state, "Some repairs to the head were visible in the form of wax between the atlas and the foramen magnum at the base of the skull, and smooth, recently applied, but solidified, resin under the chin."

Posterior Fossa Bone Thinning

The other observation of Tutankhamen's radiographs that has been used to impute a violent form of closed head trauma as the cause of his death relates to the occipital region on the lateral view radiograph. The reported thinning of the occipital bone can be easily understood by examination of the osseous floor of the posterior cranial fossa. The lateral aspects of the occipital bone expand and thin to accommodate the cerebellar hemispheres, which rest on them. Thinning of the occipital bone in this region is a normal finding. The reason that the thinning appears to be somewhat more pronounced on the lateral view radiograph of Tutankhamen is because the head is somewhat tilted laterally so that one lateral posterior fossa depression projects lower than the other. This tilt of the head also accounts for the horizontal attenuated line seen across the floor of the posterior fossa, thought by a consultant referred to by Brier (1) (who had only a photograph of the radiograph available rather than the actual radiograph) to be a calcified membrane. It is simply one side of the posterior fossa floor projecting above the other. Furthermore, if there were a calcified membrane in the posterior fossa at the time of death, the resin applied postmortem would not have crossed the margin of the membrane, which it obviously does on the lateral view radiograph. No calcified membrane was observed, and no evidence of a subdural hematoma was seen.

Cervical Spine

Likewise, no evidence of injury occurring before death to the cervical spine or the cranial-cervical junction was observed. The resin deposit obscured some of the usual anatomic landmarks in the region of the foramen magnum, but no evidence of basilar invagination or platy-basia was seen. The vertebral bodies appeared to be intact and the alignment anatomic. The bright line posterior to the vertebral bodies and the seeming lack of intervertebral spaces on the lateral view radiograph were regarded, at first glance, to be suggestive of juvenile rheumatoid arthritis or Klippel-Feil syndrome. Based on a more detailed examination of the radiographs, this conclusion could not be substantiated. The bright beaded line seen on the lateral view image of the spine posterior to the vertebral bodies and intervertebral disks most likely represents a thin deposit of resin that layered in the anterior portion of the cervical spinal canal, probably in the subdural space. We have observed on MR images of the spine, obtained after posterior fossa surgery, that the cervical subdural space may contain blood and/or CSF. We suspect that the liquid resin extended from the intracranial vault into the anterior subdural space of the spine, creating the impression of posterior spinous fusion or of a calcified membrane in the region of the posterior longitudinal ligament.

It is also probable that some of the unguents poured over the body at the time of burial were still adherent to the cervical spinous tissues at the time the radiographs were obtained. Burton's photographs taken at the time of the 1925 autopsy show that the cervical spine is rigidly attached to the skull. This can be seen in pictures of Tutankhamen's head presented by Brier (1), Harrison's BBC video documentary (2), Leek's chapters (11), Reeves's book (8), and other publications. The appearance of the spine on the lateral view radiograph that originally suggested congenital or acquired fusion of vertebral bodies is, therefore, more likely due to the resin that had glued the back of the mummy to the coffin and was removed by Carter's team only to the extent that enabled them to lift out the head. This assumption is also borne out by the report presented by Harrison and Abdalla (4) in 1972 in which it was noted that "in many places black resin still adhered to the rock-hard black tissues."

Conclusion

The radiographs of the skull and cervical spine of Tutankhamen provide no evidence for a depressed skull fracture, a posterior fossa subdural hematoma, or an injury to or congenital malformation of the cervical spine. All previously reported abnormal findings can be accounted for by postmortem artifacts and an understanding of normal skull base anatomy. We have shown that the observation of a curvilinear attenuated line in the posterior fossa does not represent a calcified membrane and can be reproduced with a skull phantom, which is slightly tilted when radiographed. Currently proposed murder theories regarding Tutankhamen's death are not supported by critical appraisal of the radiographs of the young pharaoh. Because the resin introduced at the time of embalming presents serious obstacles to a definitive evaluation of Tutankhamen's head and neck, it would be interesting to use CT for further investigation. However, the pharaoh's remains reside in his tomb in the Valley of the Kings and cannot readily be moved. Performing such an examination would present a major logistical challenge, which does not seem to be feasible in the foreseeable future. The cause of death of the famous young pharaoh remains enigmatic, but the radiographs of his skull cannot be used to support a theory of homicide.

Acknowledgment

We express appreciation to Kate Botting from Atlantic Productions, Ltd., for assisting in transport of the copies of the radiographs and the BBC videotape between England and the United States.

REFERENCES

1. Brier, B. *The Murder of Tutankhamen: A True Story.* New York: G. P. Putnam's Sons, 1998, pp. 172–73.

2. *Chronicle: Tutankhamen Post Mortem.* Atlantic Productions, Ltd.; TX: 25/10/69. VHS/NTSC.

3. Harrison, R. G. "Post Mortem on Two Pharaohs: Was Tutankhamen's Skull Fractured?" *Buried History* 4 (1971): 114–29.

4. Harrison, R. G., and A. B. Abdalla. "The Remains of Tutankhamen." *Antiquity* 46 (1972): 8–14.

5. Carter, H. *The Tomb of Tutankhamen.* London: Century Publishing, 1983, pp. 197–222, 310–19, 321–32.

6. Vandenberg, P. *Nofretete, Echnaton und ihre Zeit.* Klagenfurt, Germany: Neuer Kaiser Verlag, p. 232.

7. Atlantic Productions, Ltd. "Assassination of King Tut." VHS. Discovery Channel, 2002.

8. Reeves, N. *The Complete Tutankhamen.* London: Thames & Hudson Ltd., 1960, p. 118.

9. Harris, J. E., and K. R. Weeks. *X-raying the Pharaohs.* New York: Scribner, 1973, p. 44.

10. Harris, J. E., and E. F. Wente. *An X-ray Atlas of the Royal Mummies.* Chicago: The University of Chicago Press, 1980, p. 183.

11. Leek, F. F. *The Human Remains from the Tomb of Tutankhamen.* London: Oxford University Press, 1972, pp. 3–6, 16–19.

Appendix 4

THE INVESTIGATIVE APPROACH USED IN THE DEATH INVESTIGATION OF KING TUT

(Developed by King/Cooper: April 2001)

OVERALL SYNOPSIS OF CRIME(S)/BRIEF OVERVIEW

The first order of business in this investigation will be the compilation of all historical documents pertaining to the economic, political, social, cultural, racial, and ethnic makeup of the Eighteenth Dynasty.

A thorough review of the dates, places, and times of Tutankhamen's travels and associations must be examined, including how the information was reported or discovered and what investigative efforts may have been conducted by ancient theorists.

GENERAL DESCRIPTION OF AREA(S) WHERE CRIME(S) OCCURRED

All geographically based demographics (economic, political, social, cultural, racial, ethnic makeup) will be evaluated, including the existence of and distances to nearby cities, institutions of note, and other important locations.

An overview evaluation of the population, including growth or decline, battles or wars being waged, and the nature of any type of criminal activity in the community/area, particularly as it pertains to Tutankhamen's family.

Any recent events/incidents and trends that were generally known by, or impacted, a significant portion of the populations of the area (e.g., natural disaster, major media focus on a local event, etc.)

EVALUATION OF THE MOST PROBABLE CAUSE OF DEATH

After evaluating the historical information, we must then begin to evaluate the cause of Tutankhamen's death.

> Natural Causes
> Accident
> Suicide
> Homicide

CRIME SCENE DESCRIPTION(S)

Since there may be multiple crime scenes, for example, point of abduction, point of assault, point of disposal, and so on, each area where the pharoah would travel, including the distance from notable places, must be considered.

Evaluation of the amount of access to the areas, environmental setting, how frequently used and by whom.

Summary of evidentiary items and their location with specific examination of what is present and what is missing that should be present.

If this case is considered a homicide, a close examination of the visible injuries to victim, clothing, the manner in which the victim is discovered and cared for after discovery.

Evaluation of environmental impact on the body, normal insect/animal life around area.

SUMMARY OF VICTIMOLOGY

In order to better understand Tut, a thorough examination of who he is, is required. First, we need to hire a leading scientist to re-create Tutankhamun's head and face so that we can see behind the famous death mask.

An examination of Tut's age, sex, race, marital status and adjustment, intelligence, lifestyle, personality and demeanor will give us the much-needed glance into his personality, character, and image.

A victim assessment must be conducted in order to determine why Tut was selected as a victim if this is determined to be a homicide. What feeling was the victim experiencing and expressing before and after the assault? When was the victim last seen and where?

Complete a "risk assessment" on Tutankhamen.

MEDICAL REPORTS/RESULTS

We need to request all photos that will show the full extent of damage to his body, since the Egyptian government has been uncooperative in giving us access to his mummy. Their reasoning is sound, since Tut was so badly damaged in the initial examination and later by Harrison. In our examination, we will need closer examination of Tut's possible wounds, bruises, marks, and so forth.

Since no toxicological reports can be accomplished where we might gain a better understanding of drug, alcohol, or other toxins, we will need to rely on the historical records that indicate the method and manner of medical treatment in 1300 BCE and the mummification process.

The opinions of a medical examiner and forensic medical experts need to be requested to determine the wound causes and whether they are premortem or postmortem.

Other forensic testing as determined during the investigation.

Evaluation of the Overall Events (Crimes)

Would the data support one of the listed "most probable" causes of death?
Was the offense an organized or disorganized crime?
What risk level was determined after completing a risk assessment?

Suspect Information

After determining whether Tutankhamen was a high- or low-risk victim, establish a pool of possible suspects. As the evaluation of the risk level and the individuals within the pool of possible suspects is examined, begin to focus on the most "probable" offender first.

Once the focus has narrowed, conduct an offender profile on the suspect. Some things to consider are:
What method did the offender use to assault the victim?
What were the feelings of the offender before and during the attack?
Why did the offender make the decision to allow the victim to live or die?
What was the suspect's personality like? Who were his/her friends? What was the suspect's maturity level, interests, habits, and social or religious commitments?
Where was the suspect in relationship to the timeline of events, before, during, and after the death of Tutankhamen?

Conduct Additional Interviews with Associates of Victim, e.g., Interviews with Egyptologists, Antiquities Experts, etc.

In this stage of the investigation, we need to establish the name of person being interviewed, what is known about family of Tutankhamen (siblings, birth order, family relationships), what did Tut do in his spare time, for example, hobbies, locales frequented, and so on, and describe Tut's lifestyle, personality, and characteristics.

Further examination into what type of person Tutankhamen was will focus on his lifestyle, how he coped with problems in his life, the types of stresses he experienced, sleeping or physical ailments, and whom the pharaoh may have confided in.

Finally, it is important to evaluate from expert witnesses how they believe Tutankhamen died (suicide, accident, homicide).

FOLLOW-UP NEEDS ASSESSMENT AND EVALUATION OF WHERE TO GO FROM HERE

Additional forensic needs.
Sites and locations that need to be examined.
Interviews that need to be conducted.
Other items.

INDEX

Page numbers in italics refer to photographs